The *Qiaopi* Trade and Transnational Networks in the Chinese Diaspora

Originating in the 1820s and used for 150 years thereafter, *qiaopi* is the name given in Chinese to letters written home by Chinese emigrants to accompany remittances. Their key function was to preserve family ties. Although such correspondence focused principally on the provision of economic support, the *qiaopi* also touched on cultural, political, educational, and gender themes.

This book therefore seeks to examine the *qiaopi* from two interconnected perspectives. One views *qiaopi* from a political and institutional angle, the other from a financial and social angle. Bringing together the extensive research of a group of international scholars, this multi-authored volume sheds light on the larger significance of the *qiaopi* for modern China. Taking an empirical, evidence-driven approach, the contributors employ a wide range of primary sources in both Chinese and English and relate their findings to scholarship in both the Chinese-speaking world and in non-Chinese interdisciplinary fields. In so doing, this book helps to bridge the gap between Chinese- and English-speaking researchers in the field of *qiaopi* studies.

As one of the first books in English on the *qiaopi* trade and its significance, this book will appeal to students and scholars of Chinese history and Chinese migration, as well in Migration Studies and Diaspora Studies more generally.

Gregor Benton is Emeritus Professor of History at Cardiff University, UK.

Hong Liu is Tan Kah Kee Endowed Professor of Asian Studies and Chair of the School of Social Sciences at Nanyang Technological University, Singapore.

Huimei Zhang is the Research Fellow at Nanyang Centre for Public Administration and Centre for Chinese Language and Culture, Nanyang Technological University, Singapore.

Chinese Worlds

Chinese Worlds publishes high-quality scholarship, research monographs, and source collections on Chinese history and society. 'Worlds' signals the diversity of China, the cycles of unity and division through which China's modern history has passed, and recent research trends toward regional studies and local issues. It also signals that Chineseness is not contained within borders – ethnic migrant communities overseas are also 'Chinese worlds'.

The series editors are Gregor Benton, Flemming Christiansen, Terence Gomez and Hong Liu.

31 Consumers and Individuals in China
Standing Out, Fitting In
Michael B. Griffiths

32 Documentary, World History, and National Power in the PRC
Global Rise in Chinese Eyes
Gotelind Müller

33 Ethnic Chinese Entrepreneurship in Malaysia
On Contextualisation in International Business Studies
Michael Jakobsen

34 Chinese Student Migration and Selective Citizenship
Mobility, Community and Identity between China and the United States
Lisong Liu

35 "Mixed Race" Identities in Asia and the Pacific
Experiences from Singapore and New Zealand
Zarine L. Rocha

36 The *Qiaopi* Trade and Transnational Networks in the Chinese Diaspora
Edited by Gregor Benton, Hong Liu and Huimei Zhang

For more information about this series, please visit: www.routledge.com/asian-studies/series/SE0663

The *Qiaopi* Trade and Transnational Networks in the Chinese Diaspora

Edited by Gregor Benton, Hong Liu, and Huimei Zhang

Routledge
Taylor & Francis Group
LONDON AND NEW YORK

First published 2018 by Routledge

2 Park Square, Milton Park, Abingdon, Oxon OX14 4RN
605 Third Avenue, New York, NY 10017

Routledge is an imprint of the Taylor & Francis Group, an informa business

First issued in paperback 2021

Publisher's Note

The publisher has gone to great lengths to ensure the quality of this reprint but points out that some imperfections in the original copies may be apparent.

British Library Cataloguing-in-Publication Data
A catalogue record for this book is available from the British Library

Library of Congress Cataloging-in-Publication Data
A catalog record has been requested for this book

ISBN: 978-1-138-08106-2 (hbk)
ISBN: 978-0-367-44510-2 (pbk)

Typeset in Times New Roman
by Wearset Ltd, Boldon, Tyne and Wear

Contents

Figures

Tables

Contributors

Els van Dongen is Assistant Professor of History at Nanyang Technological University, Singapore.

Takeshi Hamashita is Professor of History at Sun Yat-Sen University, China and Executive Director and Research Department Head at Toyo Bunko, Japan.

Lane J. Harris is Associate Professor of History and Asian Studies and Director of the South Carolina Center for Teaching About Asia at Furman University, USA.

Junying Jia is Research Fellow of History at Tsinghua University, China.

Mei-fen Kuo is Research Fellow of Asian Studies at University of Queensland, Australia.

Bozi Liu is a Curator at the Museum of Quanzhou Overseas Chinese History, China.

Jin Liu is Professor of History at Wuyi University, China.

Acknowledgements

All chapters except for the first are revised versions of papers originally presented at the International Workshop on "The Qiaopi Trade in China and Overseas" (9–10 October 2015, Singapore). We gratefully acknowledge the Singapore Ministry of Education's AcRF Tier-1 research grant for "*Qiaopi* and Changing Memories of the Homeland: Emigrants' Letters, Family Ties, and Transnational Chinese Networks" (M4011208) and funding from Nanyang Technological University (M4081020 and M4081392) that facilitated the workshop organization and relevant research and editorial work. We would like to thank the workshop organizers, the Centre for Chinese Language and Culture and the School of Humanities and Social Sciences (now the School of Humanities and the School of Social Sciences) at Nanyang Technological University.

We are grateful to all the contributors who presented or submitted papers for the workshop, including Takeshi Hamashita, Lai Chi-Kong, Lane Jeremy Harris, Lee Kam Hing, Cheong Kee Cheok, Lee Poh Ping, Jia Junying, Kuo Mei-fen, Shen Huifen, Liu Jin, Kim Jong Ho, Liu Bozi, and Kua Bak Lim. We would also like to thank Els van Dongen for writing an additional chapter at our request.

The book has benefited from reviewers' feedback. We would particularly like to thank Kenneth Dean, Yow Cheun Hoe, Ong Soon Keong, Evelyn Hu-Dehart, and Koh Keng We for their invaluable comments and advice. Wang Shujuan, Tan Wee Ngar Joyce, and Low Yanling provided effective logistic support for the workshop's organization. We are grateful to the editors and colleagues of Routledge. This book would not have been possible without their professional guidance.

The views and interpretations presented in this book are solely the authors'.

Introduction

The *qiaopi* trade and transnational networks in the Chinese diaspora

Gregor Benton, Hong Liu, and Huimei Zhang

Introduction

Qiaopi 侨批 is the name given in Chinese to letters written home by Chinese emigrants to accompany remittances, in the 150 years starting in the 1820s. Archivists in China have collected around 160,000 *qiaopi*, drawn from China's major regions of outmigration and of settlement overseas, in Southeast Asia, the Americas, and the Pacific. The *qiaopi* cover a crucial and defining period in China's modern history and the history of global migration, which was a key driving force in global social and economic development. In June 2013, the *Qiaopi* Project was officially entered onto UNESCO's "Memory of the World" Register, set up in 1992 because of "a growing awareness of the parlous state of preservation of documentary heritage" in the world.

The *qiaopi* trade was run in large part by traders who also had other business interests. They combined the *qiaopi* trade with these other interests. The *qiaopi* trade – here taken to mean economic transactions carried out and facilitated through the platform of *qiaopi* – in China and overseas has been extensively researched in China and has been the subject of many Chinese-language conferences. However, it is as yet barely known to a broader international audience, including non-Chinese China experts and experts on migrants' letters and remittances. Apart from a comprehensive study by Gregor Benton and Hong Liu (forthcoming), there is no book-length study in English on *qiaopi*, and only a small handful of academic articles in English have been published.[1] This lack of studies impedes the comparative exploration of Chinese migration in the global context. Remittance played an important role in China's economic and social modernization. It was estimated that the ratio of total remittances to China's total trade deficit was 168 per cent in 1903, 98 per cent in 1909, 39 per cent in 1912, 47 per cent in 1913, 41 per cent in 1920–1923, and 108 per cent in 1928.[2] The Japanese economist Fukuda Shozo wrote in 1937 that Overseas-Chinese remittances were "the only major item that always benefits China's balance of payments."[3] Glen Peterson has demonstrated that remittances continued to play a crucial role in the Chinese economy after 1949. Between 1950 and 1957 the total value of remittances reached US$1.17 billion, which nearly cancelled the country's trade deficit in the same period (which was around US$1.38 billion).[4] A detailed analysis of *qiaopi* in interactions between the Chinese diaspora and the ancestral homeland will shed new light on the historical evolution of modern China and its linkages with globalization through the flows of capital, ideas, people, and social practices.

This multi-authored volume brings together international scholars from several countries who have undertaken extensive research on *qiaopi* and its larger significance for the Chinese diaspora and modern China. The book has two interconnected themes. One views *qiaopi* from a political and institutional angle, the other from a financial and social angle. Contributors examine the general patterns and evolution of the *qiaopi* trade and present specific case studies in it. The volume shows that the *qiaopi* trade permeated the economic, political, social, and cultural spheres in both the Chinese sending regions (the *qiaoxiang*) and the Chinese diaspora.

The key function of the *qiaopi* was to preserve family ties between emigrants and their sending places. *Qiaopi* correspondence focused principally on the provision of economic support, but it also touched on cultural, political, educational, and gender themes.

The contributors employ a wide range of primary sources in both Chinese and English, addressing relevant research questions from a comparative angle and linking up both with scholarship in the Chinese-speaking world and non-Chinese scholarship on related subjects. In so doing, they help bridge the gap between Chinese- and English-speaking researchers and open up *qiaopi* studies to non-Chinese scholars.

Structure of the book

The first chapter, "Entangled Loyalties: *qiaopi*, Chinese community structures, and the state in Southeast Asia", places *qiaopi* and the *qiaopi* trade in the larger context of China's social structure and the various ways in which *qiaopi* traders interacted with the state (including both the sending state and states in colonial and postcolonial Southeast Asia). By taking a *longue durée* approach, this chapter demonstrates how the rise and decline of the *qiaopi* trade was fundamentally shaped by state policies and Chinese social structures from the mid-nineteenth century to the mid-twentieth century. It concludes that "*qiaopi* is the broader story of the tie between Chinese communities and the home, but this early period already demonstrates that we need to understand 'home' as a spectrum of entangled loyalties".

The second chapter, "*Qiaopi* and politics in modern China and the Chinese diaspora", examines *qiaopi* from the point of view of the Chinese and foreign states and local politics. It shows how *qiaopi* connected Chinese migrants and their non-migrant families through institutionalized and transnational mechanisms that crossed oceans and political borders. This in turn contributed to the sending regions' economic development; in this process, the *qiaopi* trade shaped and was shaped by Chinese local and national politics.

Qiaopi and the *qiaopi* trade embody multiple dimensions of the network of ties between emigrants and their families, including business, social, political, and cultural networks. The third chapter, "Migration and home remittances in the financial market connecting Southeast Asia and South China", focuses on the institutional framework and networks that sustained the trade in both Southeast Asia and South China.

In the early days, *qiaopi* were delivered by individual couriers known as *shuike*. Later, when *qiaopi* deliveries became more regular, companies known as *qiaopiju* 侨批局 (remittance firm) took over the trade. They were the main form of linkage in the years before the establishment of modern postal institutions and a modern banking system. The trade grew apace in the late nineteenth century as a result of the massive increase in migration, the proliferation of shipping routes, the founding (in China and overseas) of post offices and banks, and the establishment of telegraphic communications, and it reached its acme in the first half of the twentieth century. During this period, the nation state played an increasingly important role in the evolution of *qiaopi* and in shaping the characteristics of the *qiaopi* trade. The fourth chapter, "Serving the national interest: the *qiaopi* industry, the Chinese Post Office, and the transnational practices of the state, 1937–1945", examines the historical evolution of the three-way relationship between the *qiaopi* industry, the Post Office, and the Chinese state during the War against Japan. It demonstrates how the war transformed this relationship and prompted the emergence of a new, more complicated strategy in the Chinese state's campaign to capture the overseas Chinese remittance business.

The second part of the book comprises four case studies that illustrate the complexity and multidimensionality of the *qiaopi* trade and its role in the making of transnational networks and connecting the diaspora and China.

Chapter 5, "The evolution of the *qiaopi* trade: a case study of the Tianyi firm", analyses the rise and fall of the famous Tianyi *qiaopiju* in the late nineteenth and early twentieth centuries. It argues that the *qiaopi* network was established and maintained mostly on the basis of trust. Chapter 6, "The operating modes of the *qiaopi* trade and impact on the *qiaopiju*: a case study of the Oversea-Chinese Banking Corporation", explores the operating network of the *qiaopi* trade on the basis of a study of the OCBC, which had branches throughout Southeast Asia.

In the traditional Chinese social hierarchy, women generally played only a subordinate role. The extensive overseas trade links created by the *qiaopi* trade helped transform their role in local society. Chapter 7, "Sex scandals, Gold Mountain Guests' Wives, and female roles in the Siyi *qiaoxiang*: a study of the family letters of overseas Chinese in the Republican Era", examines *qiaopi* in the light of gender relations, and focuses on a particular scandal reported both in the local press and discussed in *qiaopi* correspondence.

Chapter 8, "*Jinxin*: the remittance trade and enterprising Chinese Australians, 1850–1916", looks at the *qiaopi* trade from the Pacific by analysing how the world economy helped shape Chinese management of the remittance trade and fostered the emergence of trans-local Chinese capitalism in Australia.

In sum, the book approaches the *qiaopi* phenomenon from several different but connected angles in a number of localities under different political regimes. Vertically, it analyses individual and family ties, the operation of the *qiaopiju*, and interventions of various nation states. Horizontally, it shows that the *qiaopi* trade was founded on the basis of multiple and overlapping networks combining business, social, and cultural dimensions and operating on transnational platforms. Collectively, these vertical and horizontal mechanisms served to connect the Chinese diaspora and China throughout much of the past two centuries.

Notes

1 Cheong *et al.* 2013; Hu and Chen 2013; Harris 2015; Liu and Benton 2016.
2 Shiroyama 2008, 32–33.
3 Fukuda 1995, 192–202.
4 Peterson 2012, 67.

References

Benton, Gregor and Hong Liu. Forthcoming. *Dear China: Emigrant Letters and Remittances, 1820–1980*, Berkeley: University of California Press.

Cheong, Kee Cheok, Lee Kam Hing, and Poh Ping Lee. 2013. "Chinese Overseas Remittances to China: The Perspective from Southeast Asia", *Journal of Contemporary Asia* 43(1): 75–101.

Fukuda, Shozo. 1995. *With Sweat and Abacus: Economic Roles of Southeast Asian Chinese on the Eve of World War II*, translated by Les Oates with an introduction by J. A. C. Mackie; edited by George Hicks, Singapore: Select Books.

Harris, Lane Jeremy. 2015. "Overseas Chinese Remittance Firms, the Limits of State Sovereignty, and Transnational Capitalism in East and Southeast Asia, 1850s–1930s", *Journal of Asian Studies* 74(1): 129–151.

Hu, Shaodong and Chen Siyan. 2013. "The Co-Evolution between Remittance Business for Overseas Chinese and Institutions: The Case of Chaoshan Region During 1860–1949", *Frontiers of Business Research in China* 7(1): 138–164.

Liu, Hong and Gregor Benton. 2016. "The Qiaopi Trade and Its Role in Modern China and the Chinese Diaspora: Toward an Alternative Explanation of 'Transnational Capitalism' ", *Journal of Asian Studies* 75(3): 575–594.

Peterson, Glen. 2012. *Overseas Chinese in the People's Republic of China*, London: Routledge.

Shiroyama, Tomoko. 2008. *China During the Great Depression: Market, State, and the World Economy, 1929–1937*, Cambridge, MA: Harvard University Asia Center.

1 Entangled loyalties

Qiaopi, Chinese community structures, and the state in Southeast Asia

Els van Dongen

Introduction

Dialect, region, and lineage – these were the markers of belonging around which both Chinese emigrant communities and the *qiaopi* trade were organized. However, these local bases of identification could exist in tension with nationalist attachments, especially when crisis struck. The conflict between local and national principles of belonging in Chinese communities is reflected in the story of *qiaopi*, which concerns the local and regional bases of its operation channels, the state's efforts to incorporate these channels into state institutions such as banks and post offices, and the resistance against these efforts. This chapter discusses *qiaopi* through the lens of the main features of Chinese migration, the structure of Chinese community organizations, and the role of the state in their shaping and reshaping with a focus on Southeast Asia. The "state" in this context does not only include the sending state of China, but also the policies affecting Chinese communities before and under colonial rule and following decolonization in Southeast Asia.

Qiaopi trade developed in the nineteenth century, which was the era that witnessed mass migration and rapid developments in technology, communication, and transport. However, because *qiaopi* relied on the structural bases that were shaped in the long history of Chinese trade and emigration, and because some merchants were already engaged in the trade in the eighteenth century, a *longue durée* approach is required. This approach includes the period of early traders in Southeast Asia before the period of mass migration, as well as the period of colonial rule in the region. It also includes the period following state incorporation of *qiaopi* institutions in the mid-twentieth century, namely that of decolonization and the Cold War. Finally, it includes the period of economic reform and renewed Sino-Southeast Asian ties since the 1970s, which created the conditions for the interest in *qiaopi* in the People's Republic of China (PRC). Rather than understanding Chinese community formation and *qiaopi* channels as "traditional" markers that made room for the "modern" state, this chapter looks at the state *in* Chinese community organizations: their transformation was very much shaped by various political actors long before efforts were made to incorporate the *qiaopi* trade channels into state institutions. Similarly, the state played a central part in reviving these community forms after the Cold War.

The state and regional and local forms of community are hence not opposites, but manifestations of competing, co-existing, and entangled foci of loyalty on a wide-ranging spectrum. Nationalism, state building, and nation building are not linear processes, but complex processes of interaction in which state and nation do not necessarily coincide. The transition from empire to nation-state in Southeast Asia was equally fluid, as Anthony Reid has captured poignantly in the term "imperial alchemy", or the fact that "in essence, imperial constructs were declared to be nation-states" (Reid 2010, 1). The *qiaopi* system evolved against the background of interactions with long-existing forms of community arrangement that were transformed in the process, but that persisted nevertheless. The story of Chinese community forms, and, consequently, the story of *qiaopi* that was based on the same configurations, is a story of adaptation and resilience, one of histories that need to be "rescued" from the nation-state.

When discussing the long-term history of the Chinese presence in Southeast Asia in view of the function of the *qiaopi* trade, we first need to revisit the scholarship on Chinese business activities in Southeast Asia. Much of this has paid attention to the "business success" of the ethnic Chinese in Southeast Asia, with explanations for this "success" centring around Confucianism, ethnic entrepreneurship, capitalism, and networks (Suryadinata 2007a, 41–46). Analogous to Max Weber's argument in *The Protestant Ethic and the Spirit of Capitalism* (1905), the Confucian explanation was especially popular during the 1980s. With the rise of Japan and the "Mini-dragons" (Hong Kong, Singapore, South Korea, and Taiwan), scholars revised modernization theories that perceived of Confucianism as a "traditional" obstacle to "modernity" and development. For example, in *The Spirit of Capitalism*, Gordon Redding (1990) discussed Chinese capitalism as a distinct mode of development in which Confucian culture and familism were central.[1] Whereas this Confucian approach would emphasize the significance of the family, or values such as trust and responsibility, other works would highlight ethnic aspects, relations (*guanxi*), and networks, as for example Hamilton (1996), or as popularized in notions such as "global tribes" and "bamboo networks".

In response to this essentialist understanding of Chinese business practices, others have pointed at the importance of economic and other structural components in Chinese business success. Economist Linda Lim has dismissed notions of ethnic networks in favour of the internationalization of markets and industrialization as explanatory factors (Lim 1983). Other scholars have also argued for the inclusion of economic and sociopolitical elements to debunk simplistic understandings of cultural capitalism and ethnic entrepreneurship (Mackie 1992; Menkhoff and Gerke 2002; Gomez and Hsiao 2004). Yan Qinghuang [Yen Ching-hwang] has argued that both cultural and structural explanations have their limitations. Whereas the former lead to empty talk about "Confucian values" without taking into account the historical variations in these values, or how this connects to economic and political developments, the latter is too narrow-minded and discards cultural developments (Yan 2005, 37–38).

For our purposes, it is worthwhile to note that scholars of early Chinese traders in Southeast Asia, such as Philip Curtin (1984) or Wen-ching Chang and

Eric Tagliacozzo (2011) have referred to the concept of "trade diaspora" or networks of merchants who operated as "cross-cultural brokers". While these networks were certainly present and highly significant in trade and *qiaopi*, it is essential to rethink them as not based on "culture" or "ethnicity" in an abstract sense, but as shaped by the very markers of belonging of dialect, region, and lineage. "Ethnicity" in this context is a multi-layered concept that not only implies in-group competition, but also different levels of belonging. In addition, we also need to take into account the connection between these networks and the hometowns (*qiaoxiang*), which is also critical for our understanding of *qiaopi* (Liu 1998; Douw *et al.* 1999; Yow 2005).

The emphasis on "Confucianism" also fails to acknowledge the complex processes of identity negotiation that took place as Chinese traders remained connected to the hometown and set up families in Southeast Asia. The ideal "cross-cultural brokers" were those who had a foot in both Chinese and Southeast Asian societies – the so-called intermediate communities. Since these communities mostly had a high socio-economic status, this is also a differentiating feature that prevents us from understanding networks in any essentialized manner. Even though *qiaopi* researchers themselves note the importance of "trust" in the *qiaopi* trade, this is a highly contextualized form of trust. It was based on the trust between the emigrant and the family back home, between the emigrant and the remittance office, and between the remittance office and the sender of the *qiaopi* (Wang Weizhong 2009, 50–55). Trust in this context was also not a static concept, for it evolved from a personalized to a more systematized form (Chapter 5 in this book). As the following sections demonstrate, belonging and loyalty were multi-faceted. With these notes in mind, let us turn to the early Chinese traders, their networks, and their community organizations.

The long-term view: the early traders

Understanding Chinese community formation and the principles behind *qiaopi* requires a *longue durée* approach. We naturally turn to Chinese migration to Southeast Asia for this purpose because due to geographical proximity and trading activities, Sino-Southeast interaction goes back many centuries. Even today, around 75 per cent of the Chinese overseas – with official estimates of a total Chinese overseas population as high as 60 million in 2014 – still resides in Southeast Asia (Suryadinata 2007a; Zhang 2014).[2] Today, the largest number of ethnic Chinese in Southeast Asia can be found in the countries of Indonesia (7.7 million), Thailand (7.1 million), and Malaysia (6.3 million), according to 2007 estimates by Li and Li (2011). The smallest ethnic Chinese communities of Southeast Asia reside in Laos, Cambodia, and Brunei. Singapore is a unique case because it is the only country outside of China where the ethnic Chinese constitute the majority of the population (2.7 million Chinese in 2007) (Li and Li 2011).

Although trade between China and the "Southern Seas" (*nanyang*) goes back two millennia, it was only with the expansion of this trade in the thirteenth century that Chinese communities developed in the region (Zhu 2008; Wade

2009).[3] In the early fifteenth century, Zheng He's expeditions (1405–1433) not only reached Southeast Asia, but also South and Western Asia and the East Coast of Africa. Anthony Reid (1988, 1993) has famously referred to the period between the mid-fifteenth and the seventeenth century as the "age of commerce" in Southeast Asia, with the emergence of port cities and commerce fuelling broader economic, political, social, and cultural transitions.[4] From then onwards, state support for maritime trade and state maritime power declined, but trade was legalized in the sixteenth century (to be banned again during the Qing dynasty (1644–1911)), after which private junk trade increased. The rise of coastal ports for junk traders in Cochinchina led to an increase in emigration from South China (Wade 2009; Wang Gungwu 2009). South China, in this context, the land of the Yue, was in many ways closer to Southeast Asia, which is why Carolyn Cartier (2001) has referred to South China as a "transboundary cultural economy" in her account of Chinese emigration.[5]

Histories of trade relations and the emergence of Chinese communities vary across Southeast Asia. For example, tributary relations between China and Siam allegedly go back to the Tang dynasty (618–907 AD). Already during the seventeenth century AD, the Chinese in Siam had become economically visible as a consequence of the junk trade between China and the Nanyang. Apart from merchants and traders, the Chinese community in Ayutthaya consisted of scholars-officials, artisans, actors, doctors, and pig breeders (Skinner 1957; Tong 2010). In Malaya, Chinese settled as early as the fifteenth century under the Melaka Sultanate. From the end of the eighteenth century, they primarily engaged in urban port trade, mining, and rural agriculture (Purcell 1948).[6] As for Singapore, archaeological evidence has revealed trading links between China and Singapore during the fourteenth century, when Singapore was known as Temasek (Pan 1998). Interactions between China and Vietnam ostensibly go back to the Zhou dynasty (1046–256 BC). During the Qin dynasty (221–206 BC), Northern Vietnam was controlled by Chinese dynasties, and this remained the case for the following ten centuries (Khanh 1993). Trade between China and the kingdoms of Cambodia can be traced back to the third to sixth century AD. The Chinese community was significant in Pnom Penh since the fifteenth century and evidence suggests that it was dominant in trade before the French occupation of Cochinchina in 1859 (Willmott 1967). Apart from monopoly farming, the Chinese worked in agriculture, pepper cultivation, market gardening, and trade (Skinner 1996).

Dialect and region, and below that sub-dialect and sub-region, were crucial structural principles of Chinese overseas communities, as they were in the Chinese areas where *qiaopi* trade emerged. Chinese belonging to the five main Chinese dialect groups (Hokkien, Cantonese, Teochiu (Teochow), Hakka, and Hainanese) had been engaging in specific trades long before the start of mass migration during the mid-nineteenth century. Those belonging to the Hokkien group had been maritime traders since the 1500s, with destinations including the island of Taiwan, the Philippines, Java, Malaya, Borneo, and Siam. Many speakers of Cantonese were manufacturers and traders and could be found in great numbers in Malaya. The Teochiu (Teochow) group, many of whom went to

Thailand, was known for shipbuilding, but they also worked on plantations and were rice traders. Hakka speakers, known for mining, forestry, and agriculture, migrated to Malaya (West Borneo) and Singapore (Wang 1991; McKeown 2010). Already during the Song (960–1279) and Yuan (1279–1368) dynasties, Hokkien trading groups emerged. During the Ming (1368–1644) and Qing dynasties, Zhangzhou and Quanzhou in Fujian province, and later Xiamen, also in Fujian province, became central nodes of the Hokkien trade (Zhuang 2006, 223). Vast Chinese trading networks were formed from the thirteenth century onwards (Zhuang and Liu 2009, 3). The early Hokkien traders mostly conducted private trade and were part of a regional business network that spanned Korea, Kyushu, Taiwan, and Manila. Various principles underlay these networks, ranging from family ties, native places, lineages, guilds, and personal ties (Chin 2010). Other forms of business associations also already came into existence as the Chinese became involved in mining and plantation labour in Southeast Asia. A well-known example concerns the *kongsis* of Borneo, also found in Riau, Bangka, and Johor, a form of partnership between labourers, headmen, and those who provided capital (Zhuang and Liu 2009, 92–93).

Chinese migrants were mostly male bachelors and temporary "sojourners". Not having the intent to settle, but rather using migration as an economic strategy to support the family, *qiaopi* played a key part in the preservation of the family as an economic unit. It was common for these Chinese migrants to marry local wives, whilst at the same time maintaining a family in their place of origin, leading to a system known as the dual family system. In China, as in emigrant communities, social status was connected to family size, with larger families consisting of husband and wife, concubines in the hometown and place of settlement, and other kin of the husband. All members of the joint family were economically interdependent. The adoption of sons to assist in business and to increase male offspring was a common practice. Remittances were central in the preservation of the family: part of the money was saved for the marriage of the emigrant in the hometown; it would also be used for his burial in the hometown upon return. In addition, remittances were used for household expenditures (Chen 1978). However, remittances were also commonly recycled as investment capital and spent for commercial purposes (Chapters 3 and 8 in this book).

With the dual family system, throughout Southeast Asia, intermediate communities such as the *mestizos*, *peranakans*, and *babas*[7] gradually emerged through intermarriages between Chinese men and local women. It witnessed stable development in the seventeenth and eighteenth centuries (Skinner 1996). Members of these intermediate communities often acted as middlemen in the revenue farming policies of colonial powers, which established themselves in Southeast Asia as early as the sixteenth century. In the system of indirect rule that was the *kapitan* system, those with prestige, leadership skills, and wealth were chosen to represent the Chinese community and to act as their leaders and representatives vis-à-vis local rulers (Li 2003, 315). As revenue farmers, Chinese gained licences to operate as tax collectors for Chinese communities for products and services such as opium, spirits, gambling, and pawnshops. Farming companies engaged in competitive bidding to collect the taxes, which they kept for themselves in exchange for payment to the government (Skinner 1996). The intermediate communities, having a foot in both Chinese and local cultures, managed to fill occupational niches and to secure their economic position through tax farming under colonial rule.

In addition to being sojourners who did not receive the support of the Chinese empire – Wang Gungwu has referred to the Hokkien traders as "merchants without empires" – the Chinese were also subject to discrimination under colonial rule (Wang 1991, 79–101). In the Spanish, Dutch, British, and French colonies in Southeast Asia, Chinese were subjected to racial categorization and the exclusion from certain professions. In the Dutch East Indies, a system of collaboration between the Dutch and Chinese emerged, but already in 1740, a Chinese massacre occurred in Batavia, followed by attacks against ethnic Chinese in Java in the following years. In the 1850s, Chinese were categorized as "Foreign Orientals" distinct from both natives and Europeans, a categorization that would remain in place until the Second World War (Govaars 2005). In the Philippines, Spanish rulers made a distinction between ethnic Chinese, *mestizos*, and natives or *indios*, with the term *mestizo* becoming submerged under the "Filipino" nation towards the end of Spanish rule (Hau 2014). Here, already in 1603, a Chinese massacre took place, followed by several other attempts to curb Chinese influence. In addition, Chinese were segregated from other inhabitants and were charged taxes and residence permit fees (Zhu 2008, 35–38). Because of these policies, it became all the more relevant for Chinese communities to preserve ties with their hometowns.

The *peranakans* of Java only consisted of about 1–2 per cent of the population (around 100,000 in 1810 and 250,000 in 1890), but their economic and social status was relatively high. Although the *mestizos* in the Philippines were more numerous (4.8 per cent or 120,000 by 1810 and 5.2 per cent or 290,000 in 1890), their status was overall lower (Chirot and Reid 1997, 46). The *babas* or "Straits-born Chinese" were originally also a small group. Under the British, many *babas* migrated from Melaka to Penang and Singapore, where they grew in numbers to about 9–10 per cent of the total population of the Straits Settlements (Skinner 1996). Even though these intermediate communities were relatively small, their high socio-economic status and dominance in commerce and trade made them subject to being branded as "essential outsiders" (Chirot and Reid 1997). Several of the "classic" studies on the ethnic Chinese in Southeast Asian countries pay much attention to this aspect of their elevated socio-economic status, such as, for example Edgar Wickberg (1965) for the Philippines, and William Willmott (1967) for Cambodia.

In the various countries of Southeast Asia, Chinese managed to fill existing economic niches and to negotiate their position within the colonial or local ruling systems. They were not only active in business, trade, agriculture, and handicraft, but they also undertook mining. In trade, they sold local products to foreign traders and delivered Chinese and European products to local markets. They also set up their own shipping companies to transport goods (Yan 2006, 5). With colonial expansion in Southeast Asia and rising demand in Europe for

Southeast Asian products, Chinese gradually replaced existing traders and worked in mines and on plantations to meet demands for rubber, tobacco, coffee, sugar cane, and other products.

Apart from transformations in the global economy and the system of colonial rule that created the conditions for them to operate as tax farmers and traders, Chinese community forms also supported Chinese traders in organizing these activities. In the early Chinese migrant communities, temples functioned as the centre of political, business, and cultural life (Li 2003, 660). The early Fujian clan associations (*zongqinhui*) were based on what Yan Qinghuang [Yen Ching-hwang] calls "localized lineage", a combination of bloodline, place, and dialect. These were social and cultural bodies that, apart from mutual aid and protection, served to preserve generational continuity and foster traditional values such as virtue and piety. They also served to celebrate Chinese festivals and to arrange marriages and promote education within the clan (Yan 2006, 2–3). Temples and shrines for ancestors and gods for protection remained central in this early community formation. Already in the eighteenth century, private schools (*sishu*) appeared in Chinese overseas communities, as for example in Batavia (Wu 2004, 191).

More formalized clan organizations (*shizonghui/shigonghui*) materialized in the early nineteenth century. Their functions included mutual protection and aid, as for example those based on the "five big surnames" in Penang, all of which originated from a single county in Southern Fujian (Yan 2006, 2–3). Lineage organizations in the Philippines, for example, go back to the late Qing dynasty and consisted of both single surname and combined surname organizations for those surnames that were rare. This allowed them to join forces with other surname groups and to gain influence (Zeng 2004, 111). Some of these clan organizations are associated with the early *qiaopi* trade, such as the Chen clan in Penang, which set up a shop that also undertook remittance trade as early as 1757 (Chen 2009, 113).

The nineteenth century also saw the emergence of more formal native place organizations (*huiguan*). Some, such as the Jiaying *huiguan* and the Zhongshan *huiguan* in Penang, go back to the early nineteenth century. Others were founded after the large-scale migration in the second half of the nineteenth century, especially after the 1870s, as discussed below (Li 2003, 660–661). The *huiguan* were similar in function to the clan associations, but instead of honouring lineage ancestors or those gods of the protected lineages, they honoured regional deities (Yan 2006, 3–4). The make-up of the *huiguan* was complex. For example, *tongxiang* or "native place" could mean that members were from the same village, town, district, prefecture, or even province, or that dialect and clan lines intersected with these markers. In Southeast Asia, and particularly in Singapore, "bang" arranged around clan, native place, and dialect were prominent (Wu 2004, 186–187; Zeng 2004, 109). These markers of belonging were also crucial in the set-up of the *qiaopi* trade.

Mass migration and the development of *qiaopi*

Against this background of the existence of networks based on personal, family, and community ties along the intersecting lines of dialect, region, and lineage, the *qiaopi* trade developed in the mid-nineteenth century. This was the period of large-scale emigration from China that we need to understand in the context of the integration of Southeast Asia into a global trade system. It is estimated that one and a half million Chinese had reached Southeast Asia by the mid-nineteenth century, a number that would rise until about five million by the 1920s (Zhuang and Liu 2009, 4). In addition, vast developments in transportation and communication technology marked this period. Between the 1870s and the 1920s, the emergence of trans-oceanic shipping altered the face of migration. Also in the 1870s, the Universal Postal Union was set up. It replaced the earlier bilateral postal treaties between states and regulated and standardized international mailing rates, procedures, and services.

With the integration of Southeast Asia into a global trade system – in which the Treaty of Nanking (1842) was a significant turning point – Chinese labourers also arrived in Southeast Asia, where they worked in mines or on plantations. When Hong Kong became a British colony, the treaty ports of Xiamen (Amoy) and Shantou (Swatow) became key nodes of Chinese labour migration (McKeown 1999). As Victor Purcell (1948) notes, an important change occurred in the region when Penang was founded in 1786 and Singapore in 1819. Hong Kong also came to play a vital part in financial transactions between Southeast Asia and South China, with remittances passing through the Hong Kong exchange market (Chapter 3 in this book). Amidst these changes, during the late Qing, remittances from Chinese overseas became a crucial economic pillar in the *qiaoxiang* areas that served to balance foreign trade deficits (Zhuang and Liu 2009, 202).

The period between the mid-nineteenth and early twentieth century also saw the rise of the coolie trade, with labourers being shipped from China to Southeast Asia and the New World. Following the signing of treaties with foreign powers, the sea bans (*haijin*) of the Qing government were reversed, and large numbers of contract labourers or coolies filled the labour shortage that followed the abolishment of slavery. In Southeast Asia, recruited through special "heads" in port cities such as Macau, they worked in mines and on plantations. The contract specified the duration of the work, the salary, and the voluntary nature of the engagement. However, in practice, many stayed on because of accumulated gambling, drinking, and smoking debts, because they received very little salary, or because they had been forced or tricked into the agreement. For coolies destined for Southeast Asia, Singapore was a central collection point (Wu 2004, 9–10, 12–13). These newly arrived communities had different needs from the long-established intermediate communities. As opposed to previous migrants from the *qiaoxiang* in South China, these migrants had travelled from port cities such as Macau, Canton, and Hong Kong (Li 2003, 187).

During this period, with mass migration, new community forms or native place organizations (*huiguan*) for mutual assistance and ancestor worship expanded. The *huiguan*, which became numerous during the mid-nineteenth century, were originally based on the intersection of different "segments", namely dialect, locality, and surname. Vertically, these consisted of different levels of identification, from provincial up to local levels. Horizontally, they could spread out across provinces, such as in the case of surnames (Crissman 1967). Within dialect groups, organizations around large temples for ancestor worship could further be divided based on annual and triennial ceremonies or based on local grouping in the homeland (Freedman 1960). These arrangements were an adaptation of lineage and place associations in Ming China based on the various "human ecologies" of the respective new environments (Kuhn 2008). According to Zeng Shaocong, the main difference between these traditional organizations in China and those in Chinese overseas communities was that the former were strictly formed based on administrative divisions, whereas the latter also adjusted themselves to different natural regions (Zeng 2004, 107, 160). In general, then, both vertically and horizontally, community formats were multi-faceted, and this would also be reflected in the make-up of the *qiaopi* trade channels.

Organizations based on specific trades and crafts (*hang*), such as those for masons, carpenters, or goldsmiths, also had a long history in Chinese emigrant communities. More formalized trading organizations (*hanghui zuzhi*), however, sprang up in the nineteenth century, such as for example the *Beichenghang* in Singapore, founded in 1868. In the twentieth century, more Western-style guild organizations (*tongye gonghui*) emerged. As opposed to the traditional organizations, these newer types were broader in orientation and went beyond the interests of one specific trade (Li 2003, 666–667). Trading guilds functioned as overarching bodies for different types of other organizations, such as *huiguan* and trade organizations. In Singapore, trading guilds provided mutual aid, regulated apprentice training and wages, and established order in their respective trades. Well-known guilds were the Gambier and Pepper Society and the Sago Dealers' and Pineapple Preservers' guilds (Freedman 1960).

In colonial Southeast Asia, trading organizations and secret societies also had a wide range of functions. Secret societies were established in Singapore in the early nineteenth century and had members in the ten thousands. The *Tiandihui* (Society for Heaven and Earth) was managed along dialect lines, with an officer representing the Hokkien, Hakka, Teochiu (Teochow), and Cantonese communities (Freedman 1960). Apart from serving to protect and control the Chinese, they also regulated economic activities and smoking, drinking, and gambling practices under colonial governments (Zeng 2004, 115). Other types of organizations included money loan associations for short-term credit and friendly societies that had similar mutual aid functions as the native place organizations (Freedman 1960). Charity organizations (*cishan shetuan*) provided medical care, poverty relief, set up schools, and promoted religion and cultural activities (Wu 2004, 188).

Community composition along the lines of dialect groups overlapped to some extent with the grouping of economic interests (Freedman 1960). This was reflected in the *qiaopi* trade, where dialect groups also formed a central principle or arrangement. The corporate arrangement of the *qiaopiju* was intertwined with kinship loyalties in that some of the actors in the early *qiaopi* trade, such as the *shuike* or couriers, could work independently and relied on their networks instead. Here, the importance of *qiaoxiang* ties is revealed in the fact that newly arrived migrants would rely on couriers from the same hometown (Chapters 2 and 3). The *qiaopiju* would be arranged based on dialect groups. For example, in Singapore, in 1891, there were sixteen *shuike* with no fixed address in addition to officially ran *qiaopiju* shaped around the main dialect groups of Hokkien, Teochiunese (Teochownese), Hainanese, Cantonese, and Hakka. Each of the dialect groups would then manage a number of offices based on the needs of that respective dialect group. In early twentieth-century Batavia, for example, the Fujian "bang" had over ten different *qiaopiju* (Xu 2007, 182, 249). The *huiguan*, trade associations, guilds, and temples also played a part in the collection of remittances. In smaller Chinese communities, such as for example in Laos, *qiaopi* would often be gathered and go through places with larger and long-standing Chinese communities, such as Vietnam and Thailand, and from there to China, reflecting the transnational character of the system (Xu 2007, 138).

It is difficult to draw a clear line between the reliance of *qiaopi* traders on personalized networks and the emergence of remittance offices as main channels in the trade. Rather than operating *ex nihilo*, these offices transformed and incorporated previously existing practices (Liu and Benton 2016). The *shuike* were originally private traders who exchanged goods produced in China, such as silk and porcelain, with foreign goods. Gradually, they began to carry letters from the Chinese overseas back to their hometowns. Especially after the 1870s, with developments in transport and communication, *qiaopiju* served to handle the larger volume and frequency of *qiaopi*. However, rather than a simple standardization of practices, networks based on ties of belonging could intersect with these developments. In South China, for example, at the turn of the century, due to the increase in mail from Southeast Asia and the variation in destinations, a mail system consisting of four main areas was set up in Southern Fujian.

These *qiaopi* offices would often safeguard their business environment through native place ties (*xiangyi de guanxi*). Four big "networks" with at their centre Xiamen, Fuzhou, Xinghua, and Minxi emerged as "regional systems" (*diyu tixi*) in the Fujian *qiaopi* trade. Of these four "systems", the Xiamen system was the eldest and largest in Fujian's *qiaopi* history (Chen 2009, 114; Wang Dongxu 2009, 103–104). To take some examples from Southeast Asia that demonstrate the lack of a clear transition in practices, in Indonesia, individual *shuike* already carried *qiaopi* goods during the early nineteenth century, whilst *qiaopi* offices were numerous during the early twentieth century. In Myanmar, *shuike* were still quite vibrant in the 1920s and 1930s, but they operated in tandem with the already established *qiaopi* offices (Xu 2007, 245, 271).

With the British use of postal operations in Bangkok, Hong Kong, Singapore and elsewhere in 1867, the Chinese also started to rely on postal services to send *qiaopi* (Xu 2007, 58). Gradually, the state would increase its control of the *qiaopi* trade and challenge the long-standing organizational structures behind it. However, at the same time, there was also resistance against these efforts, as manifested in the Singapore riots following the foundation of the Chinese Sub-Post Office in 1876 (Xu 2007, 183). By the early twentieth century, the *qiaopi* trade relied on remittance offices, banks, and post offices in a complex system of interaction. Even though the control of the state increased, there is no clear and fixed linear transition to state control, a process that also differed across localities in China and across the Chinese communities in the various countries of Southeast Asia. Overall, however, political changes of a national, regional, and global nature were crucial in shaping this transition to the state overseeing the sending of remittances.

The grip of the state and the transnational imagination

Whereas the old voluntary community forms of the ethnic Chinese were local in nature and served the needs of the Chinese in their countries of destination, during the first decades of the twentieth century, in the context of growing "transnational and intra-regional activities", but also due to the rise of nationalism, these organizations moved beyond the local (Liu 2002, 50). However, the tension between local affiliation and national affinity remained. For example, around the turn of the century, Chambers of Commerce became the overarching bodies for the different types of existing community organizations in Southeast Asia. In 1904, Chinese Chambers of Commerce (*Zhonghua zongshanghui*) were set up in Kuala Lumpur, Selangor, and Manila, followed by Singapore in 1906. They served to protect the economic interests of the Chinese traders against colonial policies, liaise with Chinese communities, and act as bridges between the Qing government and the British colonial government. Chambers of Commerce could cooperate at transnational level or mobilize the existing community organizations for various purposes (Wu 2004, 188–189). It was in these Chambers of Commerce that the *shuike* and *qiaopiju* owners were key actors, not only in China but also in the Chinese communities of Southeast Asia. In the overseas communities, wealth translated into political power, and it was common practice to accumulate leadership positions in various bodies.

Since the mid-nineteenth century, overseas community leaders and businessmen had supported the construction of Chinese schools through remittances. During this period, however, schools had remained connected to the respective dialect and regional make-up of the community. During the late nineteenth century, new-style schools emerged in overseas Chinese communities, with the strongest development in Singapore, Malaya, and Indonesia (Wu 2004, 191). At the turn of the century, schools developed in tandem with political developments in China. Reformer Kang Youwei's advocacy of reform and the restoration of the emperor received much support among conservative elites in the Nanyang. The *Baohuanghui* (Protect the Emperor Society) also had a branch in Singapore. The revolutionary leader Sun Yat-sen established a branch of the *Tongmenghui* (Revolutionary Alliance) in Singapore in 1906 and visited it on several occasions in the years that followed. Several revolutionary newspapers also circulated in Singapore, such as the *Zhongxing ribao* (Resurgence Daily) (Zhu 2008, 153). Reformers and revolutionaries sought to weaken the "bang" divisions and unite the Chinese overseas behind their cause. After the 1911 revolution, the connection between politics and education became even stronger. Instead of being linked to dialect groups, the schools now became Chinese-language schools. For example, in Singapore, under the influence of the famous entrepreneur, philanthropist, and educator Lim Boon Keng, Fujianese schools gradually exchanged the Hokkien dialect (*fangyan*) for Chinese language (*huayu*) education (Yan 2006, 13–14).

Other circumstances also spurred this "re-Sinicization" process of cultural and political identification with China. Since the mid-nineteenth century, the arrival of new Chinese migrants from China had led to the formation of communities unlike the intermediate communities as discussed above. The rise of "pure" Chinese communities (with Chinese men now marrying Chinese instead of local women), in combination with the end of the revenue system, led to the decline of *mestizos* and *babas* in particular, with only the *peranakans* retaining their cultural identity (Skinner 1996). In addition, with developments in communication and transport since the 1870s, such as ocean steamers, contact between Chinese communities in Southeast Asia and Mainland China became more frequent (Li 2003, 685). *Qiaopi* is also part of this larger narrative of the waxing and waning of Sino-Southeast Asian ties and negotiation processes about Chinese identity.

In Indonesia, in the early twentieth century, with the immigration of Chinese women and the rise of nationalism, *totok* or "pure" Chinese communities with Chinese schools and newspapers emerged. The Tiong Hoa Hwee Koan (*Zhonghua huiguan*) was also founded in 1900. This community organization not only promoted Chinese-language education through modern schooling, but it was also connected to Chinese newspapers and the promotion of Confucian values (Li 2003, 669). Ming Govaars (2005) argues that this early process of "resinification" received impulses from Mainland China, Indonesian society, and colonial policies. In Siam, during the early twentieth century, the "Chinese problem" was formed with a general strike against the Chinese in 1910, the arrival of anti-Sinicism under King Rama VI, and the founding of Chinese schools, newspapers, and organizations (Skinner 1957, 155). This period, which saw massive immigration during the 1920s and the rise of the rice merchants, was followed by economic nationalist policies, political repression, and cultural assimilation, such as the "Thai-ification" of Chinese schools. In Malaya, during the early twentieth century, like elsewhere in Southeast Asia, nationalism flourished and Chinese schools emerged. The *kapitan* system was dismantled and, instead, merchant-entrepreneurs headed community organizations (Pan 1998).

Nationalist sentiment reached its peak around the 1911 Revolution and again following the Mukden Incident and the Japanese occupation of Northeast China in 1931. The latter spurred the Nanjing government to mobilize the Chinese overseas through policies (Zhuang and Liu 2009, 182). However, even during the early twentieth century, when nationalism was on the rise, it did not simply replace local identification. *Qiaokan*, magazines and newspapers that were published in the *qiaoxiang* areas but that circulated to Chinese communities globally since the 1880s, reflect the co-existence and entanglement of local affinity modes and the emergence of pan-nationalist principles. One could also argue that the nationalist sentiment that surged during the 1920s and 1930s was but an extension of the strong "clan consciousness" in Chinese culture (Zhuang and Liu 2009, 189). Relevant to note, however, is the fact that the *qiaopi* trade contributed to the strengthening of local and national affinity by using the *qiaokan* as a vehicle for advertisements. For example, already in the years after a regular ocean cruiser line was established between Hong Kong and Singapore in the 1840s, *shuike* would place business advertisements to attract remittances in Chinese newspapers when they returned to China (Xu 2007, 181). Through newspapers and *qiaokan*, it was these business interests that would become directly connected to questions of political and cultural affinity in the early twentieth century, both locally and nationally. Even though the *qiaokan* continued a tradition of local printing culture, in times of crisis, they could contribute to the formation of nationalist sentiment (Hsu 2000; Liu and Benton 2016).

This entanglement of local and national identification and forms of organization is reflected in the evolution of the *qiaopi* trade during the early twentieth century, during which it developed steadily. In Bangkok, for example, over fifty remittance offices were registered, mostly operated by members of the Teochiu (Teochow), Hakka, and Hainanese dialect groups. In addition to these, however, banks and post offices also handled remittances from Chinese communities. State efforts to control the *qiaopi* trade were hence already manifest, but older channels based on sub-divisions within communities continued to operate alongside these state institutions. Following Guangxu's 1896 edict and the signing of postal treaties with various countries that made the tariffs of the Universal Postal Union applicable within China, the Imperial Postal Administration (*Da Qing youzheng*) was set up. In 1907, in the Chinese business area of Bangkok, mail between Chinese communities and China was required to go through post office channels, but *shuike* were still operational. However, the latter were required to pay a postal fee per letter and were subjected to fines if they failed to do so (Xu 2007, 59–61).

In the early twentieth century, the *qiaopi* trade would also witness standardization. For example, in the Philippines, in the 1920s, both *qiaopi* from Manila to Fujian and *huipi* (return letters) from Fujian to Manila would be sent in a traditional Chinese-style envelope with a red banner on the left side of the envelope (Xu 2007, 159). In 1920s Myanmar, for *qiaopi* sent through postal offices, it was required to use a stamp for each individual *qiaopi* (Xu 2007, 274). Apart from postal offices, banks also became involved in the *qiaopi* trade. For example, the Quanzhou branch of the Bank of China was already engaged in managing remittances in the 1920s (Chen 2009, 112). *Qiaopi* traders, banks, and post offices co-existed in the space created by the Qing state's modernization efforts and international efforts to standardize trade and communication technology. In a later period, *qiaopi* offices of various dialect groups also organized themselves into trade associations to manage and regulate the trade in their "bangs", as for example in Singapore in the 1930s. There was even an overarching "Nanyang" association for Chinese remittance trade in 1940s Singapore (Xu 2007, 189). Overall, this was not a strict linear development: local, national, and regional loyalties intersected in various ways.

Qiaopi, the state, and community structures since the 1950s

A number of political events influenced not only the *qiaopi* trade and its institutions, but also the overall relation between Chinese and family members overseas, as well as the institutions of Chinese communities in Southeast Asia, during the second half of the twentieth century. These events included the foundation of the PRC in 1949 and the broader context of decolonization and the formation of the Cold War. Hitherto, the Chinese overseas had remained Chinese subjects; this had been institutionalized with the Nationality Law of 1909 based on *ius sanguinis*. After the Second World War, however, the ethnic Chinese in Southeast Asia were considered to be a liability – "the Chinese problem" became an area of concern in diplomatic relations between China and Southeast Asian countries (Fang 2001). Especially since the CCP rule on Mainland China in 1949, and in the context of decolonization and the Cold War, the Chinese in Southeast Asia were perceived of as a "Fifth Column" that would serve China's interests, first in an international Communist order, and later, after the Sino-Soviet split, in the form of an anti-Soviet bloc (Wang 1981, 279).

The "Chinese problem" not only implied that ethnic Chinese in Southeast Asia were politically disloyal to their host countries; they were also perceived as being wealthy and economically dominant, which connects back to the history of the Nanyang traders (Suryadinata 2007a, 4). In response to this, a vital shift occurred with the so-called Sino-Indonesian Dual Nationality Treaty of 1955. Since the earlier *ius sanguinis* had de facto led to dual citizenship under colonial rule, the 1955 Treaty ended this ambiguity. From now on, Chinese nationals abroad were asked to choose a nationality – no dual nationality was allowed. This disengagement with the ethnic Chinese in Southeast Asia continued throughout the 1960s and 1970s. During the Cultural Revolution (1966–1976), policies towards the Chinese overseas were discontinued and relatives of the Chinese overseas were persecuted because of "capitalist" associations (Fitzgerald 1972).

Against the background of these broader changes, the *qiaopi* trade declined during this period and traders made efforts to circumvent state channels. Whereas the Chinese state sought to incorporate existing channels and employ them as vehicles in class struggle (as it did for schools), the newly independent states of Southeast Asia sought to halt remittances as part of broader efforts at the protection of local economies and the economic, political, and cultural integration of Chinese communities. In the PRC, for example, by 1956, it was declared that the *qiaopi* trade had "entered socialism" (Chen 2009, 115). The degree to which the three "pillars" of the Chinese communities (native place organizations, schools, and newspapers) were being eradicated differed across the various countries of Southeast Asia, depending on factors such as the relative size of the community, its political system, and the relation with China (Wang 1981, 261–262; Suryadinata 2007a, 56). These reasons are, however, not fully explanatory; policies were also based on perceptions and prejudice.

In Indonesia, under Sukarno (1945–1967), the three pillars of the Chinese community – newspapers (apart from one, namely *Harian Indonesia*) and community organizations – were eradicated in an effort at cultural assimilation (Suryadinata 2007b). Even the celebration of Chinese cultural festivals was prohibited (Tong 2010). Economically, as in other countries, policies were designed to increase the share of the indigenous people in the economy, such as the *benteng* system during the 1950s. This system encouraged the development of indigenous Indonesian entrepreneurs and restricted certain goods to these entrepreneurs only (Suryadinata 2007b). In 1959, laws to prevent the ethnic Chinese from engaging in retail trade outside of cities were put in place. Both in 1960, following these laws, and in 1965, after the PKI-30 incident, an abortive coup d'état associated with the Indonesian Communist Party (PKI) that led to the killing of alleged Communists, many ethnic Chinese re-migrated from Indonesia (Suryadinata 2008). Under Suharto's New Order (1967–1998), the policy of total assimilation was continued and even strengthened.

Similarly, in Thailand, after the Second World War, economic nationalist policies and policies of political repression and cultural assimilation continued and were reinforced in the context of tensions in Southeast Asia (Skinner 1957; Pan 1998). Politically, in spite of some setbacks, such as the 1976 purge of Chinese students in response to the anti-government student movement, the Thai-Chinese also increasingly entered politics (Pan 1998). However, as opposed to elsewhere, and against Skinner's prediction of total assimilation (which he connects to the prospect of upward mobility in Thailand that was not present to the same extent in colonial societies) by the fourth generation, the pillars of the Chinese community were not eradicated through policies. Thailand did not forbid Chinese ethnic organizations and Chinese newspapers (Tong 2010). In addition, there was more openness towards citizenship because of *ius soli*. The third generation of ethnic Chinese (and even the second generation) was considered Thai (Suryadinata 2007b).

After the independence of Malaysia in 1957, questions of political representation and economic dominance continued to loom large. Following ethnic riots in 1969, Malaysia pursued its New Economic Policy (NEP) (1970–1990) to increase the equity participation of the Malays, followed by the New Development Policy (1991), which led to the rise of a Malay middle class. In addition, constitutionally, the Malays were privileged as *bumiputera* (sons of the soil) (Suryadinata 2007a). In the Philippines, under the Filipino First Policy (1948–1972) several industries were nationalized (Hau 2000). During the rule of President Ferdinand Marcos (1965–1986), the government actively pursued assimilation policies: Philippine Chinese schools became integrated into the national schools system, education was in the national language, and ethnic Chinese were encouraged to take up local citizenship (Suryadinata 2007b).

Against this broader background of the suppression of community arrangements, the *qiaopi* trade also became the subject of control. In the People's Republic of China, in 1952, the management of the *qiaopi* trade was formally transferred to the banking system (Wang Dongxu 2009, 104). Similar developments characterized the trade in Southeast Asia. In Thailand, for example, the foundation of the PRC was a turning point. After the Second World War, the trade had initially seen a revival, with 113 offices present in Bangkok in 1947, the majority of which were operated by the Teochiu (Teochew) dialect group. After the foundation of the PRC, the Thai state sought to control remittances, but *qiaopi* traders used private channels and continued the trade. As policies became tougher, however, some closed doors voluntarily. Government control was not the only reason for the decline of the trade in Thailand; *qiaopi* traders also faced financial losses because of the collapse of the Nationalist Government currency and fluctuating exchange rates for the Hong Kong dollar. Also, the Chinese government did promote remittances from overseas Chinese after 1949, but these were to be transferred through state banks (Xu 2007, 88–91, 95).

Overall, both in the People's Republic of China and in the newly independent states of Southeast Asia, the attempt to control the remittance trade was part of the assertion of an independent economic and political course following the foundation of the PRC and decolonization respectively, whilst the banking and postal sectors were also developed. This effort to control the trade was also part of broader efforts to shift the loyalty of the Chinese communities in Southeast Asia towards the host societies. With the 1955 Dual Nationality Treaty, ethnic Chinese were encouraged to take up local nationality and became *huaren* instead of *huaqiao*. This policy also meant a significant shift in the relation between these communities and their homeland: the idea was that they planted roots in the host societies and were sojourners no more. Apart from controlling the channels of the remittance trade, assimilation policies hence served to eradicate the very need to connect with the homeland. With community forms wiped out to different degrees, local identities could not be expressed as before. Under the influence of the state, the primary spectrum of loyalty during this period became that of the host societies.

Qiaopi research in the context of China's "rise"

With the beginning of the reform and opening-up period in the late 1970s, another transition emerged in the relation between the PRC and Chinese communities in Southeast Asia. During this period, diplomatic ties with Southeast Asian countries were resumed. The Chinese government once again reached out to the ethnic Chinese, which it no longer considered to be a liability. It particularly sought investment from the Chinese overseas. Due partly to better relations with countries in Southeast Asia that had large Chinese populations, and following the 1979 Sino-Vietnamese war specifically, the PRC promulgated the 1980

Nationality Law. This law reiterated the no dual nationality principle and served to clarify the status of the ethnic Chinese in Southeast Asia and elsewhere (Suryadinata 2007a, 99).

More recently, the long history of connectivity between China and Southeast Asia outlined in this chapter has been used under Xi Jinping to justify the "One Belt One Road" (*yidai yilu*) initiative in Southeast Asia ("Xin silu, xin mengxiang" 2014). Emphasis on the Maritime Silk Road resembles the academic discourse on "oceanic culture" that *qiaopi* researchers have put forward (Liu and Benton 2016). However, since the academic discourse emphasizes regional over national identity, it also partly challenges this official discourse. The latter neglects the contradictions involved in the promotion of trading routes because it necessarily involves questions of region, dialect, and locality. That local identity remains crucial in the interest around *qiaopi* is clear from the emergence of *qiaopi* journals in the emigrant areas since the 1990s. For example, in the inaugural journal of *Qiaopi Wenhua* (Qiaopi Culture) from Chaoshan, a major *qiaoxiang* area in Guangdong province, the editors referred to *qiaopi* as "the knot to preserve the love of blood thicker than water between the Chaoshan people overseas and the family" (Wu 2003, 8). Published by the Research Center on Chaoshan History and Culture, the journal considered Chaoshan *qiaopi* to be part of this local history and culture; *qiaopi* had "taken root in special soil" (Wu 2003, 8).

Following renewed Sino-Southeast Asian ties and global capitalism, several Southeast Asian countries manifested what has been described as a new wave of "re-Sinicization", a process that involves both China's soft power initiatives and the negotiation of Chinese identity on behalf of Chinese communities. Peter Katzenstein, for example, uses the term to refer to broad civilizational processes. These processes are not linear and one-directional and can involve both "re-Sinicization" and "de-Sinicization" (Katzenstein 2012, 7, 9). Hau (2014, 283) refers to "the revival of hitherto devalued, occluded, or repressed "Chineseness", and "the phenomenon of increasing visibility, acceptability, and self-assertiveness of ethnic Chinese in Southeast Asia and elsewhere". The paradigm of "re-Sinicization" today, as opposed to older notions of "Sinicization" that denote a one-way process of "Han-ization", hence refers to a process of interaction and negotiation regarding different understandings of "Chineseness".[8]

Hau (2014, 312) has emphasized that recent manifestations of "re-Sinicization" in countries such as the Philippines, Thailand, and Malaysia are multi-layered because they are not only mediated by different historical experiences (colonial and postcolonial policies), but also by the divided nature of "China" itself (geographically, politically, and culturally), as well as by market motives. In a recent work, Pál Nyíri and Danielle Tan (2017) also emphasize the centrality of capital in this process. Even though the PRC and Taiwan have long been involved in "re-Sinicization" efforts through policies towards the Chinese overseas, China's position in the region has altered vastly since economic reform in the late 1970s. Sino-Southeast Asian interaction received an extra impetus with the ASEAN-China Free Trade Area (ACFTA) that came into effect in 2010.

The PRC's use of soft power in the form of the promotion of Chinese culture and language is widely known. Since 2004, China has set up more than 500 Confucius Institutes and over 1,000 Confucius Classrooms under the aegis of the *hanban* of the Ministry of Education. However, local histories, practices, and sensitivities determine how Chinese culture is received in Southeast Asia. For example, in Indonesia, Confucius Institutes are called *Pusat Bahasa Mandarin* or Chinese Language Centres. Leo Suryadinata (2012, 5) argues that the name *Lembaga Khonghucu* or *Lembaga Confucius* might be avoided because of sensitivity and because Confucianism is an "organized religion" in Indonesia, which explains why it was "de-recognized" under Suharto. Specifically targeted at the ethnic Chinese are the policies towards the "Chinese overseas" (officially referred to as *huaqiao huaren*). They have received less attention in scholarship, even though China has a vast policy apparatus in place for "overseas Chinese work" (*qiaowu gongzuo*), with the Overseas Chinese Affairs Office (OCAO) being the main institution involved (Suryadinata 2017). In recent years, more efforts have been made to "go out" to the Chinese in Southeast Asia through OCAO visits to these community bodies. These organizations have continued to occupy a central place in China's efforts to reach out to the Chinese overseas. It is this re-engagement with the Chinese in Southeast Asia following the rehabilitation of the *guiqiao* (returnees) after the Cultural Revolution (1966–1976) that has created the conditions for the renewed interest in Chinese communities in the *Nanyang* among Chinese academics.

The hand of the state that was involved in the revival of *qiaopi* after 1978 through state channels was equally visible in the re-founding of the "pillars" of Chinese communities in Southeast Asia. Especially since the 1990s, many Southeast Asian countries have witnessed the arrival of large numbers of new migrants from the PRC. Whereas those Chinese who arrived in Southeast Asia before or after the Second World War were from South China and became *huaren* in the 1950s, the new migrants were from different places within China, were Chinese nationals, and many of them were highly educated. The interaction process between the old and new migrants formed a key component in the dynamics of "re-Sinicization". The influx of large numbers of new migrants in relation to smaller historical communities has particularly been the case in the countries of Mainland Southeast Asia. For example, in Laos, with the Greater Mekong Subregion (GMS) programme in 1992 that sought to create a North-South Economic Corridor (NSEC) in the region, Chinese investment in agriculture, hydropower, and mining increased, accompanied by a surge in Chinese migration (Chang 2013).

Even though Chinese community organizations once more played a pivotal part in ties between China and Southeast Asia, they became transformed under globalization. From the 1970s onward, although membership of Chinese community organizations can still be based on kinship or locality, it has become more open in practice. New types of organizations also emerged, such as those based on profession or alumni associations (Liu 1998). New migrants also set up their own organizations (Zhuang *et al.* 2010). Apart from the role of the state in this process, under the influence of globalization, local organizations became transnationalized and transformed into "global" organizations of various bents. For example, in 1983, the Global Guangxi Native Place Federation (*Shijie Guangxi Tongxiang Lianyihui*) was set up (Zeng 2004, 132). Membership hence became less restrictive and these organizations began to operate increasingly as a platform to facilitate business interactions and to connect ethnic Chinese globally through regular conventions (Liu 1998). At these conventions, ethnic Chinese from all over the world would identify with the "highest level" of lineage and place, namely that of the Chinese nation and Chinese culture rather than the more locally conceived ties of blood and place (Zeng 2004, 133).

In Indonesia, it was only after the fall of Suharto in 1998, during the *reformasi* era, that ethnic political parties and several Chinese dailies and schools emerged, even though the latter took the form of trilingual schools (Suryadinata 2012). In 2000, the official celebration of Chinese New Year or *Imlek* was reinstalled, after decades of restrictions (Hau 2014). In 2005, a "strategic partnership" between the Republic of Indonesia and the PRC was announced; in 2006, both elements of *ius sanguinis* and *ius soli* were integrated into citizenship law, but discussions on "indigenous Indonesian" identity continued (Suryadinata 2008). Against this background, and keeping in mind the presence of intermediate communities such as the *peranakans*, the culture that was re-emphasized under "re-Sinicization" impulses from Mainland China was the *totok* culture. For many *peranakans*, however, the "Chinese" culture that Beijing represents was not their Chinese culture.

In Malaysia, Chinese schools at the secondary level were not eradicated but they were subject to government control (Suryadinata 2007a). Those Chinese secondary schools that did not comply with the required monolingual education policy relied heavily on the Chinese community for funding and support (Raman and Tan 2015). Some private community-based university colleges, namely, the Southern College (*Nanyuan*), the Han Chiang College (*Hanjiang daxue xueyuan*), and the New Era College (*Xinjiyuan*), were established in the 1990s.[9] There has, however, also been resistance against renewed Chinese influence. The announcement that Xiamen University was to open a branch in Malaysia's Selangor state in September 2015 met with online criticism. The campus, estimated to cost around USD 200 million, was partially funded by a Malaysian-Chinese business leader (Ang 2013). The Chinese media referred to the Malaysia branch of Xiamen University as a matter of the "return" of history and "gratefulness" towards Malaysia because the founder of Xiamen University, Tan Kah Kee, had accumulated his fortunes in Malaya ("Xiada Malaixiya" 2014). Discussants on Facebook, however, criticized the profit motives and national interests behind the move ("Xiada haishi 'xiada'," Facebook, July 2015).[10] The case of Xiamen University reflects the different layers of negotiation regarding China's "rise" on behalf of Chinese communities in Southeast Asia – there are both opportunities and anxieties (Liu 2016).

In the Philippines, many Chinese *mestizos* who had become Filipinos, including high government officials and media figures, once again emphasized their Chinese heritage (Hau 2000; Hau 2014). As elsewhere, apart from the ethnic Chinese who are third and fourth generation descendants of immigrants, new Chinese migrants also found their way to the Philippines (Chang 2013). Here, the Chinese Filipinos have referred to new migrants as TDK (Tai Diok Ka) or "Chinese mainlanders" to distinguish themselves from these newer immigrants. In addition, renewed ties with China and increasing Chinese soft power have not been unproblematic, as the recent inflammation of the South China Sea conflict demonstrates (Hau 2014, 13).

Can we say that a pan-ethnic Chinese identity that unites ethnic Chinese beyond dialect, regional, and class divisions is on the rise? Jacobsen (2009, 69–70, 75) argues that the Chinese diaspora in Southeast Asia has been marked by "fluidity" and that the "disaggregation" of nations and states due to globalization has made room for "transnational ethnoscapes" – ethnic groups and networks that are "deterritorialized". Globalization leads to "an assertive resurgence of local identities thereby producing and increasing social and political awareness within ethnic groups". These local identities, however, are fragmented and always a response to specific historical experiences. In addition, although transnational forces play a role, the state remains a critical actor in the shaping of these identities. Identification processes take place against the background of the degree to which community pillars have been preserved, as well as against the background of the relation between the older immigrant communities and the new migrants.

Rather than understanding the rise of "ethnic" identity in Southeast Asia under global capitalism as a "deterritorialized" process, local histories and identities continue to determine the very understanding of what it means to be Chinese. In addition, the arrival of new migrants who are Chinese nationals and who are crucial actors in negotiations about Chinese identity in many Southeast Asian countries implies that "ethnic" identity can never be a "deterritorialized" process. Even though Chinese community organizations have been transformed, their transnational and global nature does not simply "replace" the local markers on which membership was initially based. Rather, these local markers have been reinterpreted in tandem with broader global developments. As noted for *huiguan*, the "native place" was never "fixed" in the first place – its scope could be one of different levels, ranging from the local to the provincial level. Similarly, the surname as a principle for community make-up did not have a clear regional connection and was combined with different levels of local affinity to demark its scope. The dialect group was always vast to begin with. The reinterpretation of locality under global capitalism is hence a reinterpretation of its meaning rooted in the very flexibility of "native place", dialect, or surname inherent in the set-up of community organizations.

In the various countries of Southeast Asia, understandings of "Chineseness" are mediated by historical experiences and the extent to which community structures were altered. The revival of community structures is hence not a monolithic process, but a multi-layered one that varies across countries and communities. The process of Chinese identity negotiation in Southeast Asia since the reform period is reflected in the renewed interest in *qiaopi* in the PRC. *Qiaopi* represents the ties between emigrants and the hometowns that are now once again emphasized following the period of ideological division of the Cold War. This process of the promotion of connectivity between China and Southeast Asia, be it in the form of "re-Sinicization" or the renewed interest in *qiaopi*, is largely driven by the Chinese state, economic investment, and the logic of capitalism. However, both in the case of "re-Sinicization" and the renewed *qiaopi* interest in the PRC, official narratives of "Chineseness" and transnational connectivity exist in tension with an emphasis on local and regional identity markers. *Qiaopi* researchers do not simply engage in *qiaopi* research in support of the "One Belt One Road" discourse, but because they consider the *qiaopi* culture to constitute part of a local trading culture rooted in special conditions. Hence, there is a clear tension between the official state narrative of unity (as also reflected in the singularity of the term "One Belt One Road") and the pluralism and locality behind *qiaopi* that we also find in "re-Sinicization".

Concluding remarks: *qiaopi* and Chinese communities in Southeast Asia

From the above, several things can be derived in terms of *qiaopi* and the broader economic, political, and cultural ties between the Chinese communities in Southeast Asia and the *qiaoxiang*.

Firstly, the long-term history of Chinese trade in Southeast Asia is relevant for grasping the development of the *qiaopi* trade in the nineteenth century. Already during this early period, dialect, region, and clan were central in the account of Chinese migration and community formation. *Qiaopi* is the broader story of the tie between Chinese communities and the home, but this early period already demonstrates that "home" referred to a spectrum of entangled loyalties. Before mass migration, Chinese traders were sojourners who did not receive support from the Chinese state, and who were also subject to discriminatory policies under colonial rule. Nevertheless, intermediate communities emerged in the Nanyang, with the Chinese filling economic niches under colonial rulers and securing their socioeconomic position. During this period, "home" was mostly the *qiaoxiang*, and dialect, region, and surname were the pillars of community life.

The *qiaopi* trade developed in tandem with developments in communication and transportation in the mid-nineteenth century. This was the period of mass migration and the emergence of the coolie trade that saw Chinese labourers shipped to Southeast Asia and the New World to work in mines and on plantations. With the arrival of large numbers of Chinese migrants in Southeast Asia, community grouping based on dialect, region, and surname became more numerous. The basis of community formation was also the basis for the set-up of the *qiaopi* trade. As local loyalties were challenged by nationalist beliefs around the turn of the century, these local markers of arrangement also had to compete with the arm of the state in the *qiaopi* trade. With new migrants arriving in Southeast

Asia, the rise in female migration, and the end of the colonial revenue system, the long-term intermediate communities were faced with new forms of Chinese identity, strengthened by the presence of Chinese officials, reformers and revolutionaries.

During this period, Chinese schools, newspapers, and community groups served to unite the Chinese beyond dialect, regional, and clan lines for the Chinese cause. In the *qiaopi* trade, this period saw efforts to regulate it through banks and post offices instead of relying on community forms. In both cases, however, this was not a narrative of linear transition, but one of entangled local and national identification. Even though Chambers of Commerce arose, they did not simply replace the *huiguan*, but operated as umbrella organizations instead. In addition, it was mostly in periods of crisis or transition, such as the 1911 Revolution or the Japanese occupation of the 1930s, that nationalist principles were dominant. Similarly, the *qiaopi* trade did not simply become incorporated by the state; resistance and circumvention of state policies based on community constellations were part and parcel of the *qiaopi* development. In addition, elements of the early *qiaopi* trade could co-exist with institutions that emerged later. For example, in some places, *shuike* or couriers would coincide with *qiaopiju*, but they would adjust to changing realities and collaborate instead of working individually.

As argued throughout this chapter, the account of the development of *qiaopi* is not one of "traditional" Chinese communities versus the "modern" state but rather one of the state *in* Chinese communities. The state was heavily involved in the creation and re-creation of these communities under changing economic and political circumstances. The decline of the *qiaopi* trade in the 1950s is part of the broader account of decolonization, the Cold War, and economic nationalist policies. In this context, national governments suppressed the pillars of Chinese communities in Southeast Asia. A policy of taking up local citizenship was encouraged during the 1950s. Against this background, with the strong politicization of loyalties, ties between the Chinese communities and the homeland diminished under the fear of persecution. A contradictory policy of encouraging remittances through state channels remained in place in the People's Republic of China. With the Cultural Revolution, ties became severed.

The renewed interest in *qiaopi* in the 1990s followed the expanding interaction between China and Southeast Asia within the broader context of global capitalism. However, during this period, instead of being a manifestation of a "deterritorialized" nationalism, the renewed emphasis on ethnic Chinese identity was directly related to state policies and state efforts to re-create Chinese community structures. The latter remained based on dialect, region, and surname, but, as in the past, the flexible nature of these markers allowed for a reinterpretation on a transnational scale. The regional identity agenda of *qiaopi* researchers also demonstrates that the spectrum of loyalties has all but made room for "the state" or "global capital". Local and national identification modes operate as a continuum rather than as a binary, with the state playing different parts in shaping and re-creating community arrangements over time. During the latest stage of migration, the dynamics between new and old migrants further complicate the picture of any linear transition, as neither the organizations, nor the migrants, nor the state are uniform agents. In other words, the spectrum of entangled loyalties has not diminished in scope.

Acknowledgements

Pookong Kee provided insightful comments on an earlier draft of this chapter. I thank Liu Hong and Wang Gungwu for their feedback to a presentation on the topic of "re-Sinicization" at the SEASIA conference in Kyoto, 12–13 December 2015. Tze-ki Hon kindly discussed the main ideas of this chapter with me and offered numerous suggestions for improvement. I also thank Liu Hong for his valid input to the revised chapter. Finally, I thank Gregor Benton for the advice and encouragement. Any remaining errors are mine alone.

Notes

1 Redding (1990). See also Yan Qinghuang [Yen Ching-hwang] (2005), pp. 23–32 in particular.
2 This number is based on estimates from the China State Council Overseas Chinese Affairs Office in 2014. Many studies cite much lower numbers. As Armstrong and Armstrong (2001, 1) note, differences in numbers are not only due to the unreliable nature of censuses in many countries, but also because of different definitions of what constitutes "Chinese".
3 On the early trade between China and Southeast Asia, see Wang Gungwu (1998 [1958]).
4 Reid (1988, 1993). See also Ptak (1998) and Reid (1996).
5 The term Yue refers both to the Yue Kingdom (sixth–fourth centuries BCE) in South China and the peoples who inhabited the territory south of the Central Plains region between the fourth and third centuries BCE. On the Yue, see Brindley (2015).
6 Whether there was a permanent Chinese settlement during the time of the Malay Kingdom (fourteenth–sixteenth century) is contested. See Purcell (1948, 18–20).
7 The terms refer to intermarriages between ethnic Chinese men and local women in this context. However, the term *mestizo* has also been used for other types of interracial marriages, whereas the term *peranakan* can also refer to *peranakan* Indians (Chitty Melaka and Jawi *peranakans*). The term *baba* is used specifically for the Straits Chinese. See Skinner (1996).
8 According to the "Sinicization School", the Manchus were "Sinicized". Mary Wright and Ho Ping-ti famously advocated this view. Since the 1990s, Evelyn Rawski, Pamela Crossley, and Mark Elliott have challenged this view. See Rawski (1996) and Ho (1998).
9 The Southern College was established in Johor state in 1990, and it was upgraded to become Southern University College in 2012; the Han Chiang College was established in Penang state in 1996; the New Era College received its first batch of students in 1998 and it was upgraded to become New Era University College in 2016. In 2004, there were plans to merge the three colleges, but these plans were abandoned because of obstacles such as the distance between the colleges and their different specializations (Raman and Tan 2015).
10 I thank Pookong Kee for pointing out this discussion on the Malaysia branch of Xiamen University.

References

Ang, Kristiano. 2013. “Chinese University Expands into Malaysia”. *New York Times*, 29 January.

Armstrong, M. Jocelyn, and R. Warwick Armstrong. 2001. “Introduction: Chinese Populations of Southeast Asia”. In M. Jocelyn Armstrong, R. Warwick Armstrong, and Kent Mulliner, eds. *Chinese Populations in Contemporary Southeast Asian Societies: Identities, Interdependence, and International Influence*, pp. 1–17. London and New York: Routledge.

Brindley, Erica. 2015. *Ancient China and the Yue: Perceptions and Identities on the Southern Frontier, c. 400 BCE–50 CE*. Cambridge: Cambridge University Press.

Cartier, Carolyn L. 2001. *Globalizing South China*. Malden, MA: Blackwell Publishers.

Chang, Amy. 2013. *Beijing and the Chinese Diaspora in Southeast Asia: To Serve the People*. NBR Special Report 43. Washington: National Bureau of Research.

Chang, Wen-Chin, and Eric Tagliacozzo. 2011. “Introduction: The Arc of Historical Commercial Relations between China and Southeast Asia”. In Eric Tagliacozzo and Wen-Chin Chang, eds. *Chinese Circulations: Capital, Commodities, and Networks in Southeast Asia*, pp. 1–17. Durham, NC and London: Duke University Press.

Chen, Ta. 1978. *Emigrant Communities in South China: A Study of Overseas Migration and Its Influence*. New York: Institute of Pacific Relations; reprint: New York: AMS Press.

Chen Xinlu. 2009. “Qiantan Quanzhou qiaopiye yu Zhongguo Yinhang Quanzhou zhihang” [A word on the Quanzhou *qiaopi* trade and the Quanzhou branch of the Bank of China]. In Chen Xiaogang, Quanzhoushi Guiguo Huaqiao Lianhehui, Quanzhoushi dang’anguan, and Quanzhouxue yanjiusuo, eds. *Huiwang Minnan qiaopi: Shoujie Minnan qiaopi yantaohui lunwenji* [Historical review of emigrant mail in Southern Fujian province: Proceedings of first symposium on Southern Fujian province], pp. 112–117. Beijing: Huayi chubanshe.

Chin, James K. 2010. “Junk Trade, Business Networks, and Sojourning Communities: Hokkien Merchants in Early Maritime Asia”. *Journal of Chinese Overseas* 6: 157–215.

Chirot, Daniel, and Anthony Reid. 1997. *Essential Outsiders: Chinese and Jews in the Transformation of Southeast Asia and Central Europe*. Seattle: University of Washington Press.

Crissman, Lawrence W. 1967. “The Segmentary Structure of Urban Overseas Chinese Communities”. *Man* 2(2): 185–204.

Curtin, Philip D. 1984. *Cross-Cultural Trade in World History*. Cambridge: Cambridge University Press.

Douw, Leo, Cen Huang, and Michael R. Godley, eds. 1999. *Qiaoxiang Ties: Interdisciplinary Approaches to “Cultural Capitalism” in South China*. London: Kegan Paul.

Fang Jinying. 2001. *Dongnanya “huaren wenti” de xingcheng yu fazhan* [The formation and development of the “Chinese problem” in Southeast Asia]. Beijing: Shishi chubanshe.

Fitzgerald, Stephen. 1972. *China and the Overseas Chinese: A Study of Peking’s Changing Policy, 1949–1970*. Cambridge: Cambridge University Press.

Freedman, Maurice. 1960. “Immigrants and Associations: Chinese in Nineteenth-century Singapore”. *Comparative Studies in Society and History* 3(1): 25–48.

Gomez, Edmund Terence, and Hsin-Huang Michael Hsiao, eds. 2004. *Chinese Enterprise, Transnationalism and Identity*. London: RoutledgeCurzon.

Govaars, Ming. 2005. *Dutch Colonial Education: The Chinese Experience in Indonesia, 1900–1942*. Trans. Lorre Lynn Trytten. Singapore: Chinese Heritage Centre.

Hamilton, Gary, ed. 1996. *Asian Business Networks.* Berlin; New York: Walter de Gruyter.

Hau, Caroline S. 2000. "Alien Nation." In idem, *Necessary Fictions: Philippine Literature and the Nation, 1946–1980*, pp. 133–176. Quezon City: Ateneo de Manila University Press.

Hau, Caroline S. 2014. *The Chinese Question: Ethnicity, Nation, and Region in and Beyond the Philippines.* Singapore: NUS Press.

Ho, Ping-Ti. 1998. "In Defense of Sinicization: A Rebuttal of Evelyn Rawski's 'Reenvisioning the Qing' ". *Journal of Asian Studies* 57(1): 123–155.

Hsu, Madeleine Y. 2000. "Migration and Native Place: *Qiaokan* and the Imagined Community of Taishan County, Guangdong, 1893–1993". *Journal of Asian Studies* 59(2): 307–331.

Jacobsen, Michael. 2009. "Navigating between Disaggregating Nation States and Entrenching Processes of Globalisation: Reconceptualising the Chinese Diaspora in Southeast Asia". *Journal of Contemporary China* 18(58): 69–91.

Katzenstein, Peter J. 2012. "China's Rise: Rupture, Return, or Recombination?" In idem, ed. *Sinicization and the Rise of China: Civilizational Processes beyond East and West*, pp. 1–38. London: Routledge.

Khanh, Tranh. 1993. *The Ethnic Chinese and Economic Development in Vietnam*. Singapore: Institute of Southeast Asian Studies.

Kuhn, Philip A. 2008. *Chinese Among Others: Emigration in Modern Times*. Lanham, MD: Rowman & Littlefield Publishers.

Li Enhan. 2003. *Dongnanya huarenshi* [History of the Chinese in Southeast Asia]. Taipei: Wunan tushu chuban gufen youxian gongsi.

Li, Peter S., and Eva Xiaolong Li. 2011. "Changes in the Chinese Overseas Population, 1955 to 2007". *Canadian Review of Sociology/Revue canadienne de sociologie* 48(2): 137–152.

Lim, Linda. 1983. "Chinese Economic Activity in Southeast Asia: An Introductory Review". In Linda Y. C. Lim and L. A. Peter Gosling, eds. *The Chinese in Southeast Asia*, Vol. 1, *Ethnicity and Economic Activity*. Singapore: Maruzen Asia.

Liu, Hong. 1998. "Old Linkages, New Networks: The Globalization of Overseas Chinese Voluntary Associations and Its Implications". *The China Quarterly* 155: 582–609.

Liu, Hong. 2002. "The Contact Zones and Socio-Cultural Interactions between China and Southeast Asia during the Twentieth Century". In Melissa G. Curley and Hong Liu, eds. *China and Southeast Asia: Changing Socio-cultural Interactions*, pp. 39–55. Centre of Asian Studies: University of Hong Kong.

Liu, Hong. 2016. "Opportunities and Anxieties for the Chinese Diaspora in Southeast Asia". *Current History* 115(784): 312–318.

Liu, Hong, and Gregor Benton. 2016. "The *Qiaopi* Trade and Its Role in Modern China and the Chinese Diaspora: Toward an Alternative Explanation of 'Transnational Capitalism' ". *The Journal of Asian Studies* 75(3): 575–594.

Mackie, James A. C. 1992. "Overseas Chinese Entrepreneurship". *Asian-Pacific Economic Literature* 6: 41–64.

McKeown, Adam. 1999. "Conceptualizing Chinese Diasporas, 1842 to 1949". *The Journal of Asian Studies* 58(2): 306–337.

McKeown, Adam. 2010. "Chinese Emigration in Global Context, 1850–1940". *Journal of Global History* 5: 95–124.

Menkhoff, Thomas, and Solvay Gerke, eds. 2002. *Chinese Entrepreneurship and Asian Business Networks*. London: RoutledgeCurzon.

Nyíri, Pál, and Danielle Tan, eds. 2017. *Chinese Encounters in Southeast Asia: How People, Money, and Ideas from China are Changing a Region.* Seattle: University of Washington Press.

Pan, Lynn. 1998. *The Encyclopedia of the Chinese Overseas.* Cambridge, MA: Harvard University Press.

Ptak, Roderich. 1998. *China's Seaborne Trade with South and Southeast Asia, 1200–1750.* Aldershot: Ashgate.

Purcell, Victor. 1948. *The Chinese in Malaya.* London; New York: Oxford University Press.

Raman, Santhiram R., and Tan Yao Sua. 2015. ISEAS Working Paper on "The Development of Chinese Education in Malaysia: Problems and Challenges". 2015.2. www.iseas.org.

Rawski, Evelyn S. 1996. "Presidential Address: Reenvisioning the Qing: The Significance of the Qing Period in Chinese History". *Journal of Asian Studies* 55(4): 829–850.

Redding, Gordon. 1990. *The Spirit of Chinese Capitalism.* Berlin; New York: De Gruyter.

Reid, Anthony, 1988, 1993. *Southeast Asia in the Age of Commerce, 1450–1680*, 2 vols. New Haven, CT: Yale University Press.

Reid, Anthony, ed. 1996. *Sojourners and Settlers: Histories of Southeast Asia and the Chinese.* St Leonards, Australia: Asian Studies Association of Australia in association with Allen and Unwin.

Reid, Anthony. 2010. *Imperial Alchemy: Nationalism and Political Identity in Southeast Asia.* Cambridge: Cambridge University Press.

Skinner, G. William. 1957. *Chinese Society in Thailand: An Analytical History.* Ithaca, NY: Cornell University Press.

Skinner, G. William. 1996. "Creolised Chinese Societies in Southeast Asia". In Anthony Reid, ed. *Sojourners and Settlers: Histories of Southeast Asia and the Chinese*, pp. 51–93. Sydney: Allen & Unwin.

Suryadinata, Leo. 2007a. *Understanding the Ethnic Chinese in Southeast Asia.* Singapore: ISEAS.

Suryadinata, Leo. 2007b. " 'Minorities' in Southeast Asian Nation-States: Ethnic Chinese as Part of the Equation". *CHC Bulletin* 10 (November): 1–7.

Suryadinata, Leo. 2008. "Chinese Indonesians in an Era of Globalization: Some Major Characteristics". In idem, ed. *Ethnic Chinese in Contemporary Indonesia*, pp. 1–16. Singapore: Institute of Southeast Asian Studies.

Suryadinata, Leo. 2012. "Recent Chinese Language Education in Southeast Asia: Some Reflections". *CHC Bulletin* 18 (October): 1–8.

Suryadinata, Leo. 2017. *The Rise of China and the Chinese Overseas: A Study of Beijing's Changing Policy in Southeast Asia and Beyond.* Singapore: Institute of Southeast Asian Studies Publishing.

Tong, Chee Kiong. 2010. *Identity and Ethnic Relations in Southeast Asia: Racializing Chineseness.* Dordrecht: Springer.

Wade, Geoff. 2009. "General Introduction." In idem, ed. *China and Southeast Asia*, pp. 1–38. Abingdon, UK; New York: Routledge.

Wang Dongxu. 2009. "Fujian qiaopi sida diyu tixi chuxi" [Preliminary study of the four major geographical systems for emigrant mail in Fujian province]. In Chen Xiaogang, Quanzhoushi Guiguo Huaqiao Lianhehui, Quanzhoushi dang'anguan, and Quanzhouxue yanjiusuo, eds. *Huiwang Minnan qiaopi: Shoujie Minnan qiaopi yantaohui lunwenji* [Historical review of emigrant mail in Southern Fujian province: Proceedings of first symposium on Southern Fujian province], pp. 103–106. Beijing: Huayi chubanshe.

Wang, Gungwu. 1981. *Community and Nation: Essays on Southeast Asia and the Chinese*. Singapore: Heinemann Educational Books.

Wang, Gungwu. 1991. *China and the Chinese Overseas*. Singapore: Times Academic Press.

Wang, Gungwu. 1998 [1958]. *The Nanhai Trade: The Early History of Chinese Trade in the South China Sea*. Singapore: Times Academic Press.

Wang, Gungwu. 2009. "Extracts from The Nanhai Trade". In Geoff Wade, ed. *China and Southeast Asia*, pp. 105–156. Abingdon, UK; New York: Routledge.

Wang Weizhong. 2009. "Chuxi Chaoshan qiaopi de chuantong wenhua jiyin" [Preliminary analysis of the traditional cultural genes of Chaoshan *qiaopi*]. In Chen Xiaogang, Quanzhoushi Guiguo Huaqiao Lianhehui, Quanzhoushi dang'anguan, and Quanzhouxue yanjiusuo, eds. *Huiwang Minnan qiaopi: Shoujie Minnan qiaopi yantaohui lunwenji* [Historical review of emigrant mail in Southern Fujian province: Proceedings of first symposium on Southern Fujian province], pp. 50–55. Beijing: Huayi chubanshe.

Weber, Max. 1905. *The Protestant Ethic and the Spirit of Capitalism*. Translated into English by T. Parsons (1930). London and Boston: Unwin Hyman.

Wickberg, Edgar. 1965. *The Chinese in Philippine Life, 1850–1898*. New Haven, CT: Yale University Press.

Willmott, William E. 1967. *The Chinese in Cambodia*. Vancouver: University of British Columbia Publications Centre.

Wu Lehua. 2004. *Nanyang huaqiao shihua* [Nanyang overseas Chinese stories]. Beijing: Shangwu yinshiguan.

Wu Qinsheng. 2003. "Chuangkan ci" [Word for the inaugural issue]. *Qiaopi wenhua* [*Qiaopi* Culture] 1(1): 8.

"Xiada haishi xiada" [Xiamen University or big scare]. Facebook, July 2015. www.facebook.com/yangguangxingdong/photos/a.445567032286968.1073741828.445563615620643/470201883156816/?Type=1&fref=nf. Accessed 5 December 2015.

"Xiada Malaixiya fenxiao zai Ma dianji, yuji mingnian jiu yue jiang kaixue" [Foundation of Xiamen University branch in Malaysia, estimated that school will open next year in September], My Xinhuanet, 6 July 2014. My.xinhuanet.com/2014–07/06c_126716208.htm. Accessed 6 December 2015.

"Xin silu, xin mengxiang" [New Silk Road, new Dreams]. *Xinhuawang* portal. www.xinhuanet.com/world/newsilkway/index.htm. Accessed 18 November 2014.

Xu Maochun. 2007. *Dongnanya huaren yu qiaopi* [Ethnic Chinese in Southeast Asia and *qiaopi*]. Man'gu: Taiguo Taihua jinchukou shanghui [Thailand Thai Chinese Import and Export Chamber of Commerce].

Yan Qinghuang [Yen Ching-hwang]. 2005. *Haiwai huaren de shehui biange yu shangye chengzhang* [Social change and commercial growth of the overseas Chinese]. Xiamen: Xiamen daxue chubanshe.

Yan Qinghuang [Yen Ching-hwang]. 2006. "Fujian ren zai Ma-Xin lishi shang suo banyan de juese" [The role of Fujianese in the history of Malaya and Singapore]. In Lin Zhongqiang *et al*., eds. *Dongnanya de Fujianren* [Fujianese in Southeast Asia], pp. 1–22. Xiamen: Xiamen daxue chubanshe.

Yow, Cheun Hoe. 2005. "Weakening Ties with the Ancestral Homeland in China: The Case Studies of Contemporary Singapore and Malaysian Chinese". *Modern Asian Studies* 39(3): 559–597.

Zeng Shaocong. 2004. *Piaobo yu genzhi: Dangdai Dongnanya huaren zuqun guanxi yanjiu* [Drifting and rooting: Research on ethnic Chinese group relations in contemporary Southeast Asia]. Beijing: Zhongguo shehui kexue chubanshe.

Zhang Hong, 2014. "Tuidong da qiaowu, buzhi da geju" [Promoting big overseas Chinese work, structuring grand framework]. *People's Daily* (Overseas edition), 11 April.

Zhu Jieqin. 2008. *Dongnanya huaqiao shi* [A history of overseas Chinese in Southeast Asia]. Beijing: Zhonghua shuju.

Zhuang Guotu. 2006. "15–19 shiji zhudao haiwai huashang wangluo de Minnan haishang" [The Hokkien sea trade that dominated overseas Chinese trading networks in the 15–19th century]. In Lin Zhongqiang *et al*., eds. *Dongnanya de Fujianren* [Fujianese in Southeast Asia], pp. 205–229. Xiamen: Xiamen daxue chubanshe.

Zhuang Guotu, and Liu Wenzheng. 2009. *Dongya huaren shehui xingcheng he fazhan: huashang wangluo, yimin yu yitihua qushi* [Formation and development of Chinese societies in East Asia: Chinese trading networks, migration, and integration trends]. Xiamen: Xiamen University Press.

Zhuang Guotu, Qing Shuichun, Pang Hongli *et al*. 2010. *Jin 30 nianlai Dongya huaren shetuan de xin bianhua* [New developments in ethnic Chinese associations in East Asia over the last 30 years]. Xiamen: Xiamen daxue chubanshe.

2 *Qiaopi* and politics in modern China and the Chinese diaspora

Gregor Benton, Hong Liu, and Huimei Zhang

Modern postal services, which Tocqueville called that "great link between minds" (John 2009, 3), were a mainstay of the modern communications revolution and at the heart of modern institutional, ideological, economic, social, cultural, and political change in probably every country (Maclachen 2011). This chapter looks at the many-layered relationship between these services and politics, at all levels, from bottom to top, including the role played in postal culture by China's *qiaopi* trade.

Throughout the world, the modern state has played a direct role in setting, or trying to set, policies and guidelines for postal services. It has sought to destroy or assimilate pre-modern postal services like the *qiaopi* system and to assert the authority of the Post Office, a state postal system that seeks to unify and monopolize the previous mix of local or private services and state-controlled offices charged with the distribution of documents, civil and sometimes military. The state's striving for a monopoly of postal services and its commitment to universal-service obligations (now a general term but one originally applied to the state postal system, and meaning uniformity in price and service) brought it into conflict with existing postal services. The later adherence by dozens of countries to the Universal Postal Union (created in 1874, under the name General Postal Union), which aimed to produce uniformity of service and equality of foreign and domestic mail, widened and internationalized the grounds for conflict. By 1914, when China joined, the Union included nearly all independent countries (Cotreau 1975).

Modern postal systems brought into the purview of central state and the mainstream economy places and classes of people previously barely touched by it, and penetrated into society more deeply and abidingly than probably any other branch of government. As a result, they have played a greater role than most institutions "in shaping the pattern of everyday life", bringing "a steady flow of information on public affairs" to the towns and villages, and enabling ordinary people to "participate in national politics" (John 2009, 4–13).

The term "postal culture" was coined by Gabriella Romani, in her book on letters in post-Unification Italy, to describe "the interconnections, influences, and overlapping of the literary representations, cultural productions, and communicative practices" that revolved around the nineteenth-century letter. She also described the "postal movements [that] provided Italians with a new geography of national identity, based on … an enhanced sense of belonging to a group, … an idealistic extension of the individual experience." According to Romani, this postal culture had a strong political edge: its primary role was to keep friends and relatives in touch, but it also created an information network that eroded distance, enhanced the sense of interconnectedness, and exposed people "to new ideas and customs [and] a world much larger than the one they inhabited" (Romani 2013, 4).

The concept of "postal culture" was extended to the United States by David Henkin, who argued that Americans became ever more aware of their participation in a network of communication that embraced the nation. Henkin defined postal culture as

> a cluster of new practices, attitudes, norms, discussions, and, crucially, habits – of communication, inquiry, and expectation – that grew up around a modern postal system, … a set of practices, discourses, and beliefs [whereby Americans] began producing and circulating in massive numbers something that had never before been an instrument of everyday sociability among ordinary people: the personal letter.
>
> (Henkin 2006, 6 and 93)

In China, letter-writing, which comprised family and non-family letters, is a "pivotal yet neglected medium of historical Chinese communication" (Kádár, 2011, 60).

However, the idea of a postal culture has not yet been widely applied to other national contexts. Lane Harris briefly mentions the term in his study on the Post Office and state formation in modern China between 1896 and 1949, but he does not analyse it in any detail, probably because his main focus is on the Post Office's contribution to forming the modern Chinese state, as opposed to its political role in broader society (Harris 2012, 181). Focusing on the years 1928–1949, Li Xiaoyan (2010) analyses remittance management by national banks and post offices, including their relations with private exchange houses, competition between the Nationalist government and the Japanese government, and overseas-Chinese and official remittance. Her study, however, does not look at the larger and comparative context of post culture and how *qiaopi* trade interacted with local politics.

This chapter explores the political dimension of the *qiaopi* trade along several different lines. It begins by looking at the political transformations wrought by the trade in the basic structure and low-level institutions of the local sending society and the overseas receiving one. Did the remitter's role in local politics at home change as a result of his remitting? Did the *qiaopi* trade's safeguarding of affective links between relatives lead to greater literacy among the lower classes and thus to greater political participation in the affairs of local society and the state by migrants' dependants? Did it contribute to progress and education among ordinary Chinese at home and abroad? What was the political effect of *qiaopi* on the women that in most cases stayed behind when the men migrated? The chapter then examines the issue of labour and politics, a perennial theme in postal studies. What was the *qiaopi* trade's political impact on regional and national official institutions in China and in Chinatown and the receiving polity and its relationship with the Chinese state and the foreign governments that strove to assert their authority over ethnic-Chinese communities? Did the *qiaopi* trade lead to the creation of new more widely based institutions, at home and abroad, capable of shaping Chinese and ethnic-Chinese politics, and to the promotion of new political attitudes and identities in the regions, in China as a whole and among Chinese overseas, in particular the idea of nationhood and national or pan-Chinese identity? Did it contribute towards producing a new-style public opinion and a larger community, like the official postal culture described by Romani and others? What was the connection between *qiaopi* and print culture – the magazines that started mushrooming in the *qiaoxiang* in the first half of the twentieth century? What was its impact on China's and Chinatown's nationalist movement and on the anti-Japanese campaigns of the 1930s and the 1940s? What role did the Communists (who had bases in and around all China's regions of outmigration and in the worldwide Chinatown for the entire course of their pre-1949 existence[1]) play in the *qiaopi* trade, in China and overseas, in the revolutionary period? Finally, in what ways did the political impact of the *qiaopi* trade resemble or differ from that of wider postal culture, in Romani's sense?

This last point is central to the rest. The *qiaopi* trade had many features in common with the wider, formal postal service, in that *qiaopi* traders carried out or arranged the physical transfer of letters and sometimes parcels, usually for payment. However, the *qiaopi* trade differed in important respects from the Post Office. *Qiaopi* letters were almost invariably an accompaniment to a transfer of "silver" (a remittance of money or some form of cheque or bill of exchange), and required a *huipi* (a reply from China) to be returned by the remittance company to the remitter, as proof of receipt. In China, and in most other countries, at least until recently, the modern mail system was a state monopoly and was internationally regulated and coordinated and run according to uniform principles. However, the *qiaopi* trade was generally private, unregulated, and variform – the Post Office did try to enter and take control of it, but it largely failed (until the 1950s), and regulation was intermittent and restricted. In fact, the *qiaopi* trade remained all along demarcated by "dialect" and region, and was further differentiated at sub-regional and sub-dialect levels. *Qiaopi* traders not only failed to develop an all-China dimension – they actively (and, for the most part, successfully) resisted nationalisation, i.e. the transformation of the remittance business into a monopolistic arm of the bureaucratic state, Chinese or non-Chinese. But that does not mean that they were without national relevance, either politically or – even more so – economically, or that the *qiaopi* trade was not swept up in the great political mobilizations of the late nineteenth and twentieth centuries.

Village-level change

By infusing wealth into their ancestral villages, remitters acquired a new political role and status in their sending places. Men (and sometimes women) previously low and junior in the village hierarchy were catapulted into its heights, disordering the village's tradition-bound hierarchies. People resident overseas could be consulted about village matters by letter, and returnees could exercise their influence directly. John Kuo Wei Tschen described the Chinese laundryman in America as "not only a mediator in personal and private affairs but also an elderman in village politics", even more authoritative than elders in the village (Siu 1987, 169). They were expected to help steer village politics, from afar, and to donate to local institutions. Back-and-forth correspondence between Ye Tang, an emigrant in the United States, and his relatives in China illustrates this process of consultation, in his case concerning the building of watchtowers and a school.[2]

The migrant went from being a villager, usually a peasant, with narrowly bounded horizons, to inhabit a wider world and, in nearly all cases, to assume a new social role, as a worker in urban industry or commerce, in a mine, or on a plantation. Overseas, he – less often, she – was exposed to new social practices and political viewpoints. The systemic racism of colonial society in Southeast Asia, of the white settler societies of North America and Australasia, and of Europe predisposed Chinese migrants to be even more sympathetic to the new nationalist and republican politics that found their readiest audiences in Chinatown.

Migrants' exposure to a society and polity further than China along the road to modernity changed the thinking of some on basic social issues such as girls' schooling, and on political issues such as democracy, freedom of assembly and expression, fair taxation, etc. Many letters were deeply conservative, especially regarding the wives, mothers, and daughters they had left behind, and instructed wives and daughters to be passive, submissive, virtuous, and filial. The culture reflected in them remained largely closed and conservative, up to and even after 1949 (Du Shimin 2004, 286–287). However, exposure to new customs, viewpoints, and institutions overseas revolutionized the thinking of some remitters, and this was reflected in letters home, particularly regarding girls' and women's rights. The new thinking was not always well received. One *qiaopi* addressed not to the mother, as custom dictated, but to the wife drew a strong reproach from the mother, who saw it as a violation of traditional propriety (Chen Hanchu 2010, 90; Zhang Guoxiong 2010, 78). Another, addressed in 1965 to the writer's mother-in-law, argued that girls should be allowed to make their decisions about marriage:

> Here in Singapore, your granddaughters are studying at college. Whenever I mention of marriage, they oppose it, saying first they'll graduate and then talk about marriage, this is reasonable. As enlightened parents, we have to agree. Moreover, living in a civilized society, children should have

absolute freedom of marriage. The parents should merely give guidance from the side, they should not have the right to oppress. That's our news, to comfort you.

(Chaoshan lishi wenhua yanjiu zhongxin 2007, 244)

Most migrants focused exclusively on hard work as a possible way out of poverty, but some not only sympathized with these new political viewpoints but proselytized for them in their letters home. There are numerous instances of such proselytizing, of family and friends, in the *qiaopi* collections, just as there is evidence of migrants' and dependants' politicization in the inscriptions painted on the houses in China belonging to *qiaojuan* and *guiqiao*. At every important political juncture in the history of modern China and the Chinese diaspora, letters home and, in some cases, letters from China to abroad (the *huipi*), as well as some of the intra-diasporic correspondence that followed *qiaopi* circuits, reflected the changes and discussed how to respond to them. This was particularly true of the Hundred Days Reform of 1898, the Emperor-Protection movement, the reformers' Business Revitalization 振兴商业 campaign, the anti-Japanese movement, the National Salvation movement, the Sino-Japanese War, the Korean War, the Cultural Revolution, and the fall of the "Gang of Four" after Mao's death.

Many letters described the emigration policies of foreign countries, and tactics to deal with them (Liu Jin 2013, 147–149). Because of the anti-Chinese Exclusion Laws, the letters that flowed either way between China and North America were likely to focus on immigration, how to deal with interrogation (on arrival), and how to get work (Pan Meizhu n.d.). One set of letters shows how a family used kinship ties to construct a migration network across the Pacific, North America, and Southeast Asia that provided family members with the information and resources (birth certificates, application forms, depositions, witness statements) necessary to circumvent the ban (Shi Jianping 2014, 308). One lineage, the Guan, from Wuyi, used letters to create a Guan diaspora several thousand strong with branches and outposts across much of the United States, Canada, and Cuba (Liu Jin 2014b).

In the United States, Li Yiquan wrote to his younger brother Li Chunyao in the "wooden huts" (where immigrants were detained at the port of entry while awaiting interrogation) in Vancouver with information about his own birth certificate, his return to China, and his subsequent return to the United States, so that his brother could successfully cope with the immigration official's questions.[3]

Some correspondence rose above the level of platitudes and clichés to deal with weightier issues, including topical political matters and the state of the world, China, and the writer's native place and place of settlement (Chen Xiaojie *et al.*, 2008, 446–447). Others described foreign customs, viewpoints, and institutions, providing a grass-roots perspective on world politics, economics, society, and culture quite different from that reported by students and government officials in their correspondence and dispatches (Zhang Guoxiong 2010, 74–78).

However, most migrants and their families did not talk much or even at all about political issues in their correspondence. Only a small minority, those active in politics overseas, wrote home about political issues. Some wrote nothing at all, but simply remitted money. Most ordinary migrants and their dependants cared about political matters only when they directly affected their daily lives. To that extent, one cannot claim on the basis of the evidence in letters that the new postal culture widened the political horizons of ordinary people.

Beyond politics in the sense of the affairs of state, there is plenty of evidence to show that, in many cases, *qiaopi* contributed to the transformation of the politics of gender and generation in the *qiaoxiang*, overthrowing established principles of power and status. This was true above all in the field of schooling.

The *qiaopi* impact on school politics was twofold. Early leaders of the *qiaopi* trade like Guo Youpin (on his role in the *qiaop*i trade, see Chapter 5 of this book) promoted Confucian values in the schools they set up, whereas their sons and heirs reformed education along modern lines. They set up hundreds of schools in the *qiaoxiang*, and funded evening classes, libraries, and other schemes. Even so, they remained part of the establishment, which vaunted their efforts. Lower down the social scale, remitters enabled their children, including many girls, and their younger relatives and in-laws to go to school, and even to universities, including prestigious foreign universities.

This promotion of schooling advanced the politicization of *qiaoxiang* society. The introduction of a modern education system and its endurance in many places for a century or more nurtured a great pool of talent that was employed at both ends and all levels of the migration chain, in education, enterprise, politics, and community leadership. Alumni associations became a main channel of international communication, and a strong sinew of diasporic and domestic community and politics (Deng Dahong 2014, 108). Migrants and returned migrants also built libraries, both for their lineages and for the general public (Wang Weizhong 2006, 63), as part of the effort to bring education and political enlightenment to the *qiaoxiang*.

The focus on schooling in the *qiaoxiang* was synchronic with political developments in wider society. In Chaoshan, the first migrant-sponsored *sishu* 私塾 (old-style private school) was founded in 1880. However, those that followed later in the nineteenth century, at around the time of the Wuxu Reforms of 1898, had as their goal the founding a modern maths- and science-based system of education. The schools movement in the *qiaoxiang* entered its heyday after the Revolution of 1911, when local schools opened their doors to the general population (Wang Weizhong 2007, 90–92). In the Hakka counties, middle and primary schools sprang up on all sides, supported by Hakkas overseas, when Qing-dynasty reformists started a campaign to promote education in the region in 1903 (Deng Rui 2010, 261–262). Like other groups, Hakka philanthropists connected to the *qiaopi* trade set up schools for girls as well as boys. Although Meixian was economically underdeveloped and remote from modern life, it was in the vanguard of modern political change in the run-up to the New Culture

Movement of the late 1910s, which led to the transformation of China's education system (Xiao Wenping *et al.* 2014). The schools movement in the *qiaoxiang* cannot be understood outside the context of radical politics in China.

After 1949, local communist officials added to the pressure on rural dependants to become literate. Mass campaigns were launched in the *qiaoxiang* to persuade women to become politically aware and learn to read and write. Remittances remained crucial for China's economic development, and local authorities believed that if migrants' wives and dependants could themselves engage in correspondence, they would be better able to solicit remittances from their menfolk overseas and thus aid both themselves and the state (Shen Huifen 2012, 90).

On occasions, changes in the mental landscape culminated in a new political mindset in some *qiaoxiang* villages. During the Sino-Japanese War, the collapse of the general economy was reflected even more acutely in villages that were no longer able to receive remittances. Government promises of protection and relief usually came to nothing, and taxes continued to rise. This led to resistance, both passive and active, and demonstrations. On one occasion, in Xinchang in November 1948, government investigators were surrounded and beaten by a mob of 200, probably organized by the *qiaopi* trade (Yuan Ding *et al.* 2014, 255–278). Over the course of many years, political protest against attempts by the authorities to restrict the trade broke out at all levels of society, in the villages, the towns, the cities, and even the national capital (both Beijing and Nanjing), as well as in Chinese communities abroad.

Protests in the villages and the smaller towns were probably in most cases organized by local powerholders intent on protecting local and their own interests, in which sense they differed little from traditional protest, and cannot count as manifestations of modern political change. But although nearly all these protest movements, particularly those closest to the villages, were deeply rooted in organizations and networks based on long-standing particularistic ties, over time they ripened in many places into a more broadly based political culture that later paved the way, both in China and overseas, for an extensive mobilization of patriotic forces.

In some cases, women, mainly *fankeshen* 番客婶 or migrants' wives, were to the fore in these movements (Shen Huifen 2012, 146–159). This is not surprising given that they made up the great majority of youthful dependants, but it was nevertheless uncommon in China and a sign of the times and of rural women's elevation into the political domain in some places.

The emergence of a postal culture in Italy and the United States led to greater literacy among the lower classes and thus created the potential for their participation in community politics and state affairs. In the Chinese case, much of the correspondence from migrants to dependants, and even more so vice versa, was written on their behalf, by others, including friends and relatives, *qiaopiju* (remittance shop) staff, professional roadside letter-writers, and (in the *qiaoxiang*) specialist teams of Party workers. However, the correspondence acted as a catalyst for the promotion of literacy. There is no statistical as opposed to anecdotal evidence of this, but in their letters home many migrants urged their female relatives and their children to learn to read and write, and funded schooling both for their children, including girls in many cases, and even, in some cases, for their wives and daughters-in-law.

Most donors were private and individual, but others were collective, organized in hometown associations, guilds, professional associations, and temples, over which Chinatown bigwigs and social luminaries held sway. At this higher end of the charity ladder, another departure from established politics, just as striking as the rise in status of the humble remitter at village level, came about. Local and regional projects that were by tradition the domain of China's gentry class devolved as a result of remittances to other social groups and classes. In China before the 1905 reforms and the 1911 revolution, the merchant was generally a despised class. However, after the collapse of the Qing, when titles and degrees became redundant, merchants – including, in southern China, merchant leaders of the *qiaopi* trade – began to assume new functions and perform new tasks in local and regional society. As benefactors, they could expect to get official positions and government jobs on retiring to their native places (Williams 2003, 97–98 and 104–105).

In the southeastern littoral politics, class structure, and class relations differed from those in other regions, and local historians talk of an oceanic culture in which trade and enterprise were valued even before the changes wrought by Sun Yat-sen's "bourgeois" revolution. The *qiaopi* trade required greater cultural and political capital than many other trades. *Qiaopi* practitioners had to be literate and to appear to be morally impeccable, in the Confucian sense, for their clients were entrusting them with hard-earned savings. So the *qiaopi* trade's strong association with promoting education in the *qiaoxiang* was in one sense a new departure, with entrepreneurs acquiring a sort of gentry status, yet in other senses it represented a continuation of local ways.[4]

Qiaopi and labour politics

Trade unions have been well represented in postal services in many countries. In Britain, agitators recruited started recruiting members of the postal staff in the mid-nineteenth century, and in China, Lu Jingshi set up a Postal Workers' Union in the early 1930s (Porter 1993, 160). But despite low wages and poor working conditions, most postal unions have, historically, lacked the bargaining power of the better organized industrial unions. Although usually among the largest workforces sharing a single employer, they were too scattered and their functions too diverse to become a united and coherent entity.

Qiaopi workers were even less likely to become class conscious and fight for their separate interests as a class. The *qiaopiju* were organized corporately, on family and sub-ethnic lines, and dominated by the owners and managers. Their organizational culture was strongly paternalistic. Their core personnel was recruited on kinship grounds, and each *qiaopiju* was presided over by a *jiazhang* 家长 (head of household) (Chen Haizhong 2013). Lowly workers had little security and earned a pittance, but even if they developed a sense of political grievance and a class identity, there was little way they could give it form. They too were usually embedded in kinship networks. They were more likely to resort to pleading than to protest.

The role of the *shuike* in the remittance process and their relationship with established *qiaopi* traders differed in some ways from that of ordinary *qiaopiju* employees and of the *pijiao* who delivered *qiaopi* to the door. Some *shuike* were part of the staff of a *qiaopiju*, but others were independent couriers who struck deals with the *qiaopiju*. *Shuike* were capable, assertive, and independent entrepreneurs in their own right. Although said to be unsociable and aloof, and to work alone, they shared ships and hostels with one another. In some places, they formed *shuike* associations to defend themselves against the intrusions of officialdom. In 1933, for example, *shuike* in the Chaoshan and Meizhou region united in a federation, the *Nanyang shuike lianhehui* 南洋水客联合会 (Federation of Southeast Asian *shuike*), which had nearly one thousand members (most of them Hakkas) (Yang Qunxi 2004, 63 and 443; Li Xiaoyan 2004, 52; Huang Ting 2008, 215). They probably also used their associations to negotiate their relationship with the *qiaopiju*, but that is a question that requires further study.

Given the need for trust, most *shuike* were men of integrity, honest and reputable, who kept their word and had no obvious vices (Zhang Shuoren 2013, 205; Xiao Wenping 2004, 255). They were better educated, more cultured, and knowledgeable than their fellow migrants, for they had to be literate and numerate, silver-tongued, entrepreneurial, and good at languages. They needed trusted networks along which to travel, and to be good at creating confidence, ties of friendship, and personal and group relations (Wu Hongli 2008, 362, 366). All these qualities would have lent them an air of political charisma in the villages in China and the foreign ports. Given that their cargo of remittances, including bullion, and exotic goods was a magnet for thieves and bandits, it is not surprising that many *shuike* practised martial arts (Huang Shaoxiong 2004, 108; Wang Weizhong 2007, 17–18), and that the father of the Communist General Ye Jianying, a Hakka, was a well-known *shuike* and martial-arts teacher (Li Xiaoyan 2004, 51).

The *qiaopiju* as a corporate body embracing both workers and employers did not survive the revolution of 1949. During the transition to state socialism, the authorities in the *qiaoxiang* engineered class differentiation in the *qiaopi* trade, by means of which the *pijiao* and other toilers were given a new designation, as *qiaopi* officers, and organized in trade unions. Thus a new labour politics was injected into the *qiaopi* system. *Qiaopi* workers now attended union meetings and spoke at *qiaopi* conferences. Praising stalwarts of the *qiaopi* trade and *qiaopi* heroes became a staple of Communist propaganda in emigrant regions, and *pijiao* were feted, Stakhanovite-style, at conferences (Wang Weizhong 2007, 55). However, the *qiaopi* union was a typical Communist-style trade union, designed to act as a "school of socialism" and a tool with which the authorities sought to mobilize labour activism rather than as an authentic voice of the workers.

Qiaopi and regional politics

The *qiaopi* trade was a local and regional phenomenon that embraced only a tiny proportion of the Chinese population. It served those parts of China – mainly in Guangdong (including Hainan, which did not separate from Guangdong until 1988) and Fujian, but also in Hubei (Tianmen), Zhejiang (Qingtian), and Guangxi (Rongxian) – from which large numbers of migrants had left to work overseas, as labourers or traders. Even within Guangdong and Fujian, only a few of the forty or so counties in each province were major sources of emigration. Although *qiaoxiang* in different parts of southern China shared similar interests and problems, Guangdong and Fujian had different provincial identities, and within each province the *qiaoxiang* were further subdivided by sub-ethnic and other loyalties and by dialect.[5]

In Singapore, members of any one particular community still tended to send *qiaopi* through remittance houses operated by members of the same community. For example, Hainanese usually used firms run by fellow Hainanese, whose businesses are all concentrated in the same part of town.[6] However, despite the trade's Chinese-ethnic diversity and the lack of direct geographic contiguity or political and cultural affinity between the counties and parts of counties it served, there were, nevertheless, practical grounds for joint action and solidarity. Nor was the fierce competition that characterized the trade necessarily a barrier to cooperation. Although *qiaopiju* and *shuike* serving the same sub-ethnic population were, actually or potentially, in rivalry with one another, those serving different places, with which they almost invariably had an ascriptive relationship, were unlikely to clash. This was particularly true of *qiaopi* traders overseas, although traders from different places were more likely – indeed bound – to be in physical proximity with one another than traders in China. The only obvious case of intra-trade conflict in China was between Hakka traders and the Teochew-speaking Chaoshanese, who controlled the ports that received *qiaopi* destined for the Hakka hinterland and used their advantage, where possible, to extend their control into the Hakka counties.

At one level, *shuike* and *qiaopi* traders in China adapted to the local landscape in order to survive. In a lawless and chaotic age, the *qiaopi* trade in China was vulnerable to thieves, pirates, local officials, warlord armies, militia, and local strongmen and gentry leaders (Jiao Jianhua and Xu Cuihong 2004, 168–171; Huang Jiaxiang 2008, 339). This led many *qiaopiju* to adopt a special form of political partnership in areas subject to bandit or official predations. *Qiaopiju* owners and managers vied to recruit local luminaries and powerholders (*shilipai* 实力派) to become their paid nominal "partners", and through the link were able to recover large amounts of remittance money stolen by criminals or pocketed by local bullies (*tuhao* 土豪) or corrupt officials. Other officials were invited to become shareholders, to the same aim (Jiao Jianhua 2005, 68).

Because of the deep segmentation of the *qiaopi* trade along sub-ethnic lines, a commonality of political and economic interest took decades to emerge, and was never fully or lastingly consummated. The eventual trigger to its formation was state interference in the trade, both in China and overseas, by governments seeking to extend to it the concept of postal monopoly. After the development of an official postal policy and the implementation of a nationalized postal service, the Nanjing Government decided in 1928 to abolish the *minxinju* (people's letter office). This decision had enormous repercussions in the Overseas Chinese community. In Singapore, a meeting of the Overseas Chinese Congress, convened by the Chinese Chamber of Commerce, set up a

> plenary assembly of all Singapore Overseas Chinese associations to petition for the retention of the *minxinju* and to negotiate with the national [Chinese] government and to force the Ministry of Communications to agree to postpone the abolition of the *minxinju*.

Not long afterwards, in 1930, the National Government demanded higher postal charges from the *minxinju*, once again to the detriment of Overseas Chinese. Thereupon, the Overseas Chinese Congress reconvened. It set up "a plenary assembly of all Singapore Overseas Chinese associations to petition for a reduction in the postal charges levied on the *minxinju*", and pleaded with the Government to force the National Government once again to make concessions and to compromise on postal charges.[7]

On the whole, these state efforts to encroach on the trade did not last long or get very far, because of the trade's vigorous resistance and intractability – its transnational nature and amorphousness (to which neither the colonial states nor the Chinese state had much of an answer). They also failed, within China, because of the state's precarious hold on society and the economy and the failure of the banks and the Post Office to establish a reliable service across the *qiaoxiang*; and, outside China, because for decades Chinese tended to live separately, in all-male ghettos, isolated from the non-Chinese around and largely impervious to the efforts of the colonial (and Thai) states to control them. However, this onslaught by predatory authorities was not repulsed without a political struggle, in the course of which the grounds for a new ethnic-Chinese political identity were greatly extended.

Politics, *qiaopi*, and the printing and dissemination of *qiaoxiang* journals

We know from research inspired by the work of Benedict Anderson that the rise of nationalism is intimately connected with the rise of print and print-capitalism, triggered by the industrial revolution (Anderson 1991). But what about the rise of nationalism in colonial and semi-colonial countries (hereafter, the Third World)? Anderson's theory has been faulted for implying that Third World countries need no sociology of nationalism because they were merely imitating, or "pirating", pre-fabricated Western models of nationhood, or (in a later version of the thesis) for arguing that "the immediate genealogy [of these models] should be traced to the imaginings of the colonial state" (p. 167). Either way, Anderson's theory rendered the study of Third World nationalism Eurocentric, and a Western construct (Chatterjee 1993; Desai 2009).

It is interesting, in light of Anderson's theory, to note that an indigenous print culture thrived in the *qiaoxiang* in the context of migration and the *qiaopi* system. Migrant and community leaders produced *qiaokan* (overseas Chinese magazines) in the villages and counties and mailed them to expatriates all over the world, to inform them of events at home and to encourage them to donate to local causes (Williams 2003, 104). They also set up other publishing enterprises to the same end. Wuyi was the main centre of *qiaokan* publishing, though *qiaokan* also appeared in other *qiaoxiang* (Liu Jin 2007, 33). Before 1949, more than 200 different *qiaokan* were published in Wuyi alone, including 127 in Taishan, 25 in Kaiping, and 26 in Xinhui. Many were monthly, and some were fortnightly and even weekly. Nearly all were migrant-funded (Mei Weiqiang and Mei Xue 2007, 6; Liu Jin 2009, 75 and 85).

These *qiaokan* included "newsletters, newspapers and magazines published by individuals, clans, schools, villages and government offices" in the *qiaoxiang*. According to an early report, four out of five were sent abroad (Liu Jin 2007, 33). The first such, *Xinning zazhi* 新宁杂志 (Xinning Magazine) appeared in Taishan in Guangdong in 1908. It was designed to meet the needs of migrants and their families and communities, by sustaining or re-establishing contact and exchanging information, particularly information about Taishan – its problems, developments, general news, and history (specified as "customs and traditions"). The *qiaokan* phenomenon peaked between 1910 and the early 1930s. In the late 1930s, new, more expressly political *qiaokan* arose to support the anti-Japanese movement and solicit donations to support national defence. Starting in 1945, most *qiaokan* resumed publication after a wartime gap. Only a minority survived China's transition to Communist government in 1949. Those that did survive played a role in attracting donations of food and materials and foreign currency remittances in the 1950s and early 1960s, before disappearing during the Cultural Revolution. They started reviving in 1978, when millions of copies were printed annually, but the government's hand was clear in the revival. The magazines lost some of their autonomy, and the emphasis in them was often on attracting capital investment (Huang and Godley 1999, 313–319; Yao Ting and Mei Weiqiang 2009).

The *qiaokan* were evidence of a vibrant local print culture in the *qiaoxiang* that strongly complemented the regional postal culture set going by the *qiaopi* trade. *Qiaokan* were a public counterpart to *qiaopi*, not private but communal, and have been called "collective family letters" by Chinese overseas (Huang and Godley 1999, 317; Liu Jin 2009, 75 and 85). Indeed, *qiaopi* and other correspondence made up much of the contents of the *qiaokan* and village newsletters.[8] The *qiaokan* had a local or regional focus. Most served townships or lineages, although a few (like *Xinning zazhi*) appeared at county level. However, during political crises they transcended particularism and made propaganda for the nation. So there is no clear dividing line between *qiaokan* and *qiaopi* culture on the one hand and a national orientation on the other.

Qiaopi traders backed the *qiaokan* financially, through donations and advertisements. Some 70 per cent of advertisements in *Xinning zazhi* were placed by *qiaopiju* and other remittance firms (Hsu 2000b, 139). *Yinhao*, *qiaopiju*, *shanghao*, and other businesses active in the *qiaopi* trade handled the overseas dispatch of *qiaokan* and acted as the publishers' agents (Liu Jin 2007, 33–34; Yao Ting 2011, 24).

Were these *qiaokan* evidence of Chinese copying in the *qiaoxiang* of Western print-culture, like the modern-style newspapers that started to proliferate in China and Chinatown in the nineteenth century? Probably they were not. Unlike the newspapers, which were distributed publicly and regularly, most *qiaokan* were distributed privately and occasionally. A much likelier model for them was the centuries-old Chinese habit of producing local and genealogical records, the so-called *jiapu* 家谱 (family records), *zupu* 族谱 (lineage records), and *zongpu* 宗谱 (clan records)[9] and the *difang zhi* 地方志 (local gazetteers), which provided information at county level and above about local history, geography, society, and economy, and were designed to aid local government and promote local identity.[10] For example, Lin Zhongbang, the son of Singapore's famous Chaoshan merchant Lim Nee Soon, was born in Singapore but his name is nevertheless recorded in the *zupu* (clan genealogy) compiled in his father's ancestral village of Maxi in Qishan in Chenghai county (Ke Mulin 1991).

The *qiaokan* replicated the same divisions as these compilations among kinship organizations and between them and the county. Traditionally, most genealogies were produced by the wealthiest sector of society, one able to defray the costs of printing. They displayed and symbolized membership of a powerful family or kinship group, and their appearance often signalled the revival of formal kinship organisation after a period of decrease. In some cases, the production of a genealogy "created the organized kinship group, rather than vice versa". Genealogies were exclusively private: their role was to transmit family or lineage history, household or lineage instructions, and standards of moral propriety to future generations and to record glorious episodes in family or clan affairs. Urbanization and internal migration, far from weakening genealogy making, strengthened it (Meskill 1970, 141–143).

So the emergence of *qiaokan* in the early twentieth century is consonant with existing, pre-modern traditions of local publishing. To produce a *qiaokan* signalled a family or lineage's achievement of wealth and power, under the special circumstances of emigration, or the elevation of a *qiaoxiang* county to higher status as a result of emigration and remittance. Like the old-style genealogies, *qiaokan* could signal or speed the further incorporation of an agnatic group newly enriched by *qiaopi*. They were distributed free, by mail in the case of overseas subscribers (Yao Ting and Mei Weiqiang 2009, 6), to anyone qualified to receive them. They were a low-level political response to emigration, and a mechanism to prevent the severing of the link between migrants and the local society they had left behind.

Abroad, the *qiaopi* trade had close connections with the new-style, modern press that sprouted alongside it, as one of the "three pillars" of overseas-Chinese society (the others being hometown associations and schools). Between 1815, when a Chinese newspaper is said to have appeared for the first time outside China (in Malacca), and 1996, at least 4,000 Chinese periodicals were published in Chinese and other languages in fifty-two countries and territories, alongside at least another 200 published by Chinese in languages other than Chinese (Benton and Gomez 2008, 192–193). In Thailand, the first Chinese-language daily was founded in 1903, and in later years sixty-five others followed. This press developed more or less hand-in-hand with the *qiaopiju* system in its heyday, and played a huge role in promoting it, through advertisements placed by *qiaopiju* owners out to recruit customers and reports on the *qiaopi* trade by journalists. The owners used the press to announce their removal to new premises (which happened frequently, as a result of expansion and shop fires), special offers, new regulations imposed either by the Chinese or Southeast Asian and other non-Chinese authorities, new currency arrangements, closures, and openings. During the early years of the War against Japan, they used the newspapers to warn Chinese and ethnic Chinese about Japanese attempts to gain control of the lucrative remittance trade (Cai Jinhe and Xu Guanghua 2014).

Qiaopi and national politics

Were the new identity created by *qiaopi* and other outcomes of migration in the *qiaoxiang* an equivalent, in the *qiaopi* sphere, of the postal culture that in Italy, North America, and elsewhere brought into being a communicative network that helped generate and was coterminous with the modern nation? Not really, for it formed in large part in opposition to Chinese national authority, with which it was in competition. It was a new-born thing, but not one that fed directly into Chinese nationalist politics. In China, it expressed a corporate regional identity: overseas, a corporate Chinese-diasporic identity. Even so, there was, at times, a strong lateral tie between *qiaopi* politics and Chinese national identity overseas.

A nationalist consciousness of the foreign threat to China arose most strongly among Chinese who experienced foreign power at first hand, along the Chinese coast and in Chinese settlements overseas. At first, the identity of Chinese overseas was chiefly cultural, and it remained deeply segmented along sub-ethnic lines. Not until the start of the twentieth century did it begin to take a political form, culminating in an attachment to the idea of Chinese nationhood. At first, Chinese politics overseas were confined to a minority of the educated elite, but in the 1920s it spread, in China and abroad, to educated youth. In the 1930s, it became a mass movement, representing all classes.

In Chinatown, *shuike* and *qiaopiju* owners were well equipped to play a part in ethnic-Chinese and diasporan politics, because of their force of character, native ability, resources, and extensive ties, in China, Chinatown, and the wider diaspora. They often took leading roles in Chinese Chambers of Commerce, the main site of political and economic activity at home and abroad, in the sending and receiving ports. They did so because of their position in the *qiaopi* trade and also because most big *qiaopi* traders had wide-ranging interests in all areas of society and the economy. This involvement of *qiaopi* traders in Chinatown politics was evident from the start. In eighteenth-century Batavia, for example, *shuike* were active in local Chinese institutions and regularly appeared before a tribunal of the local Chinese association, to defend their practices (Huang Ting 2008, 213–214).

Political mobilizations in support of the *qiaopi* trade preceded mobilizations in support of modern nationalism in China and the diaspora and, after its first full flowering, buoyed up and kept time with them. These political mobilizations could not have happened but for the prior consolidation of the trade, which came about after *qiaopi* agents were impelled on economic grounds to act together to find ways to minimize harmful competition and set common standards of conduct, in order to win the confidence of an understandably often doubting clientele. In China and the Chinese diaspora, the first trade association, the Nanyang Overseas Chinese *Qiaopi* Association 南侨批业公所, was set up in Shantou in the middle years of the Guangxu Reign (1875–1908).[11] Other associations followed, in Jieyang and Chaoyang, but the Shantou association led the trade, formulating safeguards and investigative procedures (Wang Weizhong 2007, 30–33). Abroad, similar organizations formed, sub-ethnically to start with but later along pan-Chinese lines.

These trade associations were tipped into politics by the hostile actions of the Chinese and other state authorities, which convinced the associations of the need for a unified response. Parts of the trade first struck a political stance in 1876, in protest at the Singapore Government's decision to set up a Chinese Sub-Post Office 华人小邮政局 and thus muscle in on the trade, while at the same time ridding it of what the colonial government saw as corrupt and inefficient practices. However, at that point the protest movement in Singapore (which led to days of rioting and a shop strike) was restricted to members of the Chaoshan group (Harris 2013; Li Zhixian 2013, 252–253).

The trade united on several other occasions in different places, in response to interference by the Chinese Government. In 1918, protests erupted in Shantou at Government plans to abolish both the *minxinju* and the *qiaopiju*. The protests spread to Beijing, where the Government backed down, though only in the case of the *qiaopi* trade. In 1923, 1928, 1934, and 1946, the trade again united, both in China and abroad and with varying degrees of success, against further attempts to rein it in, chiefly regarding the two issues of "clubbed packages" (the bulk delivery of bundled batches of *qiaopi*) and licensing. These movements embraced not just the *qiaopi* trade but overseas-Chinese communities and Chambers of Commerce as a whole, as well as business interests in China with overseas-Chinese connections (Chen Liyuan 2003, 98–99; Yang Qunxi 2004, 91–96; Wu Kuixin 2004, 206–207; Jia Junying 2012, 66).

Singapore was the main site of this organizing, probably as a result of its geographic centrality to the *qiaopi* trade, and because it was (and remains) the most solidly Chinese (or ethnic-Chinese) city outside China and Taiwan.[12] In May 1929, the city's Chinese Chamber of Commerce started a campaign in support of *qiaopi*, directly addressing Chiang Kai-shek and the Nanjing Government and

Southeast Asian colonial governments. The campaign broadened to encompass issues other than *qiaopi*, and created new sinews of transnational organization not just in Singapore but across the Chinese diaspora in Southeast Asia. Scarcely had the first wave subsided when a new campaign sprang up, in 1930, to oppose a rise by the authorities in the price of postage, and again supporters rallied round the movement, representing forces in both China and the diaspora. Finally, in 1935, the Chinese Government made important concessions to the overseas-Chinese pressure regarding the *qiaopi* trade (Chen Liyuan 2010, 166–179).

Even after these two movements, the three main *bang* in Singapore (Fujianese, Chaoshanese, and Hainanese) each retained its separate association (*gonghui* 公会), but in March 1946 a broadly based Nanyang Chinese Remittance Association 南洋中华汇业总汇 was formed under the leadership of Lin Shuyan (Lim Soo Gan 林树彦, 1913–1993), in principle serving the entire Malay Peninsula (Ke Mulin 2008, 470–474; Huang Qinghai and Liu Bozi 2010, 396). The occasion was the Singapore Government's renewed efforts to slap controls on the trade. The association's three main aims were to increase solidarity among the various *bang*, promote the industry, and carry out innovations and reforms. It claimed to represent *qiaopiju* workers as well as managers and owners, and organized welfare and educational activities (Li Zhixian 2014, 11–12). However, the proposed controls were relaxed after negotiations between the colonial government and the new body in which the former backed down from some of its demands (Wu Kuixin 2004, 202–203). Again, Singapore's deeply Chinese culture and demography perhaps explains its Chinese population's exceptional degree of cohesion (Ke Mulin 2008).

The *qiaopi* mobilizations in Singapore and elsewhere (notably Thailand) were part of a national and transnational (or diasporic) awakening of Chinese migrants. Although the mobilizations were in the first place economic, they also had great political potential, as well as the deeply emotional connotation of maintaining the tie to hearth and home. They not only reinforced the migrants' national identity but created a new sense of diasporic unity by fixing on an issue that Chinese migrants everywhere faced jointly and mattered to all.

On the economic front, the *qiaopi* traders, by acting unitedly, generally managed to head off the Chinese and other governments' attempts to rein them in and, ultimately, take possession of the trade and gain a monopoly of it. This was partly because the trade was too widely scattered, and the governments' resources were insufficient and they were, unlike the *qiaopiju*, incapable of acting transnationally. The Post Office had too few offices and agents, especially in rural areas, whither most *qiaopi* were bound. But most importantly, the government was unable to counter the political alliance of local and transnational interests, including emigrant organizations, Chambers of Commerce in China and abroad, the press, and the dependants that opposed or undermined government efforts (Yuan Ding *et al.* 2014, 109–133). The mobilizations set in train in Chinatowns throughout Southeast Asia were matched in vigour and extent only by the anti-Japanese mobilizations by Chinese in Southeast Asia and the world in 1937. Moreover, the transnational ties and identity created by the earlier campaigns in support of the *qiaopi* trade were a basis upon which anti-Japanese transnational movements could form, and a template for them, which took off among Chinese across Southeast Asia in the 1930s and 1940s (Chen Liyuan 2010).

In time, *qiaopi* networks stretched across regions and continents, and packed political as well as economic clout. The *qiaopi* trade in Thailand was closely linked, along particularistic ties, to its counterparts in Vietnam, Cambodia, and Laos (Chen Lie 2008, 227; Shen Jianhua 2014). Singapore was an even more important hub, handling nearly 18 per cent of all *qiaopiju* in the late 1940s. Almost from the start, it acted as a staging post for the wider region, including Borneo and Indonesia, mainly to avoid the excessive charges levied by post offices in places other than Singapore (Huang Qinghai and Liu Bozi 2010, 396–397; Jiang Ning 2010, 328–329).

The *qiaopi* trade played an important part in mobilizing overseas Chinese on a pan-Chinese basis, and this was reflected in the post-war years in their charitable giving. Diasporic philanthropy, often conducted through the medium of *qiaopi*, was to some extent synchronous with government initiatives in China and sometimes inextricable from them. This is most obvious in the case of wars, when overseas Chinese united behind the homeland effort. However, charity also chimed with government initiatives in other ways. As we have seen, the 1898 Wuxu Reforms, which aimed at sweeping social, institutional, and political change in China, though in themselves unsuccessful at the time, coincided with and inspired investment in education in the *qiaoxiang*.

Politics could also impede the *qiaopi* trade, for economic or ideological reasons. In the post-war years, colonial and other governments in Southeast Asia tried to restrict remittances to safeguard their own currencies and economies, and after 1947 some banned sending relief funds to China (Cheok *et al.* 2013, 92–94). During the Cultural Revolution, the Chinese government and local authorities discouraged remittances and stigmatized their recipients.

Qiaopi after 1937

In 1937, the Japanese invasion of northern and central China, consolidated between May and October 1938 by the invasion of Fujian and Guangdong, threw the *qiaopi* industry into panic and turmoil. During the war, the *qiaopi* trade in China had to contend with rival political authorities in what had previously been a more or less united country. However, contrary to what some historians have assumed or asserted, the barriers created by the war did not put an end to the import of remittances, although the political and military situation greatly complicated and hampered it in many places.

In the early years of the Sino-Japanese War, before the Pacific War engulfed Southeast Asia, the *qiaopi* industry supported the resistance to Japan in whatever ways it could, chiefly by donating huge amounts of its own money and of goods, remitting others' donations, and backing the call to boycott Japan, a campaign *qiaopiju* advertised on their envelopes (Jiang Ning 2008, 97; Fujian sheng dang'an guan 2013, 157). It was part of a massive political mobilization that has been called the "second overseas Chinese patriotic high tide", after the first one at the time of the birth of the Republic (Ren Guixiang 1989). Most donations went to the Guomindang Government in Wuhan and later Chongqing, but some went to the Communists, discreetly, in the form of "oral *pi*" sent via friends in China to the Eighth Route Army Office in the Nationalist capital (Wang Weizhong 2009, 52).[13]

Radical Chinese sent financial help and messages of political support to left-wing Nationalists in the 1930s and to the Communists in Yan'an after 1936. In 1931, Chinese in Vietnam donated 2,600 silver dollars to the Nineteenth Route Army in Shanghai, where it fought the Japanese at a time when Chiang Kai-shek was deemed to favour appeasement. In 1937, after the Marco Polo Bridge Incident, Chinese in Singapore immediately set about raising funds to support the Chinese resistance.[14] In 1938, young Chinese in Thailand sent 2 million guobi to the Communists' Eighth Route Army office in Wuhan (Wang Weizhong 2007, 101–102). Political donations continued after 1949. During the Korean War, *shuike* in Meixian raised more than 235 million yuan to "resist America and aid Korea" (Deng Rui 2010, 107).

During the war, the *qiaopi* trade, in so far as it survived, had to negotiate with, or evade, several different political authorities, in China and abroad. It developed closer ties than before with the Chinese Foreign Ministry and the Overseas Chinese Council, which cooperated with the Post Office and the Bank of China to simplify remittance procedures in Southeast Asia, lower the cost to remitters of remitting, reduce harmful competition, and strengthen remittance networks – all with one overriding end, to preserve the flow into China of foreign currency necessary for the war effort (Hong Lin 2006, 76; Zhang Xing 2013, 329–330).

Even in Japanese-occupied regions of southeastern China, the Post Office and its Savings Bank negotiated an agreement with the Japanese to keep remittance routes from Southeast Asia open, and for a while the volume of the trade increased. Letters were delivered across enemy lines, into occupied towns and villages. In 1942, the Japanese and the puppets even negotiated direct deals on currency transfer with the Nationalist postal authorities in Qujiang 曲江, Guangdong, where the latter had re-established their wartime headquarters. These authorities stayed in close touch with their branch in occupied Shantou. They not only supervised postal operations in occupied areas, especially regarding remittances, but issued policy directives (Yuan Ding *et al.* 2014, 134–173).

Wartime politics massively reshaped the *qiaopi* trade in the later stages of the war. The Japanese and puppet authorities were keen to keep the remittances flowing directly into areas under their control (rather than by way of Qujiang), in order to deny them to the Guomindang, help buoy up the economy and the occupation with foreign currency, and bolster the legitimacy of the puppet government, and they sought to control the *qiaopiju*, *yinhao*, and *qianzhuang* by threats and inducements. In February 1940, they organized Shantou's thirty-six surviving *qiaopiju* into a guild (*gonghui* 公会) and ordered them to cooperate with

Japanese-controlled banks in Taiwan to facilitate remittances. The guild handled remittances worth 111 million yuan between March 1940 and February 1941. However, not all *qiaopiju* stuck to the Japanese rules and some secretly delivered to villages beyond Japanese control, at great personal risk (Zhang Huimei 2004, 179–183; Zhang Xing 2013, 331).

At one time, it was widely assumed that the *qiaopi* trade largely came to a halt as a result of the invasion, but *qiaopi* studies have identified various paths along which substantial remittances continued to enter the occupied and blockaded *qiaoxiang*. Nationalist planners and Chaoshanese *qiaopiju* operators aimed to funnel remittances through Guangzhouwan (Kwangchowan), a small French enclave on Guangdong's Leizhou Peninsula ruled (anomalously) by Free France until 1943, but the plan failed, mainly because the route required a sea passage to Chaoshan, which was too hazardous at the time, and because the enclave lacked the facilities to deal with Southeast Asian currencies (Wang Weizhong 2007, 34; Jiang Ning 2008, 103–104; Wang Weizhong 2008, 205–207).

Eventually, a way into China was opened not by Nationalist administrators but by *qiaopi* entrepreneurs acting on their own initiative. They tried various land routes into China before finally settling on the border town of Dongxing (then in Guangdong, but now in Guangxi), the only established crossing still more or less open to traffic. The flow through Dongxing mitigated the Chaoshan famine of 1943, by injecting around $10 million a month, mainly in Vietnamese currency, into the *qiaoxiang* economy. At first, the town served only Vietnamese routes, but it soon incorporated Bangkok as well, and through Bangkok news of the Dongxing route spread to Cambodia and Laos. In Dongxing, the Nationalists provided a rough and ready institutional infrastructure to facilitate the trade, which they saw as a political as well as an economic triumph that they could parade as a sign of their authority.

During the war, China was broken into pieces, under rival regimes. The framework of the nation-state disintegrated and provinces and regions ceased to function as coherent units. In those years, the *qiaopi* industry survived by reviving or focusing even more intently on the traditional networks that had given birth to it, knitted together in the wider context of political and social forces, new and old associations, and competing states and parties (Zhang Huimei 2004). The war drove most *qiaopiju* to the wall, at least until after 1945. The main Chinese beneficiary was the state together with its banks and postal services. This happened because the war pitted the Chinese and the Japanese states against one another, and required the fullest possible mobilization of each side in every field. After the war, however, the Chinese state lost much of the ground it had gained during it, because of its general failings, including corruption and its inability to maintain a stable government and a modicum of prosperity and security.

After 1949, the *qiaopi* trade, born of the masses, was finally wound up by a government proclaiming itself the guide, guardian, product, and representative of the masses. However, the trade's demise did not happen all at once. It survived for two to three decades under the Communists, who, like the Nationalists before them, were deeply aware of its benefits and uses, not just for migrants' dependants but for the national economy.

The Communists' acquaintance with *qiaopi* preceded their ascent to power. Communist guerrillas controlled many of the villages in the Fujian and Guangdong *qiaoxiang* in the 1930s and the 1940s (though in many cases spasmodically), and during the Civil War of 1946–1949 they issued their own temporary local currency, the yuminjuan 裕民卷, in an effort to stabilize prices. Transfer into this currency was required of *qiaopi* brought into guerrilla areas by couriers (Zhang Mingshan 2006, 103; Chen Haizhong 2013).

We know little about Communist involvement with the internal workings of the *qiaopi* trade. Given the radical inclinations of many young overseas Chinese, especially just before, during, and after the Sino-Japanese War, and the nature of the trade, which was both financially attractive to the Party and offered it a secret path and line of communications into parts of China where it had been strongly rooted ever since the 1920s, it would not be surprising to learn that Communists did infiltrate the *qiaopiju*, but we have only one record of such infiltration. That is the case of Zhang Bogong 张伯恭, who was born in Thailand in 1921, "returned" to China in 1925, and joined the Party in 1939 in Puning in southeastern Guangdong, where he ran its liaison station. Zhang Bogong gave the Party 3,000 yuan of remittance money to fund its Chaozhou-Meixian Committee and a bookshop, and in 1942 the Party located him back to Thailand. There he ran a remittance office that was highly lucrative and employed up-to-date electronic equipment: he used some of the profit to fund the Party and used the radio to send political, military, and economic intelligence back to China (Luo Zeyang 2010). Zhang's activity is the only evidence we have so far of a Communist association with the *qiaopi* trade in the revolutionary years.

In the 1950s and the early 1960s, the *qiaopi* trade was politicized and efforts were made to re-engineer it along lines of social class, separating the workers from the *qiaopiju* owners. The Communist authorities staged conferences in Fujian and Guangdong, to sing the praises of the *qiaopi* trade and "consult" its practitioners (Fujian sheng dang'an guan 2013, 96). At the time, remittances were still one of China's two main sources of foreign currency (Peterson 2012).

For several years, the young state formulated its policy regarding "overseas Chinese", their dependants in China, and the *qiaopi* carefully and sensitively. Policy conducted under He Xiangning 何香凝, a Guomindang leftist, was not unfavourable to the dependants and their overseas relatives, who continued to remit on a relatively large scale (Jiang Guohua 2009, 56–57). At first, the Communists left in place much of the legislation and many of the practices regarding *qiaopi* that they had inherited from the Nationalist era, and the volume of remittances rose in places. The impact of land reform on wealthy families played a role in the rise, for the loss of rent and interest forced some previously landowning dependants to request additional remittances from migrants (Yang Qunxi 2004, 131–132).

Qiaopiju continued their activities throughout the early years of the new regime. *Shuike* were also encouraged to register with the authorities – several hundred did in Meizhou in 1950. The *shuike* also acquired a new official title, *qiaopiyuan* 侨批员 (*qiaopi* officer), in recognition of their incorporation into the state (Deng Rui 2004, 59–61; Xia Shuiping and Fang Xuejia 2004, 180).

But the *qiaopiju*s' days were numbered, because of political developments and changes at home and abroad. In Thailand, the Government took measures to control foreign currency in the early 1950s that radically affected their functioning (Li Daogang 2010, 128–132). In 1951, the US Foreign Assets Control Board forbade remittances to China, and most of its Southeast Asian allies quickly followed suit (Sung 1967, 19–20; Peterson 2012, 68).

Qiaopi officials in China mounted political campaigns and reverted to underground methods invented in earlier years to deal with foreign governments' attempts to ban or restrict remittances. Secret codes were revived to disguise remittances (Wang Fubing 2013, 62). In Guangdong, a special "*huipi* team" was set up to supervise the writing of *huipi* and to ensure that they maintained secrecy (Zeng Xubo 2004, 220–229; Lu Yongguang 2006, 157). *Qiaopi* officers, the *shuike* and *pijiao* of the old days, encouraged dependants to badger their relatives for money to build houses, and rival teams competed with one another to see who could raise the most. Often, team members wrote letters on the recipients' behalf – one team in Zhangzhou wrote more than 3,500 letters and traced 267 migrated relatives between 1956 and 1960, in the endless search for new sources of remittance (Ma Zhenhui 2008; Zou Qiudong and Su Tonghai 2009, 72–73). They also, as we have seen, encouraged the illiterate wives of migrants to learn to read and write, so they could request remittances themselves (Shen Huifen 2012, 90).

Despite these developments, the trade started to decline in the late 1950s, again mainly for political reasons. In some Southeast Asian countries, the authorities clamped down even more forcibly than before on remittances, and arrested traders and couriers. In Vietnam, an anti-Chinese campaign in 1956 led to persecution of the Chinese minority. In China itself, the authorities took action against currency smuggling, which revived towards the end of the decade, and placed the trade under "mass surveillance". The socialization of agriculture in the mid-1950s frightened many migrants, who feared being denounced as "class enemies" if they sent money back. Whatever Government spokespersons might say to reassure remitters, envious or radical local leaders often acted on their own authority, harassing recipients of big remittances or confiscating them (Chen Haizhong 2013). In 1956, the *qiaopi* trade was reorganized and federated, although *qiaopiju* were still allowed to operate under their old names and signboards (Yang Qunxi 2004, 195; Wang Weizhong 2007, 49). In 1958, the ownership of the remaining *qiaopiju* changed from "collective" to "of the whole people" (Jia Junying 2012, 87–88), a further move in the direction of their complete subjection to state control. In the course of the 1950s, the number of *qiaopiju* fell, by nearly half in southern Fujian, to around one hundred (Jiao Jianhua and Xu Cuihong 2004, 165). As a result of all these factors, the volume of remittances started to shrink in 1957 and fell to a new low in 1959, when Spring Festival remittances fell by more than half over the previous year (Shantou

Huaqiao zhi (chugao) 1990, 131–137). In 1962, the amount remitted through Chaoshan stood at one-fifth of the 1952 level. This was followed by a brief revival, to which the Cultural Revolution then put an end.

During the Cultural Revolution, prosperous migrants and their dependants or descendants that had bought property in the *qiaoxiang* became "objects of dictatorship" and, for the most part, stopped remitting. The dependants risked persecution and criminalization (Yang Qunxi 2004, 182–185 and 375). During land reform, the officials in charge generally restricted correspondence between dependants and their relatives overseas, to prevent the former from revealing the actual situation. Overseas Chinese also wrote home less frequently. Some letters were sent to the people in charge of the peasant association. As long as the situation at home was not clarified, Overseas Chinese were worried that their remittances would be confiscated, so in those days remittances either decreased or ceased entirely.[15] Some families in China wrote letters breaking off relations with their relatives overseas. Authorities stamped the envelopes bearing their *huipi* with strident political slogans and directives (Chen Chuangyi 2004, 305). In 1969, the *qiaopiju* were incorporated under the People's Bank, as so-called "*qiaopi* stations". It was not until the early 1970s that the hostility towards the trade abated (Wang Linqian 2008, 465; Huang Jiaxiang 2010, 506–509).

In 1979, the *qiaopi* trade was fully subsumed into the state financial system (though it seems to have lasted a little longer in some places than in others). It became an integral part of the People's Bank, which now guaranteed delivery of remittances within five days. Thus, the *qiaopiju* finally disappeared from the stage (Jiang Ning 2010, 334; Zou Jinsheng 2010, 406). At the same time, the accent in Government pronouncements (following the Third Plenum of 1978) switched from remitting to investing, as well as to donating to good causes (Deng Rui 2004, 64). The *shuike* were also decreed out of existence, in 1977 (Xia Shuiping and Fang Xuejia 2004, 181).

Politics and *qiaopi* studies

Politics have played a major role in the life of *qiaopi* studies under the Communists. Until the 1980s, few studies were done on ethnic and migrant Chinese communities abroad or their reciprocators in the sending regions, partly because of the stigmatization in the Cultural Revolution of groups with "foreign" ties. However, once the stigmatization ceased and restrictions on scholarship in China fell away in the 1980s, new methods of study and new attitudes developed. Scholarship in general became not only more diverse but more local, as monolithic models weakened in all spheres. This localism interacted with the strengthening of regional identities as the Chinese economy also "localized". Economic growth in the *qiaoxiang* and the strengthening of contacts with Overseas Chinese created a political and material base for the funding of new regional studies in which the Overseas Chinese role was often paramount. The attention of students of migration shifted from the nation-state and the provinces, long the dominant framework of its construction, to its deepest and most fundamental level, in villages, lineages, and families (Williams 2003, 86). One outcome of this was the rediscovery of the *qiaopi* trade, formally established as a school of research in November 2000 by Jao Tsung-i 饶宗颐,[16] in a lecture at the Centre for the Study of Chaoshan History and Culture located in Shantou.

China's political culture and economic system are no longer as rigidly centralized as they once were, and they were never as centralized as in the Soviet Union. Regional differences and political cultures were not wiped out by the revolution, and some new ones formed as a result of it, particularly in the southeastern provinces, which had their own revolutionary factions and traditions.[17] Since the post-Mao reforms, regional differentiation has deepened, as power in the national economy and political system is increasingly transferred downwards. Local and regional fortes are now pridefully declared rather than hidden. Different regions excel in different ways, but a strong suit of the southeast is its history of emigration. This is a particularly useful distinction in an age when China is expanding into ever more overseas markets, one that regional leaders can use to strengthen their hand in the country's national and provincial councils. The emergence of *qiaopi* studies since the early 1990s must be understood in the context of this regionalization of historiography and the political economy.

Historians of the *qiaoxiang* of Guangdong and Fujian pride themselves on the special character they claim centuries of overseas navigation and emigration have stamped on the two provinces. Like other regions and nations worldwide from which large numbers of people have left to go overseas, the tradition of venturing abroad to make a living has, according to their analysis, made sectors of the Cantonese and Fujianese population outward-looking rather than narrowly focused on the landside.[18] *Qiaopi* historians have resurrected from Hegel (a philosopher with whom they are probably familiar through Marx) the separation of the world into the potamic (rivers), the thalassic (inland seas), and the oceanic (categories he borrowed from the philosophical geography of Carl Schmitt), corresponding to Asia, Europe, and England and America (or to ancient, middle, and modern). According to Hegel, nations (like China) that shun navigation do not know freedom and sink into stagnation and superstition, whereas sea peoples are creative and industrious[19] and without limits, like the ocean, a "free element". They are wise, brave, and transcendent rather than closed and conservative (Zheng Youguo 2013).

Qiaopi historians have extended this division into coastal and non-coastal cultures to China. Pace Hegel, who saw China as "the realm of theocratic despotism", they argue that China had its oceanic culture in the past and must now reclaim it, and that sea-facing regions never lost it. One study describes China's southern peoples as "an ethnic group with oceanic characteristics", imbued with "oceanic civilisation" (Su Wenjing and Huang Qinghai 2013, 40). In applying these labels, historians implicitly assert the superiority over other parts of the country of the seaward southeast, especially Fujian, locked off until recently from the Chinese hinterland by high mountains with few passes, and also of Guangdong, furthest away from the stagnant and corrupting culture of China's landlocked heartland.

According to the newly revived regional lore, the southern Fujianese are courageous and heroic, a disposition that led Fujian's Han pioneers hundreds of years ago to climb into the region across perilous peaks. Their spirit is "daring and adventurous … and thick with sea culture" (Wu Hongli 2008, 367). The Chinese of southern Fujian are sometimes called the "Jews of China" or of Asia, a moniker scholars of the region accept with pride.[20] As for the *qiaopi* managers, they were "Robinson Crusoe-style ocean heroes".[21]

However, these historians also argue that the oceanic tradition of Fujian and Guangdong is no mere replica of foreign models but (like Deng Xiaoping's socialism) has Chinese characteristics. It is a synthesis of China's Central Plains culture, which the pioneers brought south, Fujian's pre-Han indigenous culture, and oceanic culture. The impulse to sail the world and form communities abroad broke a major taboo of Chinese culture, that one must on no account "go roaming while one's parents are alive". However, it did not lead in China to a severing of the homeland tie. In that regard, China's heroes were quite unlike the "British ocean hero". They fulfilled humanity's "eternal wish" to conquer nature, but at the same time they recognized their responsibility to their ancestors and kith and kin. Indeed, it was attachment to the family that led them to go overseas in the first place, as the family's representatives. Foreign exploration strengthened rather than weakened the tie, because of the lineage system, Chinese people's native-place orientation, and the control of emigration by senior kin, who kept the womenfolk at home. The *qiaopi* was a main link in this chain (Su Wenjing and Huang Qinghai 2013, 40–41).

The oceanic attribution is based on the unusual history of the southeastern provinces, whose inhabitants are known to have been trading and settling overseas as early as the Tang (618–907) (Mao Chujian 2008, 20), even more so after the southward refocusing of the Chinese economy in the Southern Song (1127–1279) (Wang Weizhong 2007, 4). Maritime activity was prohibited under the *haijin* 海禁 (sea bans) during much of the Ming and Qing, to curb piracy and prevent the emergence of self-sufficient regional economies. Coastal trade and shipping was declared illegal, and coastal populations were relocated inland. Although traders and emigrants did send back remittances to their families, returning to China during the bans was illegal and dangerous. Remittances were confiscated if detected, and their potential recipients were liable to severe penalties. However, during some of the Ming and Qing, ports in southern Fujian and eastern Guangdong were officially thrown open to trade, private and public, particularly with the Philippines and Thailand. Local merchants sailed around the whole of Southeast Asia and covered it with an ever growing and ever more diverse network of transnational operations (Chen Xunxian 2010, 183–186). When "sea bans" were imposed, they flouted them, and "the four oceans became their home" (Luo Zeyang 2004, 208–210). The "ocean economy" thrived most, in pre-modern days, in the thirteenth to eighteenth centuries, when Chinese merchants competed successfully with European traders in Southeast Asia, even in periods when the Chinese court "disowned" them (Su Wenjing and Huang Qinghai 2013, 40). However, it continued to influence the thinking and outlook of merchants in southern China through into modern times (Zhang Linyou 2014, 226–227).

Historians of the *qiaopi* trade claim that the region's seaward gaze and the extent of private trade in the southeast led to the creation of a political and economic culture that did not relegate merchants to the despised fourth class in the traditional division of society into scholars, farmers, artisans, and merchants usually observed in China but even admired them (Wu Hongli 2008, 362). Jao Tsung-i, the main exponent of the special nature of the southeast, has argued that Chaozhou's merchant culture "led the way" in the region's history of overseas exploration and was at the same time "a product of a seaborne *yangwu* 洋务 culture" (Chen Xunxian 2008, 168). (The Yangwu ["foreign affairs"] Movement paralleled the Self-Strengthening Movement at the time of the late-Qing reforms.)

The *qiaopi* trade was committed to upholding traditional morality and cultural values, and so were most of its customers. Although the trade was based on notions of commerce and exchange with strong modern and non-traditional associations, traditional moral values lay at its heart. This is obvious from the names adopted by the *qiaopiju*, formed by characters drawn from Confucian maxims (Wan Dongqing 2010, 294). Confucian values – of benevolence, filial piety, love and respect for one's elder brother, valuing righteousness above material gain, modesty and yielding, sincerity and trust – were reflected not only in the organization of the *qiaopi* trade but in the contents of the letters it delivered (Chen Xiaojie *et al.*, 2008, 442–443). In contemporary China, where Confucian values are once again praised after a century of vituperation, much of the commentary on the *qiaopi* trade focuses on its morality. In 2014, one group of *qiaopi* enthusiasts even went so far as to propose declaring a Day of Filial Piety and Fraternal Duty (*xiaoqin ri* 孝亲日) in honour of it (*Fujian qiaobao*, 4 July 2014). So this aspect of the trade has reacquired contemporary political relevance.

Conclusion

Benedict Anderson's genealogy of nationhood in the Third World has been criticized for asserting that Third World nationalists copied their idea of the nation from American and European models and neglecting the nationalists' creativity (Desai 2009). The emergence in the *qiaoxiang* of Guangdong and Fujian of an indigenous political and social culture, of print and post, intent (at least initially) not on stoking nationalism or overthrowing the *ancien regime* but on maintaining emotional and economic ties between migrants and their sending towns and (more commonly) their villages supports the critics' view.[22] The *qiaoxiang* case shows that Third-World nation-building was not just an iteration of American and European models but a phenomenon with deep indigenous roots.

The *qiaopi* trade was the basis for one of China's earliest excursions into the modern world economy, and it sprouted a political dimension. After progressing from the one-man operations of the early years to the *qiaopiju* that formed to take advantage of the opportunities offered by the swift growth of Chinese emigration and remittance, it eventually matured into a stable industry with its own perfected mechanisms linked to China's other modern institutions, like the banks and the Post Office, and to modern forms of communication and transport. It also gave an impetus to other forms of transnational and domestic industry and to urban growth and political change in coastal cities adjacent to the *qiaoxiang*. Initially based on networks of blood, place, and tongue, it later joined or created national, transnational, and international networks based on trade and finance. These networks, maritime and terrestrial, were not just economic but had deep cultural, political, and social dimension.

For many years, the unique role of the *qiaopi* trade in promoting the southeastern China's modernization and contributing to the economic health of China as a whole was obscured. This was partly because of the centralist political fixation of Chinese governments of all stripes, starting with the imperial court and ending with the Communists. Although China's modern revolutions either started in the south (in the Nationalist case) or retreated there in the late 1920s (in the case of the Communists, whose geography starting in the early 1930s extended, more or less uninterruptedly, through until 1949, to many *qiaoxiang*), this was forgotten or neglected under the consolidated regimes, whose political history was rewritten with a bias to reflect the hegemony of first Chiang Kaishek and then Mao Zedong, leaders whose tie to the south frayed. The neglect was also due, in part, to a relative lack of source materials. The documentary record was far more copious in the case of the Shanxi traders and bankers of the north, who founded China's modern banking system, and the banks and industries of Shanghai and Tianjin (Zhang Linyou 2014, 223).

Since the 1990s, however, the founding of *qiaopi* archives in Guangdong and Fujian has turned the *qiaoxiang* and their nearby cities into a new focus of historical, political, and sociological research. Departments of local and regional government have also begun to promote *qiaopi* studies, as a topic in "patriotic education" and an early example of transnationalism and economic expansion, a "maritime silk road", to match the northern land-based New Silk Road through Central Asia. Together, the two routes form the "One Belt One Road" initiative, Xi Jinping's signature foreign policy initiative since 2013 (Summers 2016). In September 2014, the State Council even agreed to designate Shantou's Special Economic Zone as "an important passageway to 'the Silk Road on the Sea' ", China's first such (Chen Hanchu 2014, 121). This shows that the *qiaopi* trade's political role is still not spent, some forty years after its demise in mainland China.

Chinese economic and political culture is often reduced to a single stereotype rooted in Confucian ideas about Chinese society, which supposedly could be jolted into the modern world only by exogenous shocks, but studies on the *qiaopi* trade have started to rewrite the history and geography of Chinese modernism. This rewriting, which resurrects old ideas about the special nature of China's southeastern littoral, is closely connected with new trends in regional politics, now tolerated by a system formerly more interested in homogeny than distinctions.

Over the years, *qiaopi* generated a rich culture with many regional and national variants in China and the world. In recent years, as part of the campaign to get *qiaopi* recognized as part of the UNESCO Memory of the World heritage, *qiaopi* historians in Fujian, Guangdong, and Chinese communities in many countries have worked hard to rescue this tradition from the oblivion into which it seemed destined to fade, and told the story of the trade and the letters as a special branch of China's national and transnational story, with its own strong local colours. In the course of its rediscovery and reimagining, it has become entwined with regional and diasporic identity, which has not just a cultural dimension but a solid material and financial one. As economic, administrative, and political decision-making in China becomes increasingly devolved and as old regional politics starts to regain traction and new political identities begin to emerge, the history of the *qiaopi* trade is woven into China's budding polycentric politics.

The *qiaopi* trade, from its tiny geographic base, had a profound impact on China's national economy, and was not without relevance to its politics. The focus of research on China's modern economy in the early years has been overwhelmingly on Shanghai and the eastern seaboard, but research into the *qiaopi* trade shows that Shanghai and Hong Kong were, to a much larger extent than previously thought, indebted to it: without its input, their economies would have been substantially weaker. The trade also transformed coastal parts of southern Fujian and eastern Guangdong. True, it did not lead to the creation of a sustainable modern economy in the *qiaoxiang*, because of the ubiquitous political and military chaos and other factors, including a lack of transport and modern communications, but it did fuel the development of modern cities in the southeast and lead to the introduction into economically backward regions of some modern forms of politics and administration, notably banks and a postal culture. One of its greatest achievements was to catapult the previously impoverished and marginal *qiaoxiang* to the top of regional and even national school leagues in China.

Perhaps its most important legacy to China and Southeast Asia was its creation of numerous political and economic bridges and transnational ties between China's *qiaoxiang* and their nearby cities on the one hand and migrant communities overseas. These ties extended far beyond their original scope, as conduits for remittances, and swelled over time into a broader channel for the exchange of goods and people.

Notes

1 On this point, see Benton 1992 and 1999, where the bases are listed and described.

2 Letter sent by Ye Tang in the US to his brother in the hometown in 1925.

3 Provided by City of Vancouver Archives, No. 1108141.

4 *Qiaopi* managers and the owners of remittance shops were not always willing donors. Handling *qiaopi* was a lucrative enterprise that stuck out prominently in places where prosperity was new, and it was hard to hide from powerful local factions. Authorities and local strongmen constantly demanded "donations" to "social" funds that might or might not have lived up to their name. *Qiaopi* managers had to factor in this pestering

for "donations" as a necessary expense (Yang Qunxi 2004, 467; Huang Jiaxiang 2010, 503–4).

5 The term "sub-ethnic" is questionable. Honig 1992, 10, prefers to call local attachments "ethnic".

6 Interview with Mr Wang Chunxu, Singapore, 27 April 2015.

7 *Sin Chew Daily*, 8 July 1929; 15 July 1929; 8 March 1930; 11 March 1930; 30 March 1930.

8 http://blog.sciencenet.cn/blog-415-788201.html, accessed 2 May 2015.

9 On genealogical records, see Meskill 1970, 139–161.

10 On the gazetteers, see Zurndorfer 1995, 187–195.

11 It changed its name in 1926 to Shantou Qiaopi Association 汕头侨批同业公会 and in 1931 to Shantou City Qiaopi Association 汕头市侨批业同业公会. www.chaorenwang.com/qiaopi1/content.asp?id=810, accessed 29 April 2017.

12 On Singapore's position as the nexus of ethnic Chinese social and business networks in Asia, see Liu 1999 and Liu and Wong 2004.

13 The pro-Communist remitters received a reply from Zhou Enlai and other leaders proudly described by *qiaopi* historians as a *huipi* (Chen Shengsheng 2013, 227).

14 *Sin Chew Daily*, 17 July 1937.

15 Zhang Huimei, interview with local officials in Shantou, 9 November 2005.

16 Jao Tsung-i (1917–2018) was a leading Sinologist who taught in India, Singapore, the USA, and Japan. In 1962, The Académie des Inscriptions et Belles-Lettres awarded him the Prix Stanislas Julien.

17 This is a theme of Benton 1992.

18 For example, in his preface to the multi-volume histories of overseas Chinese from Guangdong, Zhu Xiaodan, the then Governor of the province, said in 2014 that "the history and development of overseas Chinese originating from Guangdong is not only an important component of Chinese history, but also a shining chapter indispensable for the history of the world" (Liu Jin 2014a).

19 Georg Wilhelm Friedrich Hegel, *Elements of the Philosophy of Right*, § 247.

20 Huang Qinghai 2009, 55. This name is also applied to the Wenzhounese, another sub-ethnic group in southeastern China with a global trading reputation.

21 This focus on enterprise and expansion chimes with China's current efforts to establish a "new silk road" to the West, but whereas Beijing's main official emphasis is on reviving the northern route across Central Asia, strategists in the southeast talk about reviving the "maritime silk road" or "silk road on water", of which the *qiaopi* trade was an essential part (Rana and Chia 2014).

22 On this point, see also Hsu 2000a, 312, fn. 11, and 326.

References

Anderson, Benedict R. O'G. 1991. *Imagined Communities: Reflections on the Origin and Spread of Nationalism*, revised and extended edition, London: Verso.

Benton, Gregor. 1992. *Mountain Fires: The Red Army's Three-Year War in South China, 1934–1938*, Berkeley: University of California Press.

Benton, Gregor. 1999. *New Fourth Army: Chinese Communist Resistance along the Yangtze and the Huai, 1938–1941*, Berkeley: University of California Press.

Benton, Gregor, and E. T. Gomez. 2008. *Chinese in Britain, 1800–2000: Economy, Transnationalism, Identity*, Basingstoke: Palgrave.

Cai Jinhe 蔡金河 and Xu Guanghua 许光华. 2014. "Shilun Taiguo Huawen bao dui Taiguo qiaopi ye de gongxian" ("On the contribution of Thailand's Chinese-language press to Thailand's *qiaopi* trade"), in Zhongguo lishi wenxian yanjiu hui, eds, 2014, pp. 365–370.

Chaoshan lishi wenhua yanjiu zhongxin, eds, 2007. *Chaoshan Qiaopi Jicheng* [Collection of Chaoshan *Qiaopi*], vol. 1, no. 1, Guilin: Guangxi Normal University Press.

Chatterjee, Partha. 1993. "Whose Imagined Community?" in Chatterjee, *The Nation and Its Fragments: Colonial and Postcolonial Histories*, Princeton: Princeton University Press, pp. 1–13.

Chen Chuangyi 陈创义. 2004. "Qiaopi: Fengge dute de qunti shuxin" [*Qiaopi*: Collective letters with a special character], in Wang Weizhong, ed., 2004, pp. 303–306.

Chen Haizhong 陈海忠. 2013. "Lishi jiyi zhong de Chaoshan qiaopi yu xiangcun shehui" [Chaoshan *qiaopi* and village society in historical memory], in Zhongguo qiaopi shijie jiyi gongcheng guoji yantao hui zuwei hui, eds, 2013, pp. 296–307.

Chen Hanchu 陈汉初. 2010. "Chaoshan qiaopi de dang'an wenxian jiazhi" [The documentary value of the Chaoshan *qiaopi* archive], in Wang Weizhong, ed., 2010, pp. 82–93.

Chen Hanchu 陈汉初. 2014. "Qiaopi toudi: Dute de 'haishang sichou zhi lu'" [*Qiaopi* delivery: A unique 'maritime silk road'], in Zhongguo lishi wenxian yanjiu hui, eds, 2014, pp. 109–122.

Chen Lie 陈列. 2008. "Guanyu Chaoshan qiaopi wenhua ruogan wentide qiantan" [Some observations on some questions concerning Chaoshan *qiaopi* culture], in Wang Weizhong, ed., 2008, pp. 225–236.

Chen Liyuan 陈丽园. 2003. "Jindai haiwai Huaren de kuaguo zhuyi yanjiu" [Research into transnationalism among today's overseas ethnic Chinese], in Li Zhixian 李志贤, ed., 2003, pp. 85–101.

Chen Liyuan 陈丽园. 2010. "Qiaopi yu kuaguo Huaren shehui de jiangou" [*Qiaopi* and the construction of transnational ethnic-Chinese society], in Wang Weizhong, ed., 2010, pp. 164–180.

Chen Shengsheng 陈胜生. 2013. "Cong kangzhan houqi de 'Dongxing huilu' shixi qiaopi de shijie yiyi" [Analysing the world significance of *qiaopi* on the basis of the 'Dong xing remittance route' of the later period of the War of Resistance], in Zhongguo qiaopi shijie jiyi gongcheng guoji yantao hui zuwei hui, eds, 2013, pp. 219–240.

Chen Xiaogang 陈小钢, ed. 2009. *Huiwang Minnan qiaopi: Shoujie Minnan qiaopi yantao hui lunwen ji* [Looking back on Minnan *qiaopi*: Collection of papers of the first Minnan *qiaopi* conference], Quanzhou: Huayi chuban she.

Chen Xiaojie 陈晓杰 *et al.*, 2008. "Fengge dute de Chaoshan qiaopi" [The special style of Chaoshan *qiaopi*], in Wang Weizhong, ed., 2008, pp. 442–449.

Chen Xunxian 陈训先. 2008. "Qiaopi ye yu Chao shang wen hua yuan" [The *qiaopi* trade and the origins of Chao merchant culture] in Wang Weizhong, ed., 2008, pp. 167–171.

Chen Xunxian 陈训先. 2010. "Lun 'yinxin hefeng'" [On 'silver and letter in one envelope'], in Wang Weizhong, ed., 2010, pp. 181–189.

Cheok, Cheong Kee, Lee Kam Hing, and Poh Ping Lee. 2013. "Chinese Overseas Remittances to China: The Perspective from Southeast Asia", *Journal of Contemporary Asia*, 43(1): 75–101.

Cotreau, James D. 1975. *The Historical Development of the Universal Postal Union and the Question of Membership*, Boston: n.p.

Deng Dahong 邓达宏. 2014. "Lüelun guoji yimin shuxin dui qiaoxiang jiaoyu de ying xiang" [On the influence of international migrants' letters on *qiaxiang* education], in Zhongguo lishi wenxian yanjiu hui, eds, 2014, pp. 99–108.

Deng Rui 邓锐. 2004. "Cong Meizhou shi qiaohui de fazhan guocheng kan qiaopiju xingshuai" [Looking at the rise and fall of *qiaopi* offices from the point of view of the development of overseas remittances in Meizhou], in Wang Weizhong, ed., 2004, pp. 57–64.

Deng Rui 邓锐. 2010. "Qiantan qiaopi de zhongyao zuoyong ji kaifa liyong" [On the important role and uses of *qiaopi*], in Wang Weizhong, ed., 2010, pp. 103–117.

Desai, Radhika. 2009. "The Inadvertence of Benedict Anderson: Engaging Imagined Communities", *The Asia-Pacific Journal*, 16 March.

Du Shimin 杜式敏. 2004. "Chaoshan qiaopi de funü guan chutan" [On the view of women in Chaoshan *qiaopi*], in Wang Weizhong, ed., 2004, pp. 286–293.

Fujian sheng dang'an guan 福建省档案馆, eds. 2013. *Bainian kuaguo liangdi shu* [Hundred years of letters between two transnational places], Xiamen: Lujiang chuban she.

Harris, Lane Jeremy. 2012. *The Post Office and State Formation in Modern China, 1896–1949*, PhD dissertation, University of Illinois at Urbana-Champaign.

Harris, Lane Jeremy. 2013. "The 1876 Post Office Riot in Singapore", *The Newsletter* (IIAS), no. 63.

Henkin, David M. 2006. *The Postal Age: The Emergence of Modern Communications in Nineteenth-Century America*, Chicago: University of Chicago Press.

Hong Lin 洪林 2006. "Jianshu Chaoshan lunxian qianhou yu Xianluo qiaopi ye" ["On Chaoshan before and after its fall [to Japan] and the Siam qiaopi trade"], in Hong Lin and Li Daogang, eds., 2006, pp. 73–77.

Hong Lin 洪林 and Li Daogang 黎道纲, eds. 2006. *Taiguo qiaopi wenhua* [Thailand's *qiaopi* culture], n.p.: Taiguo xuehui congshu.

Honig, Emily. 1992. *Creating Chinese Ethnicity: Subei People in Shanghai, 1850–1980*, New Haven, CT: Yale University Press.

Hsu, Madeline Y. 2000a. "Migration and Native Place: *Qiaokan* and the Imagined Community of Taishan County, Guangdong, 1893–1993", *The Journal of Asian Studies*, 59(2): 307–331.

Hsu, Madeline Y. 2000b. *Dreaming of Gold, Dreaming of Home: Transnationalism and Migration Between the United States and South China, 1882–1943*, Stanford: Stanford University Press.

Huang, Cen, and Michael R. Godley. 1999. "A Note on the Study of *Qiaoxiang* Ties", in Leo Douw, Cen Huang, and Michael R. Godley, eds, *Qiaoxiang Ties: Interdisciplinary Approaches to "Cultural Capitalism" in South China*, London: Kegan Paul, pp. 306–338.

Huang Jiaxiang 黄家祥. 2008. "Zhaoan qiaopi ye chutan" [Preliminary investigations into the Zhaoan *qiaopi* trade], in Wang Weizhong, ed., 2008, pp. 337–344.

Huang Jiaxiang 黄家祥. 2010. "Zhaoan qiaopi ye liubian" [Flow and change in the Zhaoan *qiaopi* trade], in Wang Weizhong, ed., 2010, pp. 502–510.

Huang Qinghai 黄清海. 2009. "Cong Quanzhou qiaoxiang jingji fazhan guiji kan Minnan qiaopi baohu de yiyi" [Looking at the meaning of the preservation of *qiaopi* from the point of view of the trajectory of the development of the southern Fujianese economy], *Haiwai chuanzhen*, 2: 53–55.

Huang Qinghai 黄清海 and Liu Bozi 刘伯孳. 2010. "Qiantan Xinjiapo qiaopi zhongxin" [On the Singapore *qiaopi* centre], in Wang Weizhong, ed., 2010, pp. 392–401.

Huang Shaoxiong 黄少雄. 2004. "Chao ji qiaopi lishi tan yuan" [Exploring the origins of Chao *qiaopi* history], in Wang Weizhong, ed., 2004, pp. 107–110.

Huang Ting 黄挺. 2008. "'Gongan bu' suo jian zaoqi qiaopi ye yunying de yixie wenti" [Some questions in the operations of the *qiaopi* trade in the early period encountered in the 'public ledgers'], in Wang Weizhong, ed., 2008, pp. 208–217.

Jia Junying 贾俊英. 2012. Qiaopi shi yanjiu: Yi Tianyi ju wei gean de kaocha [Research into the history of *qiaopi*: An investigation using the Tianyi office as a case study], MA thesis, Huaqiao University.

Jiang Guohua 蒋国华. 2009. "Qiaopi ye wei guojia waihui shouru zuochu zhongyao gongxian" [The *qiaopi* trade's important contribution to national foreign-currency income], in Chen Xiaogang, ed., 2009, pp. 56–58.

Jiang Ning 江宁. 2008. "Qiaopi yu kuaguo jinrong de hudong" [The interaction between *qiaopi* and international finance], in Wang Weizhong, ed., 2008, pp. 95–110.

Jiang Ning 江宁. 2010. "Bu tong zhengzhi tongzhi xia de qiaopiju" [Remittance offices under two different political control systems], in Wang Weizhong, ed., 2010, pp. 328–336.

Jiao Jianhua 焦建华. 2005. "Zhidu chuangxin yu wenhua chuantong: Shixi jindai pixinju de jingying zhidu" [System creation and cultural tradition: Analysing the management system of the modern remittance company], *Zhongguo shehui jingji shi yanjiu*, 2: 64–70.

Jiao Jianhua 焦建华 and Xu Cuihong 徐翠红. 2004. "Jindai pixin ju tese tanyuan" [Origins of the special features of modern remittance offices], in Wang Weizhong, ed., 2004, pp. 164–173.

John, Richard R. 2009. *Spreading the News: The American Postal System from Franklin to Morse*, Cambridge, MA: Harvard University Press.

Kádár, Daniel Z. 2011. *Historical Chinese Letter Writing*, London: Continuum.

Ke Mulin 柯木林. 1991. "The Finding of Chengyi Maxi Village Lin's Clan Genealogy and its Historical Values", *Journal of Southeast Asian Affairs*, 1: 70–76.

Ke Mulin 柯木林. 2008. "Xinjiapo minxinye lingxiu Lin Shuyan" [The Singapore remittance trade leader Lin Shuyan], in Wang Weizhong, ed., 2008, pp. 470–477.

Li Daogang 黎道纲. 2010. "Wushi niandai chu Taiguo qiaopi pin xian kunjing yuanyou" [The reason Thailand's *qiaopi* frequently fell into difficulties in the early 1950s], in Wang Weizhong, ed., 2010, pp. 128–133.

Li Xiaoyan 李小燕. 2004. "Kejia diqu de shuike yu qiaopiju" [*Shuike* and *qiaopi* offices in Hakka regions], in Wang Weizhong, ed., 2004, pp. 51–56.

Li Xiaoyan 李小燕. 2010. *Zhongguo guanfang hangju jingying qiaohui yewu zhi yanjiu (1937–1949)* [A study of overseas Chinese remittance through Chinese national banks and Post Offices, 1937–1949], PhD dissertation, National University of Singapore.

Li Zhixian 李志贤, ed. 2003. *Haiwai Chao ren de yimin jingyan* [The emigration experience of Chao overseas], Singapore: Xinjiapo Chaozhou bayi huiguan.

Li Zhixian 李志贤. 2013. "Gongtong jiyi, kuayu wangluo: Ershi shiji Xinjiapo Chao ren qiaopiju de tese" [Shared memories, supra-regional networks: Special characteristics of Singapore Chao people's *qiaopi* offices], in Zhongguo qiaopi shijie jiyi gongcheng guoji yantao hui zuwei hui, eds, 2013, pp. 247–261.

Li Zhixian 李志贤. 2014. "Shijiu zhi ershi shiji qijian Xinjiapo ge bang minxin ju de yingyun yu tongye zuzhi" [The operation and professional organisation of the remittance houses of the various *bang* in Singapore from the nineteenth to the twentieth century], in Zhongguo lishi wenxian yanjiu hui, eds, 2014, pp. 1–15.

Liu, Hong. 1999. "Organized Chinese Transnationalism and the Institutionalization of Business Networks: Singapore Chinese Chamber of Commerce and Industry as a Case Analysis", *Southeast Asian Studies* (Kyoto), 37(3): 391–416.

Liu, Hong, and S. K. Wong. 2004. *Singapore Chinese Society in Transition: Business, Politics and Socio-economic Change, 1945–1965*. New York: Peter Lang Publishing.

Liu Jin 刘进. 2007. "Minguo shiqi Wuyi qiaokan zhong de yinxin guanggao" [Remittance advertisements in Wuyi *qiaokan* in the Republican period], *Wuyi daxue xuebao*, 9(1): 33–37.

Liu Jin 刘进. 2009. *Wuyi yinxin* [Wuyi silver and letters], Guangzhou: Guangdong renmin chuban she.

Liu Jin 刘进. 2013. "Jiazu shuxin yu Huanan qiaoxiang de guoji yimin" [Family letters and south China's international migration], in Zhongguo qiaopi shijie jiyi gongcheng guoji yantao hui zuwei hui, eds, 2013, pp. 143–150.

Liu Jin 刘进 ed. 2014a. *Bijiao,jiejian yu qianzhang: Guoji yimin shuxin yanjiu* [New perspectives: International symposium on transnational migration letters], Guangzhou: Guangdong renmin chuban she.

Liu Jin 刘进. 2014b. "Minguo shiqi beiMei Huaqiao yu Huanan xiangcun shehui zhuanxing" [Overseas Chinese in North America and social transformation in the South China villages], in Liu Jin, ed., 2014a, pp. 319–337.

Lu Yongguang 卢永光. 2006. "Wo kao qiaopi zhangda" [I grew up on *qiaopi*], in Hong Lin and Li Daogang, eds, 2006, pp. 155–157.

Luo Zeyang 罗则扬. 2004. "Qiaopi wenhua yu haiyang wenhua" [*Qiaopi* culture and oceanic culture], in Wang Weizhong, ed., 2004, pp. 208–214.

Luo Zeyang 罗则扬. 2010. "Dixia dang can yu qiaopi (hui) shiye de lishi yuanyou" [The reasons in history why the underground Communist Party joined in the *qiaopi* (and remittance) trade], in Wang Weizhong, ed., 2010, pp. 518–522.

Ma Zhenhui 马祯辉. 2008. "Qiantan qiaopi yu jinrong de guanxi" [Observations on the relationship between *qiaopi* and finance], in Wang Weizhong, ed., 2008, pp. 90–94.

Maclachen, Patricia L. 2011. *The People's Post Office: The History and Politics of the Japanese Postal System, 1871–2010*, Cambridge, MA: Harvard University Asia Center.

Mao Chujian 马楚坚. 2008. "Chao bang pixin ju yu qiaohui liutong zhi fazhan chutan" [Preliminary investigation of the Chao *bang* remittance offices and the development of the circulation of overseas remittances], in Wang Weizhong, ed., 2008, pp. 19–40.

Mei Weiqiang 梅伟强 and Mei Xue 梅雪. 2007. *"Jiti jiashu" lian Wuzhou-Wuyi qiaokan xiangxun yanjiu (1978–2005)* ["Collective family letters" and research on Wuzhou-Wuyi *qiaokan* and village newsletters], Hong Kong: Xianggang shehui kexue chuban she, p. 6.

Meskill, Johanna M. 1970. The Chinese Genealogy as a Research Source", in Ai-li S. Chin and Maurice Freedman, eds, *Family and Kinship in Chinese Society*, Stanford: Stanford University Press.

"On the abolition of the *minxinju and* the Congress declaration", *Sin Chew Daily*, 8 July 1929.

"On the Congress called by the Chinese General Chamber of Commerce", *Sin Chew Daily*, 15 July 1929.

"On the official correspondence regarding the preservation of the *minxinju*", *Sin Chew Daily*, 8 March 1930.

"On the Congress's appeal to the Government to reduce postal charges", *Sin Chew Daily*, 11 March 1930.

"On the Congress called to support the reduction in postal charges", *Sin Chew Daily*, 30 March 1930.

Pan Meizhu 潘美珠 (Joanne Poon). n.d. *Huagong shuxin* [Chinese labourers' letters], unpublished manuscript.

Peterson, Glen. 2012. *Overseas Chinese in the People's Republic of China*, Abingdon: Routledge.

Porter, Robin. 1993. *Industrial Reformers in Republican China*, Armonk: M. E. Sharpe.

Rana, Pradumna B., and Wai-Mun Chia. 2014. The Revival of the Silk Roads (Land Connectivity) in Asia, *RSIS Working Paper* No. 274, Singapore, May.

Ren Guixiang 任贵祥. 1989. *Huaqiao di er ci aiguo gaochao* [The second overseas Chinese high tide], Beijing: Zhonggong dangshi zialiao chuban she.

Romani, Gabriella. 2013. *Postal Culture: Reading and Writing Letters in Post-Unification Italy: Reading and Writing Letters in Post-Unification Italy*, Toronto: University of Toronto Press.

Shantou Huaqiao zhi (chugao) 汕头华侨志 (初稿） [Shantou overseas Chinese gazetteer (draft)] 1990, Shantou shi renmin zhengfu qiaowu bangong shi, eds, in Yang Qunxi, ed., 2004, pp. 131–137.

Shen, Huifen. 2012. *China's Left-Behind Wives: Families of Migrants from Fujian to Southeast Asia, 1930s–1950s*, Singapore: National University of Singapore Press.

Shen Jianhua 沈建华. 2014. "Tansuo Liaoguo pixin ju de jingying fangshi" [Investigating the management methods of Laos' remittance office], in Zhongguo lishi wenxian yanjiu hui, eds, 2014, pp. 162–167.

Shi Jianping 石坚平. 2014. "Siyi yinxin zhong de xiangzu niudai yu haiwai yimin wangluo" [The tie of consanguinity in Siyi's remittance letters and overseas emigrants' networks], in Liu Jin, ed., 2014a, pp. 307–318.

Siu, Paul C. P. 1987. *The Chinese Laundryman: A Study in Social Isolation*, edited by John Kuo Wei Tchen, New York: New York University Press.

Su Wenjing 苏文菁 and Huang Qinghai 黄清海. 2013. "Quanqiu hua shiye xia de qiaopi ye: Jian lun qiaopi wenhua de haiyang wenming shuxing" [On the *qiaopi* trade in the perspective of globalization: And also on the oceanic civilisational quality of *qiaopi* culture], *Minshang wenhua yanjiu*, 7(1): 33–47.

Summers, Tim. 2016. "China's 'New Silk Roads': Sub-national Regions and Networks of Global Political Economy", *Third World Quarterly*, 37(9): 1628–1643.

Sung, B. L. 1967. *The Story of the Chinese in America*, New York: Collier Books.

Wan Dongqing 万冬青. 2010. "Touguo Minyue bianqu qiaopi kan qiaoxiang chuantong wenhua" [Looking at the traditional culture of the *qiaoxiang* from the angle of the Fujian-Guangdong *qiaopi*], in Wang Weizhong, ed., 2010, pp. 292–310.

Wang Fubing 王付兵. 2013. "Qiaopi dang'an wenxian de jiazhi" [The documentary value of the *qiaopi* archives], *Dongnan Ya zongheng*, 7: 58–62.

Wang Linqian 王琳乾. 2008. "Qiantan jiefang hou Chaoshan de huobi liutong yu qiaopi ye huodong he qiaohui wuzi gongying" [On the circulation of money in post-Liberation Chaoshan and the activities of the *qiaopi* trade, together with materials provision by remittances], in Wang Weizhong, ed., 2008, pp. 461–469.

Wang Weizhong 王炜中, ed. 2004. *Shou jie qiaopi wenhua yantao hui lunwen ji*, Shantou: Chaoshan lishi wenhua yanjiu zhongxin.

Wang Weizhong 王炜中. 2006. "Taiguo qiaopi yu Chaoshan qiaoxiang de miqie guanxi" [The close relationship between Thailand's *qiaopi* and Chaoshan's *qiaoxiang*], in Hong Lin and Li Daogang, eds, 2006, pp. 61–72.

Wang Weizhong 王炜中. 2007. *Chaoshan qiaopi* [Chaoshan *qiaopi*], Guangzhou: Guangdong Renmin chuban she.

Wang Weizhong 王炜中. 2008. "Chaoshan qiaopi yuan heri yu Huizhou qiyue pimei" [The *qiaopi* origins rival those of the Huizhou contracts], in Wang Weizhong, ed., 2008, pp. 195–207.

Wang Weizhong 王炜中. 2009. "Chuxi Chaoshan qiaopi de chuantong wenhua de jiyin" [Preliminary research into the genes of Chaoshan's traditional *qiaopi* culture], in Chen Xiaogang, ed., 2009, pp. 50–55.

Wang Weizhong 王炜中, ed. 2010. *Di san jie qiaopi wenhua yantao hui lunwen xuan* [Third symposium on research into *qiaopi* culture], Hong Kong: Tianma chuban youxian gongsi.

Williams, Michael. 2003. "In the Tang Mountains We Have a Big House", *East Asian History*, 25–26: 85–112.

Wu Hongli 吴鸿丽. 2008. "Chuxi Minnan qiaopi wenhua" [Preliminary investigation of southern Fujian's *qiaopi* culture], in Wang Weizhong, ed., 2008, pp. 358–369.

Wu Kuixin 吴奎信. 2004. "Qiaopi chuandi guandao de gengzu yu shutong" [The blocking and dredging of the channels through which *qiaopi* were delivered], in Wang Weizhong, ed., 2004, pp. 200–207.

Xia Shuiping 夏水平 and Fang Xuejia 房学嘉. 2004. "Meizhou keshu diqude shuike ye shulüe" [Discussion of the *shuike* trade in the Hakka region of Meizhou], in Wang Weizhong, ed., 2004, pp. 179–186.

Xiao Wenping 肖文评. 2004. "Kejia shancun de shuike, qiaopi, yu qiaoxiang shehui" [*Shuike*, *qiaopi*, and *qiaoxiang* society in the Hakka mountain villages], in Wang Weizhong, ed., 2004, pp. 253–263.

Xiao Wenping 肖文评, Tian Lu 田璐, and Xu Ying 许颖. 2014. "Cong qiaopi kan minguo shiqi Meizhou qiaoxiang yu Yinni diqu jindai jiaoyu de fazhan" [Looking at the development of modern education in the Meizhou *qiaoxiang* and the Indonesian region in the Republican period from the point of view of *qiaopi*], in Zhongguo lishi wenxian yanjiu hui, eds, 2014, pp. 31–45.

Yang Qunxi 杨群熙, ed. 2004. Chaoshan diqu qiaopi ye ziliao [Materials concerning the *qiaopi* trade in the Chaoshan region], Shantou: Shantou shi tushu guan.

Yao Ting 姚婷. 2011. "Qiaokan zhong de qiaoxiang shehui yu 'qiao' 'xiang' wangluo – jiyu 1949 nian qian *Xinning zazhi* 'guanggao' lanmu de fenxi" [*Qiaoxiang* society and '*qiao*' and '*xiang*' networks in *qiaokan* – based on an analysis of the advertisements columns in *Xinning zazhi* before 1949], *Huaqiao Huaren lishi yanjiu*, 4: 21–30.

Yao Ting 姚婷 and Mei Weiqiang 梅伟强. 2009. *Bainian qiaokan: "Xinning zazhi" lishi wenhua lun* [One hundred years of *qiaokan*: *Xinning zazhi* and historical culture], Taishan: Zhongguo Huaqiao chuban she.

Yip Sang letters, Vancouver Archives.

Yuan Ding 袁丁, Chen Liyuan 陈丽园, and Zhong Yunrong 钟运荣. 2014. *Minguo zhengfu dui qiaohui de guanzhi* [The Republican government's control of remittances], Guangzhou: Guangdong renmin chuban she.

Zeng Xubo 曾旭波. 2004. "Lüetan anpi de chansheng ji caozuo de fangfa" [On the birth and way of operating secret *pi*], in Wang Weizhong, ed., 2004, pp. 219–231.

Zhang Guoxiong 张国雄. 2010. "Guangdong qiaopi de yichan jiazhi" [The heritage value of Guangdong *qiaopi*], in Wang Weizhong, ed., 2010, pp. 68–81.

Zhang Huimei 张慧梅. 2004. "Zhanzheng zhuangtai xia zhi jinrong yu chuantong renwen wangluo: 1939–1945 nian Chaoshan yu dongnan Ya jian qiaohui liutong yanjiu" [Finance and traditional human networks in a war situation: Studying the circulation of remittances between Chaoshan and Southeast Asia, 1929–1945], in Chaoshan lishi wenhua yanjiu zhongxin, eds, *Chaoxue yanjiu*, no. 10, Guangzhou: Huacheng chuban she, 2004, pp. 157–192.

Zhang Linyou 张林友. 2014. "Qiaopi dang'an yu Minyue jindai jinrong shi yanjiu: Jiyu shiliao bijiao de fenxi kuangjia" [Research on the *qiaopi* archives and the modern financial history of Fujian and Guangdong: An analytical framework on the basis of a comparison of historical materials], in Zhongguo lishi wenxian yanjiu hui, eds, 2014, pp. 223–227.

Zhang Mingshan 张明汕. 2006. "Qiaopi ye zhe jianfu lishi shiming" [*Qiaopi* traders shoulder a historical responsibility], in Hong Lin and Li Daogang, eds, 2006, pp. 101–104.

Zhang Shuoren 张朔人. 2013. "Minguo shiqi Hainan qiaohui wenti shulun" [On some questions regarding Hainan overseas remittances in the Republican period], in Hainan wenhua yanjiu zhongxin, eds, 2013, *Hainan yimin lunwenji* [Collection of essays on Hainan emigration], Singapore: Xinjiapo Hainan wenhua zhongxin.

Zhang Xing 张行. 2013. "Kangzhan shiqi de Minyue qiaopi ye yanjiu" [Researching the Fujian-Guangdong *qiaopi* trade in the period of the War of Resistance], in Zhongguo qiaopi shijie jiyi gongcheng guoji yantao hui zuwei hui, eds, 2013, pp. 326–337.

Zheng Youguo 郑有国. 2013. "Heigeer 'haiyang wenhua' chanshi" [Expounding Hegel's notion of 'oceanic culture'], *Minshang wenhua yanjiu* [Studies on southern Fujian's entrepreneurial culture], 7(1): 60–69.

Zhongguo lishi wenxian yanjiu hui, Shantou shi Chaoshan lishi wenhua yanjiu zhongxin 中国历史文献研究会，汕头市潮汕历史文化研究中心, eds, 2014. *Shijie jiyi yichan: Qiaopi dang'an yanjiu hui lunwen ji* [World memory heritage: Collection of papers from the *qiaopi* archive symposium], Shantou: n.p.

Zhongguo qiaopi shijie jiyi gongcheng guoji yantao hui zuwei hui 中国侨批世界记忆工程国际研讨会组委会, eds, 2013. *Lunwen ji* [Conference papers collection], Beijing: n.p.

Zou Jinsheng 邹金盛. 2010. "Chenghai ren kaishe de qiaopiju" [The *qiaopi* offices opened by Chenghai people], in Wang Weizhong, ed., 2010, pp. 402–412.

Zou Qiudong 邹求栋, and Su Tonghai 苏通海. 2009. "Shuo 'huipi'" [About '*huipi*'], in Chen Xiaogang, ed., 2009, pp. 70–74.

Zurndorfer, Harriet Thelma. 1995. *Chinese Bibliography: A Research Guide to Reference Works About China Past and Present*, Amsterdam: Brill.

3 Migration and home remittances in the financial market connecting Southeast Asia and South China

Takeshi Hamashita

Introduction

This chapter focuses on financial and regional aspects of home remittances (in the form of *qiaopi*) by looking at the debate between Robert Hart and H. B. Morse of the Chinese Maritime Custom on the trade imbalance at the beginning of the twentieth century and at the role of remittances in balancing China's statistical excess of imports, followed by the issue of the fluctuation of foreign exchange on the Hong Kong financial market and its influence on homebound remittances. Historical relations between Singapore and Hong Kong have mattered greatly in the management of the financial market as a result of home remittances (*qiaopi*) from Southeast Asia to South China.

Throughout the history of Southeast Asia, many Chinese have migrated, particularly from Guangdong, Fujian, and Hainan. Most were men who went to work as labourers, leaving their families behind in their home villages. Some migrants soon became entrepreneurs by establishing commercial firms and investing in rubber manufacturing, tin mining, and rice processing. The Chinese overseas kept close contact with their families by sending letters and money home through remittance houses (*qiaopiju*).

Remittance houses across the whole of Southeast Asia specialized in money exchange and postal communications between emigrants and their home villages. They not only transmitted money (often in very small amounts) but also wrote letters for the labourers, thus rendering a valuable service. Once an official postal system was established in 1896 by the Qing government under the Chinese Maritime Customs, the number of these remittance houses decreased due to new regulation in 1896, although their services remained important for small-scale transfers by labourers overseas.

Chinese overseas wanting to send money gave the remittance house their name and address and that of the recipient in the home village in China, to ensure smooth delivery. There was no limit to the amount of money sent. It took about two weeks for each bill to reach China. Remittance houses maintained close ties with money changers, the primary financial agents in the large cities in South China. These money changers cashed the remittances, which were dispatched by bank transfer.

Groups of rich Chinese traders combined the remittance business with their other businesses. They were trusted by compatriots from their own villages. Their inter-regional trading activities facilitated the delivery of customers' bills to China. These people later developed their businesses into a modern banking system.

Many remittance-house owners engaged in a wide range of commercial interests. The remittance business, which was akin to operating a small bank, usually made a healthy profit. The owners bought and sold bills and exchanged currency, alongside the routine delivery of remittances. They used the remittances as an investment fund to support their trading activities rather than send the remittances directly to Hong Kong from Southeast Asia. They controlled networks that consisted of themselves, their relatives, and their partners in Singapore, Hong Kong, and South China, who assisted them by organizing various types of business network, including joint associations (*lianhao*) and joint investment schemes (*hegu*).

Remittance by overseas Chinese

Chinese went abroad to earn money and send it home, rather than to settle permanently in a new country. Thus an individual's wages were considered part of household income. Migrants also remitted funds to agents, to pay for their own passage overseas. Migrants were overwhelmingly from Fujian and Guangdong. Their remittances helped to finance transactions across the whole of the South China–Southeast Asia trade zone. In addition, some money was remitted for investment purposes.[1]

Remittances were not entirely consumed in the form of household expenditure. Recycled as commercial payments and investment capital, they became a vital element in China's international financial ties. When Britain, France, the United States, and Japan developed economic interests in Southeast Asia, all of them utilized this financial network.

Chinese immigrants could get money back to China in the following five ways: by mail, by hand, through private remittance agents, through remittance houses, and through foreign banks (Lin Jinzhi 1983).

a *Mail:* The Universal Postal Union was created in 1878, but the Chinese government did not sign up to the convention until 1917. Foreign countries set up branch post offices in China that handled international mail, but few overseas Chinese used them (Shijie shuju youxian gongsi, n.d., 1959, 624–633).

b *Hand-carried:* H. B. Morse, of the Statistical Department of Shanghai's Maritime Customs, described in a report how overseas Chinese personally brought back gold and silver, foreign drafts, and local paper currency, or entrusted funds to a returnee to do so on their behalf.

c *Private remittance agents:* The agents provided various services. They recruited migrants, lent them passage money, booked their passage, and handled commercial transactions. They stayed in close touch with immigrants, visiting each Chinese community every few months. The newcomers invariably dealt with an agent from the same hometown in China when sending money and personal letters. In areas not serviced by remittance houses, agents were the main conduits.

d *Remittance houses:* Immigration to Southeast Asia reached significant proportions in the fifteenth century and steadily increased despite the Ming dynasty's ban on overseas settlement. Chinese merchants abroad sold rice, sugar, raw cotton, foodstuffs, and handicrafts to China, and imported sundries, handicrafts, and tea. In addition, Siam, Vietnam and Burma made a profit from tributary trade relations with China, and this activity also helped to create a trade zone between South China and Southeast Asia. In the seventeenth century, the European powers moved into the region in search of certain Asian products. Based on this well-established prior commerce, Western merchants were able for the first time to buy highly prized goods such as tea, silk, pepper, and cotton by using profits gained from the entrepôt trade.[2]

The remittance house, the principal instrument by which Chinese sent money home, was the financial lynchpin of trade between South China and Southeast Asia. Called "silver remittance houses (*yinxinju*)", "Guangdong and Fujian silver houses (*Yue Fu yinxinju*)", and other names, remittance houses were a combination of post office and foreign exchange bank. Many houses also engaged in trade, financed trade deals, and dealt in gold and silver. This exchange and remittance network attracted the arrival of foreign banks, which also competed for the exchange and remittance business as a source of capital. Tianyi Ju, one of the largest remittance houses in the early twentieth century, was based in Xiamen and had branches or agents in Manila, Saigon, Penang, Singapore, Medan, Batavia, Bandon, Semarang, and Rangoon. With sub-units throughout Fujian, including in Quanzhou, Chaozhou, Dongan, Anxi, Jinmen, and Huian, Tianyi Ju handled most of the remittances sent home by Fujianese (see Chapter 5 in this book).

There were numerous remittance houses throughout Southeast Asia. Most had their headquarters in Singapore, Bangkok, Malacca, Batavia, or Manila, with branches or agents in Hong Kong and across Guangdong, Fujian, and Hainan. The approximately four million Chinese living in Southeast Asia in the early twentieth century sent home about $57 million dollars annually (Kanji Saito 1914).

Remittance houses transferred money in several different ways – as cash, drafts, and commercial goods. A customer purchased a draft for a given amount in Chinese dollars. Rather than send the money immediately, the houses waited until individual transactions had mounted up or until the exchange rate was favourable. In some cases, in lieu of actual transfers, they purchased goods for sale in China or bought gold and silver. Some transactions were denominated in yuan, while others done by way of Hong Kong were in Hong Kong dollars (Kanji Saito 1914). (See Figure 3.1.) The Hong Kong dollar was the main currency for commercial activity between China and Southeast Asia. Although the final destination of most remittances was a family in a rural village, the money remitted was used for trade, finance capital, and investment in various forms (Zheng Linkuan 1940, 67–84).

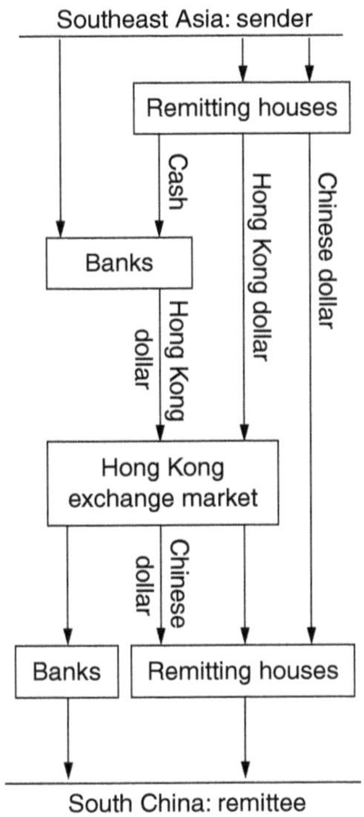

Figure 3.1 Flow of money in home remittance from Southeast Asia to South China.

e *Foreign banks:* Starting in the mid-nineteenth century, when Hong Kong gained in importance as a financial intermediary and Singapore emerged as a supplier of rubber and tin to European markets, foreign banks became a serious force in the financial field in the region. Chinese exchange banks also began operations in Southeast Asia in the same period.[3] These so-called modern banks enlarged and reshaped the channels originally formed by the remittance houses to create an Asian financial region around the Singapore–Hong Kong artery. Far from being supplanted by the banks, the remittance houses used the exchange rates set by foreign banks (especially the Hongkong and Shanghai Bank) and entered new fields of business activity (Hamashita 2008, 39–56, 145–166). (See Table 3.6.)

Remittances and China's international balance of payments

Towards the end of the nineteenth century, China's increasing excess of imports over exports became a matter of concern. As shown in Table 3.1, imports exceeded exports by almost one-third at the turn of the century.

Table 3.1 The value of merchandise and treasure, 1894–1903 (unit: 1,000 Haikwan taels)

	Merchandise year		*Recorded movement of treasure*	
	Imports	*Exports*	*Import*	*Export*
1894	139,569	144,690	13,613*	…
1895	150,244	160,697	30,061*	…
1896	177,631	146,929	…	6,394*
1897	177,915	181,770	…	6,870*
1898	184,487	177,165	…	2,982*
1899	233,954	217,610	…	6,368*
1900	185,871	176,680	16,645*	…
1901	237,872	187,955	14,362	27,036
1902	300,909	236,107	18,437	41,692
1903	310,453	236,205	27,001	33,047

Source: China, the Maritime Customs, *Documents Illustrative of the Origin, Development, and Activities of the Chinese Customs Service*, Vol. 7, Shanghai, 1940, 184.

Note
* Net import or export.

With particular reference to this point, Robert Hart, Inspector General of Customs in Beijing, wrote to H. B. Morse, Secretary of the Statistical Department of Customs in Shanghai, as follows:

> The imports appear to have been in excess of exports, in both 1902 and 1903, to the extent of some seventy million taels each year. How does China pay for them, or how is the difference accounted for? There must be an explanation, and it would be well to study the question and record results clearly and tersely in one dispatch. A cognate question arises in connection with payment of indemnity, and interest on loans. China pays out annually some forty million taels; where does all that silver come from? Where does it go to? How is it made up for? Does it remain in the Banks at Shanghai, or go in specie to foreign countries? Or is it remitted in Bills of Exchange, and how? And what are the inner processes in this complex and complicated proceeding?[4]

Hart asked Morse to explain (a) how China was able to offset the trade imbalance and (b) to cast light on the silver situation. This issue was also crucial for Chinese officials. One reflection of its importance was a meeting between the President of the Board of Revenue, Chao Erh-hsun, and Hart, at which Chao enquired about balance of trade.[5]

The issue was, in fact, not new. Questions about the imbalance had already arisen at the end of the 1880s. Table 3.2 shows the imbalance for 1888 and 1889, with net import value derived from market value by an F.O.B. base adjustment[6] and export value derived from market value by a C.I.F. base adjustment.[7] In explaining the adoption of the F.O.B. and C.I.F. basis calculations, E. McKean, Statistical Secretary at the time, reported:

Table 3.2 Adjustment of trade value, 1888 and 1889

1888			
Net imports, market value	Hk. Tls. 124,782,893	Exports, market value	Hk. Tls 92,401,067
Deduct duty and likin	Hk. Tls. 8,395,263	Add duty, estimated at	Hk. Tls. 6,499,839
Net imports, minus duty	Hk. Tls. 116,387,630	Exports, plus duty	Hk. Tls. 98,900,906
Deduct charges. 7 per cent	Hk. Tls 8,147,134	Add charges, 8 per cent on market value	Hk. Tls. 7,392,085
Net imports, value at moment of landing	Hk. Tls. 108,240,496	Exports, value at moment of shipment	Hk. Tls. 106,292,991
1889			
Net imports, market value	Hk. Tls. 110,884,355	Exports, market value	Hk. Tls. 96,947,832
Deduct duty and likin	Hk. Tls. 7,628,263	Add duty, estimated at	Hk. Tls. 6,389,045
Net imports, minus duty	Hk. Tls. 103,256,092	Exports, plus duty.	Hk. Tls. 103,336,877
Deduct charges 7 per cent	Hk. Tls. 7,227,926	Add charges, 8 per cent on market value	Hk. Tls. 7,755,826
Net imports, value at moment of landing.	Hk. Tls. 96,028,166	Exports, value at moment of shipment	Hk. Tls. 111,092,703

Source: *Report on the Foreign Trade of China for the Year 1889*, 2.

> Now, those of Imports are based on, as far as can be ascertained, the prices of the commodities in the various markets of the ports at which the Imports enter China, and those of Exports on the prices in the markets of those ports at which the Exports quit China. Anyone can understand that the market price of any article must, as a rule, reimburse the seller all outlay incurred on it up to the time of sale, and must exclude all prospective outlay. Thus, such price of an Import includes not only the prime cost of the thing when it was about to land, but also costs incurred by it after landing, namely, the expenses of landing, storing, and selling, and the Duty paid on it; so also the market price of an Export excludes the cost of buying (i.e., the exporter's profit or commission), the expenses of packing, storing, and shipping, and the Export Duty-increments of value all of which accrue to it in China and have to be added to the market price to ascertain the value of the article at the moment of its quitting China. And for the purposes of comparison it is the value of the Imports at the moment of landing and of the Exports at the moment of shipment that I have to estimate.
>
> (China Imperial Maritime Customs 1890, 1)

The trade balance problem continued to raise similar issues regarding a trade imbalance at the beginning of the twentieth century, although by then the lower price of gold and the consequent changes in foreign-exchange rates boosted exports. In the circumstances, it was necessary to seek other factors of a much more fundamental nature in order to explain the phenomenon from a wider point of view, that of Chinese external economic relations. Morse attempted to explain the problem as follows:

> Until the end of the war with Japan, China had incurred practically no Foreign debt. As a consequence of that war she was burdened with a debt of £50,000,000 (or, say, Hk. Tls. 400,000,000), and the periodic payments abroad under this head were further increased by the indemnities to be paid to Foreign Powers for their rescue operations in 1900–01; the annual payments under these two heads now amount to upwards of Hk. Tls. 45,000,000 a year. The natural effect of this increase in the national indebtedness should be a compulsory increase in the shipment of merchandise to cover the indebtedness; but in this land of paradox it has happened that it is the imports which have increased, until they are now a third greater than the exports; and it is the object of this inquiry to throw some light on the anomaly thus presented.
>
> (China Imperial Maritime Customs 1937–1940, 184)

In an attempt to arrive at a balance, Morse drew up a list of items belonging to what is now routinely known as invisible trade (a term that Hart strongly favoured), as shown in Table 3.3.

Table 3.3 shows, most notably, that loans and indemnities were the second largest element in China's liabilities. Here we will consider two items of "invisible trade", those specified by Morse as (f) and (m), about which Hart sought clarification. It will be evident that Morse did not distinguish between resident and non-resident foreigners in category (f), which sets out the amount of remittance from China to other countries. Although he calculated the amount by adding up two factors, we may question whether the sum total of net rentals from real estate in the various ports and dividends of all local companies may be taken as representative of the remitted savings of foreigners in China presented (China Imperial Maritime Customs 1937–1940, 188–190). Morse, incidentally, included Hong Kong as "essentially a part of commercial China".

Morse was the first person to attempt to pin down all the factors relevant to external economic relations in one comparative table, and the inclusion of invisible factors in it is one of his most important contributions.

Besides his calculation of profit remittances by foreigners, the item "remittances from and money brought in by Chinese emigrants" in the assets column is another of Morse's significant additions to China's international balance of payment tables. The item accounts for a sizeable portion of total assets.

Table 3.3 Liabilities and assets of China in international trade (by H. B. Morse)

	Liabilities	*Haikwan taels (1,000)*
A.	Value of merchandise imported into the treaty ports of China, 1903, at moment of landing	310,453
B.	Value of bullion and coin imported into the treaty ports, 1903	37,001
C.	Principal and interest of loans and indemnities	44,210
D.	Expenditure on Chinese Embassies and Consulates abroad	1,320
E.	Expended by Chinese students and travellers abroad	3,000
F.	Net profits of foreigners remitted to home countries	16,000
G.	Net freights and net premia of insurance (fire and marine) collected by foreign companies	6,750
	Munitions of war, not included in value of merchandise imported	5,000
Total		423,734
	Assets	*Haikwan taels (1,000)*
a.	Value of merchandise exported from the treaty ports of China, 1903, at moment of shipment	236,205
b.	Value of bullion and coin exported from the treaty ports, 1903	33,047
c.	Excess of exports over imports of unrecorded trade over land frontiers of China	4,000
d.	Expenditure on development of railways, mines, etc.	27,000
e.	Expenditure on Foreign Embassies and Consulates, etc., in China	5,000
f.	Maintenance of foreign garrisons	7,500
g.	Expended on maintenance of foreign war vessels, including money spent by crews	15,000
h.	Expended on maintenance of foreign merchant vessels, including money spent by crews	2,000
i.	Repairs to foreign vessels at Shanghai and elsewhere	10,000
k.	Expenditure on foreign missions, hospitals, and schools	6,000
l.	Expended by foreign travellers in China	6,000
m.	Remittances from and money brought in by Chinese emigrants	73,000
Total		424,752

Source: China, the Maritime Customs, *Documents Illustrative of the Origin, Development, and Activities of the Chinese Customs Service*, Vol. 7, Shanghai, 1940, 187.

In Tables 3.4a and 3.4b, Morse examines remittances from Chinese emigrants abroad more closely, basing his estimates on the Chinese population in each relevant country and their living conditions, and presenting minimum and maximum calculations. For Indo-China he explains as follows:

> Indo-China. – Chinese population, 150,000. The huge rice trade of Saigon is in the hands of Chinese. Chinese residents are not so well received or so

> well treated as further south, and for this payment has to be made; and wages of Chinese servants are good. A safe estimate, therefore, would be Hk. Tls. 100 a head, or, in all Hk. Tls. 15,000,000.
>
> (China Imperial Maritime Customs 1937–1940, 197–198)

It is, of course, difficult, if not impossible, to calculate the exact volume of remittances from abroad given the vagueness of the data, so Morse also indicated the major sources of remittances through banks in Tables 3.5a and 3.5b.

Table 3.4a Remittances from emigrants abroad

	Minimum Haikwan taels	*Maximum Haikwan taels*
1. United States and Canada	14,000	38,000
2. Hawaii	1,500	3,250
3. American Hemisphere	2,000	5,000
4. Australia	5,000	10,000
5. Japan	1,500	2,750
6. Siberia and Korea	1,000	2,000
7. Philippines	3,000	4,000
8. Indo-China	5,000	15,000
9. Singapore and Malay Peninsula	–	–
10. Dutch Indies (including Borneo)	–	–
11. Siam: Remittances by bank paper	12,500	25,000
Remittances in coin	5,000	10,000
12. British India	2,500	10,000
13. Formosa	2,000	5,000
Total	55,000	130,000

Source: China, the Maritime Customs, *Documents Illustrative of the Origin, Development, and Activities of the Chinese Customs Service*, Vol. 7, Shanghai, 1940, 195.

Table 3.4b Remittances from emigrants abroad

Place whence remitted	*Mexican dollars (1,000)*
New York	6,000
San Francisco	15,000
Saigon	700
Bangkok	5,000
Batavia	1,280
Samarang	360
Soerabaya	120
Singapore	6,155
Penang	4,400
Rangoon	1,230

Source: China, the Maritime Customs, *Documents Illustrative of the Origin, Development, and Activities of the Chinese Customs Service*, Vol. 7, Shanghai, 1940, 200.

Table 3.5a Import and export of treasure at Hong Kong, 1904 (values in Haikwan taels)

	Import		*Export*	
	Gold	*Silver*	*Gold*	*Silver*
Chinese ports*	1,286,656	22,750,458	192,999	16,764,221
Non-Chinese ports	1,503,765	9,659,940	9,630,465	3,137,450
	2,790,421	32,410,398	9,823,464	19,901,671
Total	45,200,819		29,725,135	

Note
* Including inconsiderable quantities to and from Macao.

Table 3.5b Import and export of treasure of China, 1904 (values in Haikwan taels)

	Import		*Export*	
	Gold	*Silver*	*Gold*	*Silver*
Chinese ports*	9,737,851	6,754,415	197,779	14,377,910
Hong Kong	11,503,765	9,659,940	9,630,465	3,137,450
	21,241,616	16,414,355	9,828,244	17,515,360
Total	37,655,971		27,343,604	

Source: *Report on the Foreign Trade of China for the Year 1904*, 1905, xi.

Note
* Excluding inconsiderable quantities to and from Macao.

We can quickly ascertain from this table that the amount of remittances was not a direct function of the Chinese population in any given place, so we can surmise that the remittances from each country flowed into China not necessarily with the individual nation as a unit but, more probably, through the financial centres in each region, in the intermediate form of trade settlements, investments, and foreign exchange business, before finally finding their way to China.

The role of Hong Kong finance

Judging by the number of financial centres in Southeast Asia dealing with home remittances and by the fact that most overseas Chinese in the region were from southern provinces of China like Guangdong and Fujian, it is appropriate to deal with these remittances as a part of the South China regional economy. Morse also reported on the Hong Kong economy. In 1904 he wrote as follows:

> Hong Kong is always our element of statistical confusion, receiving as it does Foreign goods for distribution to the ports of South China and Chinese produce for shipment to all ports of the world, including China itself.
>
> (China Imperial Maritime Customs 1905, iv)

Morse's allusion to the complexities of Hong Kong from a statistical viewpoint relates to Hong Kong's financial role as an exchange centre and an intermediate centre of trade settlement. Table 3.5, which outlines the import and export of treasure through Hong Kong, shows that the silver trade with Chinese ports and the gold trade with non-Chinese ports was a major function of the Hong Kong financial market, and contributed to Hong Kong's reserves to the tune of around 15 million Haikwan taels, of which nearly 80 per cent was in silver. Morse explains that this difference between treasure export and import represented a gain for the colony's banking reserves (China Imperial Maritime Customs 1905, xi).

Morse evidently faced a dilemma in treating Hong Kong, statistically, as part of the Chinese economy. In fact he oscillated between including and excluding it. His dilemma, together with the problem of how to calculate the volume of the junk trade between the China coast, Hong Kong, and Southeast Asia, reveals the difficulties that contemporaries faced in understanding the Chinese economy in its full complexity, i.e. by taking into account all aspects of the local economy.

In connection with these "invisible" factors affecting the Chinese economy, Morse further pointed to the problem of fluctuating exchange rates. In its various stages of development, Chinese trade was conducted using different monetary means, so that a series of exchanges became necessary – trading with foreign merchants was done in gold, China's wholesale currency was silver, and the currency used by local people was copper. Every consignment of foreign products, in the course of its movement from place of production to the ultimate consumer, and every Chinese product moving between the producer and the foreign market was subject to a bewildering series of exchange conversions, in which anyone handling the goods had to allow a margin sufficient to cover all possible fluctuations along the chain. These fluctuations could amount to as high as 16 per cent in the period it took for goods to move from their starting point to their ultimate destination (China Imperial Maritime Customs 1905, i–ii).

The problem of exchange was crucial in trade settlement both internationally and domestically in the latter half of the nineteenth century. This was due to the sudden fall in the price of silver in relation to gold, as a result of the increase in silver production and the abandonment of the double-standard currency system by many European countries. Neither phenomenon resulted in an increase in exports and a decrease in imports by the silver-standard countries of the sort that might have been expected (Hamashita 1984, 227–255).

Morse's argument about the relationship between exchange and balance of trade is important both when taking the whole Chinese economy into consideration and when dealing with more localized or limited economic relationships such as that between South China and Southeast Asia. Hart frequently wrote to tell Morse that Chinese officials were eager to get the statistical data gathered by the foreign inspectorates in each open port, so Morse's introduction of the concept of invisible trade was clearly viewed as leading to a better method of narrowing the trade imbalance and a better analysis by Chinese officials of the composition of the Chinese economy.

In the financial market between Southeast Asia and South China, the huge volume of drafts passing through Hong Kong involved a double conversion – first into Hong Kong dollars and then into Chinese dollars. Remittance houses at first used the money sent home in the form of remittances to offset bills paid in Hong Kong for export/import transactions; some turned a profit on the price differential in gold and silver bullion between Singapore and Hong Kong. There was thus a synergistic interplay of trade and foreign exchange dealing.

Factors affecting remittance fluctuations

The volume of overseas-Chinese remittances varied from year to year and the economic transaction greatly affected these fluctuations, which were either sudden or gradual. The fluctuations were closely linked with the economic fortunes of South China. A massive influx of remittances energized the finances of all the affected provinces, invigorated trade, and caused the market to thrive, but if the volume of remittances suddenly decreased, finances slackened, trade declined, and domestic commerce contracted. The impact of remittances was even greater in centres like Amoy, Quanzhou, Shantou, and Guangzhou, where remittances were concentrated, and stimulated the market (Zheng Linkuan 1940, 67–84). The factors underlying these fluctuations are numerous. Here, we examine the various types of fluctuation.

a The earning power of Chinese overseas: Remittances mainly derived from income from labour and enterprise profits. Fluctuations in these two components directly affected the capacity to remit, which was an expression of the earning power of Chinese overseas. The ability to remit varied, even within a single area, according to the remitters' occupations and earning power. Remittances by business people exceeded those of peddlers, given their greater earning power.
b Overseas economic conditions: Business conditions overseas directly affected the fortunes of overseas Chinese. This type of influence was extremely marked in times of war. Before the outbreak of the First World War, economic conditions were particularly good everywhere outside China and remittances by overseas Chinese increased massively. However, the subsequent protracted conflict depressed the global economy. When the market for Southeast Asian products was flourishing, businesses and small landowners in Southeast Asia made fortunes from rubber, tin, rice, coconuts, and the like. High wages due to labour shortages caused major dips in business profits. There were also many extra-economic causes of fluctuations. Examples include instability in the value of silver (before China's

currency reforms of 1935) and changes in customs policy and currency systems in various countries, all of which had a direct or indirect impact on the level of remittances.

c The magnitude of investment profits: If the greater part of overseas Chinese remittances is regarded as investment funds, the magnitude of investment profits in China will clearly be reflected in fluctuations in the volume of remittances. When a large profit could be gained, Chinese remitted whatever they could from their small earnings and invested the remittance in houses and land. As a result, remittances increased.

d The relationship with channels of investment: The greater the opportunities for investment, the higher the concentration of funds. When there were numerous channels for investment, investors could choose at leisure. This often happened in the case of idle capital. Some remittances, for example, were deposited in Hong Kong banks in the expectation of such an opportunity. Once opportunities arose in China, large amounts of capital were mobilized.

e Interest: Interest rates on the money market also influenced the capacity of the economy to absorb overseas-Chinese remittances. On the international market, short-term capital is held in money markets in different geographic area and different types of financial market. When a loss is incurred in the course of exchange, it can thus be offset, or capital can be placed where interest rates are high. This type of capital normally moved to those places where interest rates were higher. If they were higher on the domestic market than abroad, overseas Chinese capital was remitted to the home country.

f Currency control policies: The freer the flow of international capital, the greater the concern for its security, so that many countries applied currency controls. In extreme cases they even imposed controls on money transfers. Foreign-exchange transfers were restricted and permission was necessary in certain circumstances. These artificial restrictions inconvenienced remitters, causing or assisting in a rapid fall in the volume of remittances by Chinese residents overseas.

g Seasonal variation: Among economic activities, monthly fluctuations in the course of a single year were referred to as "seasonal variation". There were two reasons for seasonal variation. One arose from natural causes. For example, rice prices normally fluctuated in line with the harvesting and planting seasons. The other was artificially induced, for example at New Year or during other festivals that caused consumption to increase and prices to rise. Seasonal variation was cyclical and periodic. Its intervals were generally constant but their size and configuration was not necessarily the same each year (Zheng Linkuan 1940).

Fluctuation of exchange rates and its influence on remittances

As money transfers between countries happen in different currencies, the exchange rates between countries to some extent offset both the causes and the results of overseas-Chinese remittances. Speaking only of Southeast Asia, remittances received fluctuated as a result not only of differences in domestic and foreign monetary systems but also of the fluctuation of exchange rates on the international currency market. Before November 1935, when China created the legal tender currency (*fabi*), currency exchange between China and other countries was subject to complex relationships in the relative value of gold and silver, quite apart from domestic changes in the exchange rate. China was, at the time, on the silver standard, so when silver appreciated in value, China's external exchange rate rose and the rate of foreign to domestic currencies declined. Then the funds for home remittance were invested abroad and, as a result, the volume of overseas-Chinese remittances inevitably decreased, even if there was no particular decrease in terms of foreign currencies. Conversely, when silver falls in value, the exchange rate of foreign to domestic currencies will rise.

The huge one-way flow of remittances by overseas Chinese into South China might have affected exchange rates. A fall in Southeast Asian exchange rates was prevented by offsetting the receipts of gold/silver and imports, which increased liabilities to Shanghai and Hong Kong. This trade pattern strengthened financial ties, through foreign banks, among Southeast Asia, Europe, the United States, and East Asia. Britain's financial interests in Asia, anchored in Singapore and Hong Kong, depended on trends in China, Southeast Asia, and India. British colonial banks were a vital cog, extending the financial grid to Europe and Japan.

Shanghai's commercial ties increased the amount of capital in Shanghai and strengthened Shanghai's connections with East Asia and Southeast Asia, as the Hongkong and Shanghai Banking Corporation started up both in Hong Kong and Shanghai in 1865. Consequently Hong Kong, an important player in trade, increasingly became a financial entrepôt for settling accounts and transferring remittances.

Foreign banks opened branches in commercial centres created by overseas Chinese (Table 3.6). The Chartered Bank of India, Australia and China, incorporated in 1853, which opened its first branches in Asia in 1858, was strongest in India and the Malay Peninsula, whereas the Hongkong and Shanghai Bank (established in 1865) was strongest in Hong Kong and China, and the Banque de l'Indochine (established in 1875) was strongest in Indochina. All three institutions had branches or agents in the main historical business hubs and trade ports of Southeast Asia.[8]

The Asian trade zone, stretching from India to South China, which was facilitated by Hong Kong and Singapore, was also linked to Europe and the United States. The lifeblood of this regional trade was formed by the business activities of Chinese merchants and immigrants and by remittances and exchange transactions. For example, the finances of the Banque de l'Indochine had, as of 31 October 1905, extended the following amounts of credit (current accounts, drafts, merchandise collateral, etc.): to Europeans, 4,030,000 dollars (piastres); to Chinese, 3,330,000 piastres; to Chettiars (mercantile castes in South India), 610,000 piastres; and to Annanese, 640,000 piastres (Ministere des Finances

Table 3.6 Branches and agents of foreign banks in Asia

Year created	*Chartered banks*	*Hongkong and Shanghai Bank*	*Banque de l'Indochine*
1858	Calcutta, Bombay, Colombo, Shanghai		
1859	Hong Kong		
1861	Singapore, Rangoon		
1863	Hankow, Batavia		
1865		Hong Kong, Shanghai, Canton	
1866	Yokohama	Yokohama, Saigon	
1867		Calcutta	
1868		Hankow, Tianjin	
1869		Bombay	
1870		Kobe, Nagasaki	
1872	Manila	Osaka	
1875	Penang	Manila, San Francisco	Paris, Saigon
1877	Surabaya	Singapore	Pondicherry
1880		New York	
1881		Lyon	
1883	Ilo Ilo	IloIlo	
1884	Medan	Penang, Jakarta, Surabaya, Semarang	
1885		Peking	Tonkin, Haiphong
1887		Haiphong	Hanoi
1888	Taiping, Kuala Lumpur	Bangkok	Numea (New Caledonia)
1889		Hamburg	
1891			Phnom Penh
1892		Rangoon, Colombo	
1894	Bangkok		Hong Kong
1895	Kobe, Tianjin		
1897			Bangkok
1898			Shanghai
1900	Madras, Cebu		
1902	New York		Hankow, Canton
1903	Saigon		
1904	Hamburg		Battambang
1905			Singapore, Papeete
1906	Karachi		
1907			Peking, Tianjin
1908			Djibouti
1909	Kurangu, Phuket		
1910	Seremban, Amurisuku		
1911	Malacca, Delhi, Canton	Dalian, Harbin	Mengzi
1912	Ipoh	Changchun, Qingdao	

Source: Compiled from C. Mackenzie, *Realms of Silver*, London, Routledge and Kegan Paul, 1954; Maurice Collis, *Wayfoong*, London, Faber and Faber Limited, 1965; and Gonjo Yasuo, *Furansu Teikoku Shugi to Ajia* [French Imperialism and Asia], Tokyo University Press, 1985.

1901–10). More than half of the bank's loans were to local borrowers, and the lion's share went to Chinese. Indochina was typical of the credit extended by foreign banks in Asia – most went to local entrepreneurs.

Foreign banks also used the Asian trade and remittance network to acquire funds for colonial enterprises. The 1910 Shanghai rubber panic dealt a blow to Chinese who had invested in rubber and sugar plantations and in tin mining in Southeast Asia. Nevertheless, capital for such ventures continued to be raised in Shanghai, and in 1912 a particularly large number of new companies was launched. These companies were active in the Malay Peninsula and the Netherlands East Indies, chiefly in gambia, sugar, and tin. Compared to other stocks, share prices were very low. Some stocks fell below the issue price, leaving shareholders at risk, yet large amounts of money were invested.

The capital raised in Shanghai stemmed from remittances and account settlements. Large amounts of Southeast Asian drafts were sold in Hong Kong and Shanghai. Because payment settlements did not fully offset the currency inflow, there was a danger that exchange rates would drop, thus depreciating the drafts. Goods from the interior were shipped abroad from Shanghai and money from all over China accumulated in Shanghai for short periods. This capital tended to be invested, through foreign banks and Chinese financial institutions, either in Shanghai-based ventures or in Southeast Asia, where business was booming. The money circulated around Southeast Asia, South China, and Shanghai; much of it passed through Hong Kong, inbound and outbound, thus generating new investment opportunities.

Regarding finance in the Asian region, also noteworthy is the complementary nature of intra-regional ties and ties with Europe and the United States. The decline in the value of silver starting in the 1870s had a major impact on financial transactions between Asia, a silver region, and the rest of the world.[9] Although the depreciation led to a steady increase in investment in the Asian colonies, given that capital could be raised cheaply in London, and enhanced the role of foreign banks for fund raising, it also led to violent fluctuations in the prices of goods, such as tea and silk, exported to Europe and the United States. The foreign powers used the gold standard in their colonies in an attempt to stabilize exchange markets, whereas silver continued to be used in China's economic sphere. The problem was how to offset the resulting exchange differences.

The Singapore dollar was pegged to London's silver price, so the price of rubber and tin exported to Europe and the United States rose or fell (with some deviations) in response to changes in foreign-exchange rates. Although pound-denominated prices were generally stable after 1906, the price of rice, the largest commodity traded in Asia, moved in inverse proportion to prices for exports to Europe. This reverse ratio reflected both shifts in supply and demand for the commodities and the depreciation of Asian currencies on exchange markets as a result of the fall in the value of silver. There was probably a selective investment in commodities, as a hedge against adverse movements in the price of gold or silver (Chiang Hai Ding 1978).

Conclusion

Hong Kong and Shanghai were the twin gateways to China's external economy, with Hong Kong especially important in the fields of currency and finance. At the 1902 general meeting of the Hong Kong General Chamber of Commerce, the colony was described as a "non-producing commercial port, ... a commercial medium between the world and China". Hong Kong's trade was actually foreign trade with China, as one member observed. Since more than "90 percent of the world's monetary standard is gold and China's is silver", it was irrelevant to which standard Hong Kong's currency was tied.

These comments also attested to Hong Kong's vital financial role. Some chamber members feared that if Hong Kong adopted the gold standard, merchants in China would bypass the colony and trade directly with other countries. One member countered that businesses in China inconvenienced by the settling of accounts in Hong Kong dollars – a two-stage foreign exchange system – might want to simplify the process to just one stage, but no nearby port could compete with the advantages derived from such a "magnificent distributing port as Hong Kong" (Hongkong General Chamber of Commerce 1911, 347–349). The dual exchange process, in which transactions were conducted in Hong Kong dollars and in gold and silver, enabled Hong Kong to process gold- and silver-denominated bills as well as settlements in gold, silver, and local currencies. This capacity enhanced the colony's ability to attract and circulate capital, including local currencies and silver and gold from Japan. For trading purposes, Japan minted a silver yen patterned after the silver Mexican dollar, the international currency in Asia in the late nineteenth century. About two-thirds of the 106 million silver yen produced were circulated chiefly in Hong Kong and Singapore (Matsukata Masayoshi 1899, 310, 503–526). Foreign banks in Japan used the currency to make import exchange payments, and surplus yen capital was invested in Shanghai and Hong Kong from Kobe and Yokohama.[10]

Hong Kong had strong connections with Singapore. In 1858, the British East India Company, having lost its trade monopoly, also lost control over the Straits Settlements. Penang, Singapore, and Malacca were established as crown colonies in 1867. In the late nineteenth century, rubber plantations and tin mines attracted large numbers of Indian and Chinese labourers to the Malay Peninsula. During this same period, Singapore became a transit point for immigrants (as did Hong Kong), as well as an entrepôt for Western capital and trade and a point for settling financial transactions. A new, more complex Asian trade zone was emerging around Singapore and Hong Kong.[11]

Singapore and Hong Kong faced new problems in the closing decades of the nineteenth century and the early twentieth century. These were brought on by the slump in and the volatility of silver prices. Although the Chambers of Commerce in the two colonies recognized the advantages of a common approach, strong advocates of silver or gold in both places ruled out a joint policy. In 1906, Singapore adopted the gold standard, while Hong Kong kept its dollar linked to silver until 1935, when China abandoned the silver standard. Nonetheless, both cities shared a common history. They were commercial centres built by Chinese merchants, strategic footholds for foreign merchants' houses and for banks engaged in trade, finance and investment, and both were British colonies administered from London. We may think of Singapore and Hong Kong as simply performing complementary financial functions. In other words, they were the "contacts" and "transformers" that connected the various regional economies throughout Asia.

By passing through the layered procedures from local to regional and international, described in this chapter, remittances from overseas Chinese, based essentially on family and local ties, functioned to organize and expand inter-regionally facilitating financial markets through trade settlement and investment. They were also influenced by fluctuations in foreign exchange between Southeast Asia and South China, with Singapore and Hong Kong as the two major centres of the financial market. The flow of remittances promoted the development of the regional financial market, but this market was also influenced and shaped by foreign-exchange fluctuations on the regional and world financial markets.

Notes

1 Home remittance has been studied as domestic labour movement and household expenses (Qian Cai 2000).
2 Though China's modern postal system began in 1896 and operated through the Maritime Customs network, it had already started functioning in the 1870s, through Maritime Customs networks.
3 Many banks were established in Singapore in the early twentieth century – they included Guangyi Bank (Guangdong capital) 1903; Sihaitong Bank (Chaozhou capital) 1907; Huaqiao, Bank (Fujian capital) 1912.
4 Hart to Morse, Peking, 26 April 1904. The unpublished letters of H. B. Morse are held by the Houghton Library, Harvard University.
5 *Ibid.*, 6 December 1904.
6 F.O.B. (Free on Board or Freight on Board) means the cost of delivering the goods to port is included but the buyer is responsible for onward shipping and other costs associated with getting the goods to their destination.
7 C.I.F. (Cost, Insurance, and Freight) requires the seller to arrange for the carriage of goods by sea to their destination, and provides the buyer with the documents necessary to obtain the goods from the carrier.
8 Yokohama Specie Bank started in Yokohama in 1880 (Bank of Taiwan 1914).
9 On the increased influence of foreign banks as a result of dealing in interest-bearing promissory notes for the Orient, see Ishii Kanji (1979).
10 On the remittance of gold to Shanghai, see Kojima Jin (1981). According to Morse, most of the gold remitted to Hong Kong was from Japan. See China Imperial Maritime Customs (1905).
11 From the late nineteenth century through to the early twentieth century, the Chambers of Commerce in Hong Kong and Singapore debated currency problems and exchanged views on the issue. Hong Kong settled on silver relatively soon, whereas there was no consensus in Singapore. See the "Currency" section in the annual reports of the Singapore General Chamber of Commerce (from *Annual Reports of Singapore Chamber of Commerce*).

References

Bank of Taiwan. 1914. *Nanyo ni okeru kakyo, fu kawase kankei* [Overseas Chinese in the South Pacific: The foreign exchange business], Bank of China.

Chiang Hai Ding. 1978. "Chapter IX: The effect of exchange rate depreciation". *A History of Straits Settlements Foreign Trade 1870–1915*. Singapore: National Museum.

China Imperial Maritime Customs. 1890. *Returns of Trade and Trade Reports for the Year 1889*. Shanghai: The Custom Press.

China Imperial Maritime Customs. 1905. *Returns of Trade and Trade Reports for the Year 1904*. Shanghai: The Custom Press.

China Imperial Maritime Customs. 1937–1940. *Documents Illustrative of the Origin, Development, and Activities of the Chinese Customs Service*, Vol. 7. Shanghai: Statistical Dept. of the Inspectorate General of Customs.

Hamashita, Takeshi. 1984. "International Financial Relations Behind the 1911 Revolution; The Fall in the Value of Silver and Reform of the Monetary System". In S. Eto and H. Z. Schiffrin, eds. *The 1911 Revolution in China*. Tokyo: University of Tokyo Press.

Hamashita, Takeshi. 2008. *China, East Asia and the Global Economy: Regional and Historical Perspectives*. London: Routledge.

Hongkong General Chamber of Commerce. 1911. *Brief History of the Hongkong General Chamber of Commerce from its Inception: 29 May, 1861, to Date*, in *Report of Hongkong General Chamber of Commerce for the Year 1910*.

Ishii Kanji. 1979. Lgirisu shokuminchigun no saihen (part 2) [The transformation of British colonies], *Keizaigaku kenkyu*, 45(3).

Kanji Saito. 1914. *Nanyo ni okeru kakyo, fu kawase kankei* [Overseas Chinese in the South Sea: The foreign exchange business]. Research Department, Bank of Taiwan, chapter 4.

Kojima Jin. 1981. *Nihon kinhonisei jidai (1897–1917)* [Japan and the gold standard, 1897–1917], chapter 3, Tokyo: Nihon Keizai Hyoronsha.

Lin Jinzhi 林金枝. 1983. *Jindai Huaqiao touzi guonei qiyeshi yanjiu* 近代华侨投资国内企业史研究 [A history of modern Chinese investment in domestic enterprises]. Fuzhou: Fujian renmin chuban she.

Matsukata Masayoshi. 1899. *Meiji sanjunen heisei kaikaku shimatsu gaiyo* [The 1897 monetary system reform]. Ministry of Finance, in Meiji zenki zaisei keizai shiryo shusei [Compilation of historical materials on finance and the economy in early Meiji], 11(1932): 310, 503–526.

Ministere des Finances. 1901–1910. "Finances Banque de l'Indochine, 1901–1910". *Indo-chine*, 27: 120.

Qian Cai. 2000. *Remittances, Networks and Migration in Hubei Province, China*. PhD diss., Department of Sociology at Brown University.

Shijie shuju youxian gongsi. n.d. "Xingma qiaohui yu minxinye" 星马侨汇与民信业 [Overseas Chinese remittances and private remittance agencies in Singapore and Malaya] in *Xingma tonjian* 星马通鉴 [Encyclopaedia of Singapore and Malaya]. 1959. Singapore: Shijie shuju youxian gongsi.

Zheng Linkuan 郑林宽. 1940. *Fujian Huaqiao huikuan* 福建华侨汇款 [Remittances by overseas Chinese from Fujian]. Fuzhou: Fujian sheng zhengfu mishu chu tongji shi.

4 Serving the national interest

The *qiaopi* industry, the Chinese Post Office, and the transnational practices of the state, 1937–1945

Lane J. Harris

In the early twentieth century, the Chinese Post Office participated in a nation-building project to forge a territorially bound national community out of the disparate elements of the multi-ethnic Qing empire, but it also intervened in the transnational social spaces occupied by overseas Chinese during the War of Resistance against Japan (1937–1945). The first half of the twentieth century saw several migrant-sending states, like China and Italy, utilize discursive practices to secure the emigrant's political loyalty and financial support in exchange for diplomatic protection in often hostile foreign environments (Choate 2007). The exigencies of war, however, provoked a more radical response by the Chinese state. With the Japanese threatening the flow of capital and remittances from abroad, the wartime Chinese state resourcefully pursued an agenda to disarticulate itself from its national territory, effectively deterritorializing itself, by constructing a state-run transnational network as a safe and reliable channel for the transmission of overseas Chinese remittances. It also encouraged overseas Chinese to support the wartime state financially by fostering a deterritorialized cultural identity of Chineseness that affirmed the global extent of the Chinese nation by naming immigrants and sojourners as national ethno-subjects or *huaqiao guomin* 华侨国民 (overseas citizens), who had a vital, if largely economic, role to play in the anti-Japanese national salvation movement. If recognizing that the territorial state was not coterminous with the ethno-nation was easy, the wartime state still faced the challenges of circumventing international law by extending itself outside its borders, creating a transnational remittance network through cooperative agreements between state and private institutions, and convincing the overseas Chinese to use this network to transmit the remittances that would help financially sustain the war effort, all challenges made more difficult by the domination of the overseas Chinese remittance industry by the *qiaopiju*.

When the war began, the *qiaopiju* 侨批局 had been dominating the flow of *qiaohui* 侨汇 (overseas Chinese remittances) to the homeland for nearly a century. *Qiaopiju*, or overseas Chinese letter offices, were business firms that emerged in the mid-nineteenth century to specialize in transporting labour overseas, shipping goods throughout the diasporic network, handling private and business correspondence, and providing remittance and other banking services to overseas Chinese. In the mid-nineteenth century, they initially utilized geo-consanguineous ties as part of the organizational process of transnationalization, allowing them to make connections across land, border, and ocean. By the 1870s, the economic limitations inherent in relying exclusively on such ties coupled with the advent of new technologies and institutions allowed *qiaopiju* owners to create a more profitable business model. Rather than profit on remittance fees, *qiaopiju* owners took advantage of the accelerated time and economic incentives offered by telegraphs and steamships to use the remittances as short-term loans to engage in other economic activities – currency speculation, trans-shipping, securities trading, or arbitrage – in the time lag between accepting the remittances and the customer's expectation of its delivery. To make their businesses run efficiently, the *qiaopiju* owners also pioneered a flexible, decentralized, rhizomatically organized network densely connected through interfirm relations that expanded the scope of their businesses and allowed them to operate in the interstitial gaps between nation-states, empires, and colonies. The organization of *qiaopiju* firms, their business practices and profit-making strategies, and the structure of their network all helped them to dominate the overseas remittance industry from the mid-nineteenth century until the war (Harris 2015).

Most scholarship on the overseas Chinese remittance industry focuses on the successful business practices of the *qiaopiju* in the pre-war period. These studies concern overseas Chinese investments in local development and economic reconstruction in Fujian and Guangdong, approach the *qiaopiju* from a network perspective to emphasize their innovative institutional structure and culturalist customer services, or examine the numerous clashes between the government and firms over control of the industry (Jiao 2006). The few existing works on the wartime *qiaopi* industry, by contrast, usually emphasize the strenuous efforts of the firms to overcome the challenges presented by the Japanese occupation of southeastern China and Southeast Asia, but generally overlook the efforts of other institutions to capture overseas Chinese remittances (e.g. Jiao 2014). The value of international remittances to the domestic Chinese wartime economy, I argue, led the Chinese state to engage in a historically contingent process that resulted in the development of a vast financial and administrative system, eventually known as the *qiaohui jinrong wang* 侨汇金融网 (overseas Chinese remittance financial network). Within that financial network, the Chinese Post Office played a vital role not simply as the only state institution that could distribute the remittances to every household in the southeast, a unique feature of wartime postal arrangements that will be discussed below, but more importantly as an institution capable of utilizing its vast financial, administrative, and human resources – the Post Office was the largest civilian state institution (Harris 2012) – to temporarily move into the space occupied by the *qiaopiju* when the Japanese interfered with their networks.

The Post Office and broader Chinese state always understood the importance of overseas Chinese remittances to the domestic economy. By the 1920s, overseas remittances almost balanced China's international trade deficit (Remer 1933, 205–214; Wu 1967, 16). While the inflow of international remittances bolstered the Chinese domestic economy, the *Youzheng zongju* 邮政总局 (Directorate General of Posts), to give the Chinese Post Office its formal name, long believed *qiaopiju* practices prohibited the Post Office from profiting as much as it should from the industry. Very early in the history of the *qiaopi* trade, overseas Chinese remittance firms utilized a *zongbao* 总包 (clubbed package) system in which they "clubbed" a large number of individual letters from different remitters into a single package. Under this system, registered *qiaopiju* firms only paid a partial postage charge on the total weight of their clubbed package to the Post Office rather than on the individual remittance letters. Frustrated by the refusal of the firms to abandon the clubbed package system and pay the full letter rate on each remittance letter, the Post Office adopted aggressive tactics to hinder or shut down the *qiaopiju* in 1922, 1926, 1928, and 1930 (Harris 2015, 141–145). Each time the Post Office's threats were countered by *qiaopiju* owners throughout the southeast littoral zone and archipelagic Southeast Asia, who mobilized support among the transnational Chinese community, founded modern trade associations, and sent delegations to confront postal officials across the region, thereby emerging as a powerful voice in a developing overseas Chinese transnational civil society. Pressure from this transnational civil society always convinced the government to back away from the industry, but once the war began economic pressures forced the Post Office and Chinese state to formulate a new strategy.

At the beginning of the war, the Chinese state acknowledged the limited economic resources available within its borders. In 1937, H. H. Kung 孔祥熙, President of the Executive Yuan, called on the nine million overseas Chinese to fund one-quarter of China's military expenses (Akashi 1970, 126). In response, overseas Chinese, who only represented 2 per cent of the worldwide Chinese population, contributed some CN$664 million in 1938 to sustain the war effort, of which 528 million came in the form of remittances from overseas Chinese to their families (*The China Press* 1938a; Qiaowu 1957, 43). That same year, however, the Japanese invaded the southeast coast and occupied key nodal points in the *qiaopiju* network, thus seriously hampering the ability of the firms to deliver their remittances. The overseas Chinese remittance firms fought to sustain their businesses by moving inland and developing overland smuggling routes from Southeast Asia, but Chinese state concerns about a rapid decrease in the flow of remittances and Japanese interference in the industry provided a new opportunity for the Chinese Post Office and its subsidiary the *Youzheng chujin huiye ju* 邮政储金汇业局 (Directorate General of the Postal Remittance and Savings Bank).

As the *qiaopiju* system struggled to survive the Japanese onslaught, the Post Office and Postal Remittance and Savings Bank developed their own state-run transnational remittance network. Although broadly designed to ensure the continued flow of remittances to bolster the broader Chinese state, the Post Office's primary institutional purpose in creating its own transnational network was to capture a portion of the overseas Chinese remittance market, which would increase profits on postage by circumventing the clubbed package system and, more importantly, allowing the Post Office to collect lucrative remittance charges, a source of income previously untapped by the Post Office. Whether they were petty remittances to support overseas Chinese families, bulk remittances by overseas businessmen to their branches in China, or wartime donations by patriotic overseas Chinese to the state, they all profited the Post Office by allowing it to collect full postage charges and remittance fees on each individual remittance. For example, the Post Office collected CN$130,000 on *qiaopiju* clubbed packages between January and November 1938 (Second Historical Archives of China, Nanjing [SHAC] 1938a).[1] After it created its own transnational remittance network in 1939, the gross revenue on petty remittances alone (if bulk remittances were included the figure would be much higher) was CN$355,000 (SHAC 1939a). For a cash-strapped postal administration trying to overcome its own wartime financial difficulties, these additional profits were motive enough to invest in the creation of an overseas remittance network.

The portion of the overseas remittance financial network created by the Directorate General of Posts and the Directorate General of the Postal Remittance and Savings Bank consisted of a system of domestic distribution centres across the southeast, a specially trained cadre of remittance workers, and a series of mutually profitable agency contracts with international banks, local companies, and various other overseas firms engaged in foreign exchange and remittances. The creation of this state-run transnational network that linked together diasporic communities, transnational corporations, and global financial markets with the Chinese state required various structural changes within the state, the deployment of new technologies and culturalist services, and the discursive reconfiguration of social relations between the state and overseas Chinese communities. The purpose of these various practices was to dramatically accelerate the time, and narrow the space, separating overseas Chinese communities from the Chinese state in order to move capital and remittances quickly to the mainland by out-manoeuvring the *qiaopi* firms, the entrenched middlemen, who had been dominating the industry for more than a century.

The men behind the creation of the state-run transnational remittance network, long aware of the financial importance of overseas Chinese remittances, were able to step outside the idea of the national state through a willingness to circumvent international law and violate the comity of nations – something done quietly and secretly – to create a new kind of relationship between overseas Chinese and the state. Although many were involved in these practices, the primary group consisted of a managerial elite within the Post Office and Postal Remittance and Savings Bank, including Director General of Posts Guo Xinsong 郭心崧, Deputy Director Xu Changcheng 徐昌成, and foreign postal directors H. S. Kierkegaard, C. E. Molland, J. Jouvelet, and W. D. Murray, who had the support of high-level state actors like T. V. Soong 宋子文 and H. H. Kung, and who worked with the managing directors of international banks like Lee Kong Chian 李光前 of the *Huaqiao yinhang* 华侨银行 (Oversea-Chinese Banking Corporation). Together, this transnational group of men formed a powerful nucleus of economic and political elites who viewed state interests in a transnational rather than national framework. The small group behind these wartime practices, however, also highlights that such practices were a contingent and temporary response, a wartime measure designed and implemented to secure vital economic resources to sustain the national state. Those economic resources never seemed more important than in the summer of 1937.

The national salvation movement in overseas Chinese Communities

One of the keys to the survival of the National Government during the first year of the War of Resistance was the *jiuguo yundong* 救国运动 (national salvation movement) and its fundraising efforts in overseas Chinese communities around the world (Akashi 1970; Leong 1979; Huaqiao xiehui zonghui 1999; Koh 2013; Lu 2014). Ever since 1909, when the Qing government promulgated its nationality law, successive Chinese states had embraced the concept of *jus sanguinis*, that anyone born, no matter where, of a Chinese parent was considered Chinese and a member of the state-defined nation (Shao 2009). The concept of blood-line descent helped Chinese governments understand overseas Chinese settlers or sojourners as deterritorialized "overseas citizens". The Nanyang Chinese often reciprocated those feelings and participated in many of the major political movements of the early twentieth century, including the 1911 Revolution, the May Fourth Movement, the 30 May Movement, and anti-Japanese protests after the Ji'nan (1928) and Mukden (1931) incidents.

When Jiang Jieshi (Chiang Kai-shek) established the Nationalist party-state in Nanjing in April 1927, the party opened branches throughout the Chinese diaspora, where they sponsored schools for overseas Chinese children to inculcate them with official views of Chinese language, culture, and national identity. The *Qiaowu weiyuanhui* 侨务委员会 (Overseas Chinese Affairs Commission), founded in 1932, also maintained regular contact with overseas Chinese businesses as well as social and philanthropic organizations by establishing branch offices in major cities throughout the southeast, publishing a variety of overseas Chinese-related magazines and newspapers, and engaging in extensive propaganda work (Zhang 2008). Although frequently understood as "cultural" endeavours, these pre-war efforts to extend government influence into overseas Chinese communities served to keep Peranakans, Straits-born babas, and Sangleys in a Chinese state of mind, one inflamed by the Japanese invasion.

Shortly after news of the Japanese attack on Beiping reached overseas Chinese communities, national salvation associations, boycott committees, and anti-Japanese resistance organizations sprang up in Singapore, Malaya, the Philippines, the Dutch East Indies, Thailand, and Hong Kong, all helping to turn the growing Sino-Japanese conflict into a war with global dimensions. In the United States, representatives from more than ninety organizations met to form the *Lü-Mei huaqiao tongyi yijuan jiuguo zonghui* 旅美华侨统一义捐救国总会 (China War Relief Association of America) while in Europe overseas Chinese established the *Quan-Ou huaqiao kangri jiuguo lianhehui* 全欧华侨抗日救国联合会 (All-European War of

Resistance National Salvation Association of Overseas Chinese). Throughout July and August 1937, individual contributions to the Nanjing "war chest" began pouring in from Chinese in New Zealand, San Pablo Leguna, Vancouver, Melbourne, Johannesburg, and San Francisco – totalling 3.3 million yuan by mid-September (*The China Press* 1937a). Relief and fund-raising organizations appeared in rapid succession all across the Chinese diaspora to raise voluntary contributions, purchase liberty and national salvation bonds, and to collect funds for the Red Cross and innumerable other causes. By December 1940, there were more than 900 overseas national salvation and fund-raising organizations around the world (Council of International Affairs 1943, 319). The heart of the national salvation movement in the diaspora emerged in Singapore where Tan Kah Kee 陈嘉庚 (1874–1961), maybe the most prominent businessman in Southeast Asia, began raising "comfort sums" for the troops in North China through the *Xinjiapo chouzhen hui* 新加坡筹赈会 (Singapore Chinese Relief Fund Association) (*The China Press* 1937b; Tan 1994, 61–118). By early October, overseas Chinese in Singapore and across Malaya had raised CN$6.5 million for the war effort with Tan Kah Kee projecting a total of CN$100 million "as a great devotion to the mother country in her time of trouble" (*Straits Times* 1937).

The National Government actively supported the national salvation movement among overseas Chinese communities. Several dozen prominent Nationalist party, state, and military officials, with connections to Guangdong or Fujian, visited cities throughout the Chinese diaspora to promote wartime contributions, including H. H. Kung, Chen Shuren 陈树人 (1884–1948), the head of the Overseas Chinese Affairs Commission, Cai Tingkai 蔡廷锴 (1892–1968), the Guangdong-born hero of the 19th Route Army, Sa Zhenbing 萨镇冰 (1859–1952), the most famous admiral in the Chinese navy and former governor of Fujian (1922–1926), and Teo Eng Hock 张永福 (1872–1957), the Singapore-born former mayor of Shantou. The continued flow of remittances was such a matter of vital concern that H. H. Kung cabled Tan Kah Kee after the fall of Xiamen in May 1938 and asked him to organize a more coordinated fund-raising drive. In October, Tan called together 165 overseas Chinese representatives from across Southeast Asia to establish the *Nanyang geshu huaqiao chouzhen zuguo nanmin zonghui* 南洋各属华侨筹赈祖国难民总会 (Federation of China Relief Fund of the South Seas). By the end of 1938, as mentioned earlier, overseas Chinese had contributed some CN$664 million to sustain the war effort.

These fundraising efforts during the national salvation movement were a temporary boon for the *qiaopiju*. With their business model designed to operate in the transnational spaces between China, Hong Kong, and Southeast Asia, the decentralized and rhizomatically organized *qiaopiju* network continued to operate smoothly as the southeast coastal ports of Xiamen and Shantou became primary nodes in an emerging network for moving war supplies, foodstuffs, and international remittances into China. The number of remittances sent by overseas Chinese to support their families at the beginning of the war is astonishing. In July 1937, the Post Office handled a total of 108,224 *pixin* 批信 (remittance letters) – each letter represented one transaction – for *qiaopiju* firms through the clubbed package system (SHAC 1937a). So many remittances were sent that Shantou-based *qiaopiju* found it difficult to locate enough currency to cash them all (*Jinrong zhoubao* 1937, 8; *Singapore Free Press and Mercantile Advertiser* 1937). In September 1937 alone, Xiamen-based *qiaopiju* distributed a total of 45,000 remittance letters through the Post Office (SHAC 1938c). By early 1938, the Post Office was handling approximately 250,000 *qiaopi* transactions per month (SHAC 1937a). This golden period for the *qiaopiju*, however, soon came to an end.

Although *qiaopiju* owners had declared they would carry on their business for the duration of the war "for love of country and hometown", most were forced to fundamentally alter their business model when the Japanese invasion of the southeastern provinces began in early 1938. Once the Japanese occupied the southeastern ports, *qiaopiju* firms had to abandon their most profitable strategies and start charging higher remittance rates to pay for their expensive smuggling operations (*Nanyang Siang Pau* 1938a). By late summer 1938, Xiamen-based *qiaopiju* had either moved to Jinjiang 晋江 to operate out of Quanzhou Bay, or to Gulangyu Island 鼓浪屿, just across the harbour from Xiamen; in both instances, the firms had to pay dearly to smuggle their remittances inland (SHAC 1940a). On Hainan Island, Haikou became another active market for overseas remittances, but those *qiaopiju* had to soon evacuate to Guangzhouwan 广州湾, a French leased territory on the mainland directly across from Hainan (*Dongnan ribao* 1939). After the fall of Shantou in June 1939, many *qiaopiju* firms in northern Guangdong were forced to move inland to Meixian 梅县 or Jieyang 揭阳 and transmit their remittances through Shayuchong 沙鱼涌 or Shanwei 汕尾 and thence overland. Although *qiaopiju* were often successful in getting the remittances through, and many individual *qiaopiju* survived and even thrived during the war, the government's concern that overseas Chinese remittances might fall into Japanese hands led it to begin developing its own state-run transnational remittance network in 1938. The Post Office, however, had already begun pioneering such a system eighteen months earlier.

Origins of the Post Office's overseas remittance network, 1936–1937

Although the *qiaopiju* had defeated numerous Post Office efforts to take control of the remittance industry in the 1920s and early 1930s, the Directorate General of Posts continued to study their operations, network, and business model. In September 1930, the Post Office issued the "Provisional Regulations for *Minju* Registered Licenses" (SHAC 1930). From the licence applications, the Post Office gained detailed information about the number of *qiaopiju*, demographic information about the owners, and the size and extent of the various inland and international networks, which allowed postal officials to regulate and track remittance flows. The Directorate began ordering frequent counts of the number of *qiaopiju* and their branches, dispatched inspectors to study their business practices, assigned accountants to tabulate remittances, sent postal delegations abroad to investigate local conditions, and assigned statisticians to accumulate all sorts of figures about the industry. Between late 1936 and early 1938, the Directorate began using this information to form its own transnational remittance network.

There had long been a sentiment in the Directorate that the Post Office "has an almost perfect … organization for handling overseas remittances" with its 71,000 offices in every city, town, and village of import, its uniformed army of 40,000 workers criss-crossing the country, and its post road network of 371,000 miles, but legal difficulties and the strength of the *qiaopiju* kept the Post Office from effectively engaging in competition for the remittances (SHAC 1940b).[2] One might claim, as *qiaopiju* owners frequently did, that their firms served the diaspora "better" than the Post Office, but once the war broke out stories began circulating about *qiaopiju* firms charging exorbitant exchange rates. The fall of the coastal ports, one writer argued, has "given these agencies an extra-ordinary opportunity" to exploit their compatriots with ridiculous remittance fees (Tung 1939, 102). "Unscrupulous exchange merchants", another reporter wrote, are using the war to "soak poor and ignorant victims" with high exchange rates (*Straits Times* 1939). The Directorate felt the *qiaopiju*'s lack of an "ethical model of business" – their profit motive – worked against the larger purpose of overseas remittances to support the wartime Chinese state against annihilation (SHAC 1941a). As one Directorate employee put it, "it is hoped that these Overseas Chinese [firms] will not spoil the good name of patriotism because of a little personal gain at the sacrifice of National Interest" (SHAC undated[a]). Remitting from abroad through the Post Office might be a bit more expensive for overseas Chinese, postal officials admitted, but its "state-run character" meant "the Post Office does not take profit as its raison d'être" and is therefore more suitable in "assisting our overseas compatriots" (SHAC 1940b).

The first step in developing the Post Office's overseas remittance network was to find overseas agents to collect the remittances. In finding such agents the Directorate was very careful to skirt a number of international legal restrictions prohibiting state activities in postal matters outside national borders. The conventions of the Universal Postal Union prohibited any state from engaging in postal activities within the borders of another state (Universal Postal Union 1907, 3). The Directorate had also signed international money order agreements with many Southeast Asian countries that prohibited them from dealing in international remittances, except through the other signatory postal administration. As the Directorate understood very well, a Chinese state-run transnational remittance network operating in Southeast Asia would be "strongly opposed" by local postal administrations and colonial officials (SHAC undated[b]). The only way for an overseas bank or company to act as an agent for the Directorate, and thus avoid the complications of international law, was to carefully avoid words such as "international" or "remittance" in their formal agreements (SHAC 1938b).

In the fall of 1936, Director of Posts Guo Xinsong quietly dispatched Deputy Director Xu Changcheng to Saigon to meet with prospective agents and discuss the possibilities of expanding the Post Office's international remittance business to capture several hundred thousand in postage on overseas Chinese remittances by developing a state-run transnational remittance network (SHAC 1938d). In early 1937, Xu's work bore fruit when he signed the first agency agreement with the *Dongya yinhang Xigong fenhang* 东亚银行西贡分行 (Saigon branch of the Bank of East Asia) and another with the local branch of the *Zhongguo yinhang* 中国银行 (Bank of China). To the vexation of the Directorate, the two banks showed little enthusiasm for this new branch of business and costs were prohibitively expensive for remitters; the two branches collected very few remittances. It quickly became apparent that unless the Post Office and its agents developed a remittance procedure virtually identical to the one offered by *qiaopiju* firms, and lowered their postage and handling charges, their efforts would be futile.

In April 1937, R. de Sercy, a Deputy Commissioner in the Guangdong Head Post Office, began negotiations with representatives of the *Guangdong sheng yinhang* 广东省银行 (Guangdong Provincial Bank) to have the bank's Bangkok branch collect overseas Chinese remittances. This particular contract was worded "to avoid international postal complications" by making it appear as though the Post Office only had a relationship with a domestic Chinese bank. It should appear, the negotiators agreed, that "we are endeavouring to urge banks abroad to obtain a greater share of this remittance business for this country". The fees to be collected by the bank – their profits – would be 1 per cent on all transactions with a minimum of $0.20. The remitter would also pay a total of $0.26 in various postal fees plus postage on the *pixin* and *huipi* at full postage rates for a total of $0.76 – very high for a small remittance of under $10 (SHAC 1938c). With such high fees and fewer services than the *qiaopiju*, the Directorate and its agents still had trouble collecting remittances.

In October 1937, Guangdong Postal Commissioner C. E. Molland tried to resolve some of these problems by recommending the elimination of all postal fees in order to lower costs. Molland admitted that the Post Office would still not be offering the same services as the *qiaopiju*, but at least the basic cost would be the same (SHAC 1937b). The crux of the problem, as Molland admitted, was the lack of something like a free *pixin* and *huipi* service for the remitters. The Post Office had an *huizhi* 回执 (Acknowledgement of Payment) service, CN$0.25 per letter, but without an accompanying personal letter from the remittance recipient, overseas Chinese were still loath to trust the Post Office (SHAC 1937c). In their negotiations with Molland, representatives of the Oversea-Chinese Banking Corporation finally suggested the system that was eventually adopted – it was essentially the *qiaopiju*'s *pixin* and *huipi* system, except with different names (SHAC 1938d). A few months later, in July 1938, the Postal Remittance and Savings Bank began offering overseas Chinese remittance services in coordination with the opening of "petty remittance" departments in the branches of the Oversea-Chinese Banking Corporation throughout Southeast Asia (*Nanyang Siang Pau* 1938b; *Sheng hang tongxun* 1938, 15–17). In the midst of these negotiations, however, the Ministry of Finance of the National Government had, without informing the Post Office, begun discussing the possible creation of its own overseas remittance network, including a prominent role for the Post Office and Postal Remittance and Savings Bank.

The Post Office and the overseas Chinese remittance financial network, 1937–1941

In expectation of the Japanese invasion of the southeast coast – Fuzhou, Xiamen, Shantou, and Guangzhou all fell between May 1938 and June 1939 – the National Government slowly began planning a multi-front strategy to ensure the continued flow of remittances to the mainland in late 1937. Immediately after the war started, Minister of Finance H. H. Kung ordered central and provincial banks throughout the southeast to develop international remittance operations to guarantee that the valuable funds of overseas Chinese handled by the *qiaopiju* did not fall into Japanese hands (Council of International Affairs 1941, 495–497). A few months later, in early 1938, a Japanese-trained economist from Taishan named Huang Yuanbin 黄元彬, who was serving as a special advisor to the Military Affairs Commission, outlined a "movement to mobilize overseas Chinese remittances" that began to frame government policy. Huang called on all overseas Chinese to remit their money through official government banks; on the banks to lower their remittance charges; and for propaganda efforts be made throughout the Chinese diaspora to explain the importance of overseas remittances to the war effort (Huang 1989, 412–414). H. H. Kung's Ministry of Finance embraced Huang's suggestions in a circular letter addressed to Chambers of Commerce across the Chinese diaspora. The letter announced the Ministry's efforts to secure reduced remittance rates from the Bank of China (*Nanyang Siang Pau* 1938c; *The China Press* 1938b).

Over the remainder of 1938, the Ministry of Finance, the Overseas Chinese Affairs Commission, the Bank of China, and the Post Office began issuing and promulgating a host of new government laws, policies, and methods to attract overseas Chinese remittances that culminated in what H. H. Kung, in his 1 January 1939 speech to the fifth plenary session of the Fifth Nationalist Party Congress, called the "Overseas Chinese Remittance Financial Network" (Kong 2006, 7). In late January, Kung continued to develop the idea of the network in the Ministry of Finance's *Xishou qiaohui hezuo banfa* 吸收侨汇合作办法 (Cooperative Method for Attracting Overseas Chinese Remittances), promulgated on 28 January 1939 (Caizheng pinglun she 1940, 95–96). Finally, in March 1939, Kung revealed the full details of the network: the *Zhongyang yinhang* 中央银行 (state-run Central Bank), controlled by H. H. Kung, and the Bank of China, managed by Kung's brother-in-law T. V. Soong, were ordered to establish new domestic and overseas branches. These branches would work with the Fujian and Guangdong Provincial Banks, who would also establish new branches in smaller towns throughout Guangdong and Fujian. All of them would, in turn, work with the Post Office and the Directorate General of the Postal Remittance and Savings Bank to organize the international remittance network (Kong 1994, 30–31). In the Overseas Chinese Remittance Financial Network, the Post Office and Postal Bank were charged with signing agency agreements with international banks or private companies in countries and cities not served by the Bank of China or Central Bank; the Postal Bank would also receive and clear some of the remittances from the state and provincial banks; and the Post Office would be solely in charge of effecting the delivery and dispatch of the remittances and accompanying letters passing back and forth between the overseas remitter and his or her family members in China (Cao 1979, 196). For its part, the Overseas Chinese Affairs Commission would develop and implement the propaganda plan to spread knowledge of the new system to overseas Chinese communities (Chen 1940, 5–6).

Although the Post Office had already begun developing its own transnational remittance network, it accepted the new arrangements and began carrying out the Ministry's plan. The mid-1938 contract with the Oversea-Chinese Banking Corporation covered remittances from overseas Chinese in Malaya, the Dutch East Indies, Burma, and Hong Kong. In March 1939, following the Ministry of Finance's February promulgation of the *Yinhang zai guowai sheli fenhang xishou qiaohui tongyi banfa* 银行在国外设立分行吸收侨汇统一办法 (Unified Method for Banks to Establish Domestic and International Branches to Attract Overseas Remittances), the Postal Bank signed a formal contract with the Central Bank and Bank of China and agreed to the *Xishou qiaohui hezuo yuanze* 吸收侨汇合作原则 (Principles for Cooperation in Attracting Overseas Chinese Remittances) (SHAC 1939b; Zhongguo yinhang 1991, 551, 554). By early 1941, the Bank of China had established 209 domestic branches and 18 more abroad, including offices in Singapore, London, New York, Batavia, Surabaya, Penang, Haiphong, Osaka, and Rangoon (Zhongguo yinhang 1991, 429). The managing director of the Guangdong Provincial Bank Gu Yiqun 顾翊群 (Y. C. Koo), with T. L. Soong 宋子良, T.V. Soong's brother, on the Board of Directors, opened branches in more than ninety cities and towns along China's southeast coast. The chairman of the Fujian Provincial Bank, the economist Dr Zhang Guowei 张果为, travelled to Singapore in October 1938 to announce plans to rapidly develop the bank's facilities for overseas Chinese remittances, after which he expanded the number of its branches to ninety-four (a process that was completed in late 1939) (*Nanyang Siang Pau* 1938d).

In accordance with Kung's outline, wherever the state or provincial banks were not represented, or were underrepresented, the Post Office signed agency contracts with local companies in overseas Chinese communities. In Hong Kong, the Post Office was represented by Feng Minde/Fung Manter 冯民德, an amateur inventor and author, who ran *Xinhang jinyin gongsi* 信行金银公司 (Kam Koam Tsing and Co.). In Thailand, the military-dominated Phibun government's broad anti-Chinese political programme forced the Directorate to sign agency agreements with the Banque de l'Indochine, the private Chinese merchant Ah Kim Phong, who ran the general merchandise firm of *Guangya gongsi* 光亚公司 (Kwang Ah Co.), and *Malifeng jinyin gongsi* 马丽丰金银公司 (Lee Hong Goldsmiths & Jewellers). In Macao the Directorate worked with the *Minxin yinhao* 民信银号 (Ming Shun Cash Shop), while in Manila the agents were the *Tonghui huidui gongsi* 同辉汇兑公司 (Tiong Hui Exchange & Trust Company) in downtown Manila and the newly established *Feilübin jiaotong yinhang* 菲律宾交通银行 (Philippine Bank of Communications), a branch of the state-run Bank of Communications. In New York, the Directorate's representative was the Bank of China (SHAC 1941b). Shortly after signing its agency agreements, the Post Office announced its new remittance service across the Chinese diaspora (*Nanyang Siang Pau* 1939a).

In concert with their overseas efforts, the Post Office and the Postal Remittance and Savings Bank began setting up a domestic distribution system for overseas remittances. For such a system to work, however, the Directorate had to be able to maintain control of post offices in Free China as well as in Japanese-occupied areas throughout the southeast. In the months following the Marco Polo Bridge Incident, the Directorate ordered most employees to flee inland but to reopen operations in the nearest free area adjacent to the occupied zones. In each of the occupied postal districts, the Directorate left behind a skeleton staff controlled by a foreign postal director, since the Japanese would not arrest or execute foreign postal staff, and authorized the creation of *banshichu* 办事处 (General Affairs Offices) in the occupied postal districts to serve as intermediaries with offices in Free China.[3] The Directorate also created the *Guangzhou youju zhu Gang fenxinchu* 广州邮局驻港分信处 (Hong Kong Sorting Office of the Guangzhou Post Office), under the administration of W. D. Murray, a British subject, in early 1939 and a *Haifang youjian zhuanyunchu* 海防邮件转运处 (Transmission Office in Haiphong) controlled by the Frenchman Jean Jouvelet, in May 1940. In addition to handling regular mail matter, these two offices also funnelled overseas remittances either directly to the Distribution Centres or through Mongcay 芒街 on the Indochinese border (SHAC 1938e; SHAC undated[c]; SHAC undated[d]). For the entire period from 1937 until 1943, when the abolition of the Unequal Treaties removed extraterritorial protection from foreign postal officials, the Directorate largely retained control of post offices in the occupied zones (Harris 2012, 78–91).

The domestic side of the Post Office's transnational remittance network was based on the *qiaohui fenfaju* 侨汇分发局 (Overseas Chinese Remittance Distribution Centre). Although Chen Liyuan has argued that the Post Office was unable to deliver overseas remittance to 88 per cent of small villages in the rural southeast, thus embracing the argument of the *qiaopiju* themselves, the Post Office had introduced *mianfei toudi weishe youju chusuo* 免费投递未设邮局处所 (rural free delivery) in 1935 so that "all places in China are finally drawn into the postal net" (SHAC 1935; SHAC 1936a; Chen 2006, 45–46). In other words, rural postmen and remittance couriers delivered to every home in China thanks to continued control of those offices through the wartime *banshichu*, whether the town or village had its own post office or not – something that the Directorate understood was essential for their overseas remittance business (SHAC 1936b). Each of the Distribution Centres, under the control of a *fenfaju juzhang* 分发局局长 (Distribution Centre Director), was an office specializing in the handling, sorting, and delivery of overseas remittances in one of twelve *fenfaqu* 分发区 (distribution areas) in Free China and the occupied zones. Distribution Centres were usually fairly small offices, but it was important to separate them from regular postal establishments because of the specialized paperwork, provided by their own *qiaohui gongyingju* 侨汇供应局 (Supply Departments), and the need to situate the centres close to the Japanese lines. The Directorate placed the first Distribution Centres in Guangzhou, Shantou, Minhou, and Xiamen, which began handling overseas Chinese remittances in mid-1939 (SHAC 1939d). As the network matured, additional centres were established throughout Fujian and Guangdong – in Fuzhou, Jinjiang, Longxi, Haikou, Qianshan, Jiangmen, Suixi, and Huiyang. The Taishan Distributing Centre was of particular importance for the "hard workers and money makers in the New World" who came primarily from the Four Counties and migrated to Canada, the United States, and the Philippines (SHAC 1941c). Beneath the Distribution Centres was an extensive network of sub-offices and branches specializing in handling overseas remittances. For example, the Guangzhou Distribution Center had seventy-one offices under its control, the Shantou Center had forty-seven, and the Jiangmen Center had forty-five (Yuan *et al.* 2014, 141). (See Table 4.1.)

To mimic the *qiaopiju*, the Directorate also created a number of new positions to staff the Distribution Centres. Under the Distribution Centre Director was the indoor staff, which included a *Kuaiji guzhang* 会计股长 (Head of Accounting, a small group of *Qiaohui zhuanyuan* 侨汇专员 Overseas Remittance Specialists, and *Qiaohui tebie shujiyuan* 侨汇特别书记员 Overseas Remittance Special Recorders). In November 1941, the Specialists and Recorders were amalgamated into the single position of *Qiaohui shiwuyuan* 侨汇事务员 (Overseas Remittance Clerk). Overseas Remittance Clerks had three primary duties: (1) escorting overseas remittances; (2) spot-checking remittance stamps and their delivery; and (3) assisting in all office matters relating to remittances

Table 4.1 Overseas petty remittances handled through the distribution centres, July–November 1941[a]

Distributing centre 分发局	*Total amount= N$ (National dollars)*
Guangzhou 广州	8,504,724.12
Shantou 汕头	3,459,292.00
Jiangmen 江门	13,294,359.73
Qianshan 前山	865,573.03
Suixi 遂溪	4,782,675.25
Haikou 海口	6,470,945.03
Huiyang 惠阳	22,911,202.61
Fuzhou 福州	3,818,088.52
Jinjiang 晋江	12,100,557.35
Xiamen 厦门	4,988,319.55
Longxi 龙溪	1,483,561.90
Kunming 昆明	501,083.94
Total	83,180,383.03

Note

a Statistics, including petty and bulk remittances, compiled from monthly reports entitled "Overseas Petty Remittances Reports" (SHAC 1941d). For a list of all places served by Distribution Centres, see (SHAC 1940c).

(SHAC 1941e). As for couriers, they were originally called *Qiaohui paochai* 侨汇跑差 (Overseas Remittance Runners), which was later changed to *Qiaohui zhuanchai* 侨汇专差 (Overseas Remittance Couriers) (SHAC 1941e).[4] Couriers, much like postmen, delivered remittances but not other mail matter. Unfortunately, I could not locate all the employment records to determine the total number of special overseas remittance workers, but the representative figures from Fujian and Guangdong give us some idea of their importance. In 1941, there were 15 remittance specialists, 23 remittance recorders, 97 remittance couriers, and 301 temporary remittance couriers in Fujian; in Guangdong, there were about 240 remittance clerks and 400 remittance couriers (Lin 1995, 666). These overseas remittance clerks and couriers received roughly the same benefits as middle-ranking postal clerks and postmen in terms of salary, rice allowances, bonuses, and leave time (SHAC undated[e]). In addition to clerks and couriers, there were also *Qiaohui xunyuan* 侨汇巡员 (Overseas Remittance Inspectors), whose duty was to constantly traverse the overseas remittance networks in China to ensure the smooth functioning of the system (SHAC undated[f]; SHAC undated[g]).

The Directorate's remittance procedure worked essentially in the same way as the *qiaopiju*'s system. Agent banks or companies collected remittances and family letters. Once these were collected, the banks telegraphically transferred the remittances to the appropriate Distribution Centre, often through Hong Kong. The Distribution Centre then turned the funds into *huipiao* 汇票 (overseas remittance stamps), which contained a serial number, remittance amount, and recipient's name and was chopped with a postal dater and signed by a remittance clerk. The remittance stamp also had a receipt attached that was torn off upon delivery. Accompanying the remittance was a return letter blank and envelope, to be filled out by the remittance recipient and sent back through the Post Office. Throughout the whole process the Directorate emphasized the speed of delivery, the probity of the couriers, and the simplicity of its procedure (SHAC undated[a]).

The Post Office's transnational network saw moderate success in late 1938 and early 1939 but received unexpected support when various foreign countries began placing currency exchange controls on overseas Chinese remittances after the outbreak of the war in Europe, controls either actively encouraged or passively accepted by the Nationalist Government. In September 1939, the British governments of the Straits Settlements and Federated Malay States passed the Defence (Finance) Regulations, which included legislation on foreign exchange control. On 1 February 1940, the Straits government ordered all *qiaopiju* to apply for permits in order to ensure that their family remittance business was not a cover for capital flight. At the same time, the colonial government lowered the amount an individual could remit from $500 Straits dollars a month to $250, with an overall total for the colonies set at $500,000 a month (*Jingji huibao* 1941, 91–93; *Singapore Free Press and Mercantile Advertiser* 1940a; *Straits Times* 1940a). Shortly thereafter, the government began threatening to cut the monthly amount from $250 to between $15 and $50, a threat immediately contested by the Singapore Chinese Chamber of Commerce (*Straits Times* 1940b; *Singapore Free Press and Mercantile Advertiser* 1940b). After several months of argument between overseas Chinese in Singapore and the colonial authorities, the Foreign Exchange Controller officially reduced the monthly remittance limit to $50 per person per month (*Xingdao ribao* 1940; *Xinhua ribao* 1940). The Dutch East Indies followed suit with its own Foreign Exchange Control Ordinance in early 1940, which restricted the family remittances of individual overseas Chinese to 100 guilders a month (*Maoyi yuekan* 1941, 34).

Across the Pacific, Canada fully cooperated with the Nationalist state in forcing remittances into the overseas Chinese remittance financial network. In September 1939, the Canadian government, under its War Measures Act, created the Foreign Exchange Control Board. The Board administered the permits required to remit money and set the individual amounts remitters could send. In a decision that destroyed the remittance branch of many Canadian Chinese businesses, the Board set the family remittance rate to China at US$25 a month. It set the rate in US dollars because the Board required remittances to China to pass through the government-controlled Bank of China in New York City, an agent of the Chinese Post Office. In 1940, the Chinese state also convinced the Canadian government to allow the Chinese Consulate in Vancouver to review all remittance applications, which gave the Nationalist state full control over who could remit and how much they could send (Mar 2010, 114–117).

In the United States, similar restrictions were placed on remittances to China. In July 1941, following an appeal by Jiang Jieshi to President Roosevelt, the US Treasury Department froze all financial transactions between China and the United States, ostensibly to stop Japanese in the occupied areas of China from trading with the United States. Shortly thereafter, the Stabilization Board of China was established to protect confidence in China's national currency by setting international exchange rates (Young 1965, 247–260). The Stabilization Board and the US Treasury quickly worked out what was known as the "China Program", a group of "general licenses" granting certain corporations the right to handle trade between China and the US (Treasury Department 1943, 15). The Treasury Department's General License No. 75, issued on 12 November 1941, prohibited all remittances to China except those sent through a "designated agent". The officially designated agents included all the banks in the overseas Chinese remittance financial network as well as the Chinese Post Office's agents – the Bank of China in New York, the Philippine Bank of Communications in Manila, and the Oversea-Chinese Banking Corporation in Singapore (Federal Reserve Bulletin 1941, 1220–1221).

The combination of the Post Office's system of domestic distribution centres, well-trained staff of remittance workers, and profitable agency contracts coupled with a variety of wartime exchange controls placed on overseas Chinese remittances by allied countries allowed the Post Office to improve its market position in the overseas remittance industry (see Table 4.2). In its first full year of operation, the Post Office's transnational remittance network secured approximately 4 per cent of the market. These were not the hoped for results, but with modest

Table 4.2 Overseas Chinese remittances received by the Post Office as a percentage of total overseas remittances, 1938–1941[a]

Year	*Post Office*	*Total remittances*	*Percentage*
1938	6,734,111.00	644,074,000	1.04
1939	50,370,001.00	1,270,173,000	3.96
1940	114,558,188.00	1,328,610,000	8.62
1941	155,721,703.00	244,000,000	63.82

Note

a Figures for international remittances sent through the Post Office, which include petty and bulk remittances, can be found in SHAC (1941f), which includes a month-by-month breakdown. The statistics on total remittances, including those handled by Qiaopi firms and the Post Office for 1938–1941, are estimates and can be found in Chen (2014: 13).

improvements in the system, and increasing Japanese interference with *qiaopiju*, the Post Office's market share increased to 8.6 per cent in 1940. Considering the dominance of the overseas remittance trade by *qiaopiju* firms for nearly a century, and the various challenges that had to be surmounted to build a state-run transnational remittance network, the Post Office's network was a moderate success through to 1940. Although the figures for total remittances sent in 1941 are probably dramatically underestimated, once the foreign exchange controls began slowing *qiaopiju* operations and funnelling remittances to the agents of Chinese state, the Post Office appears to have secured a major percentage of the overseas remittance market. When the broader Pacific War began in late 1941, however, external events and domestic inflation quickly began to sap the strength of the Post Office and the overseas remittance financial network.

The Pacific War and the decline of the overseas Chinese remittance financial network, 1942–1945

By March 1942, the Japanese had occupied the Philippines, Malaya/Singapore, Thailand, and the Dutch East Indies. During the invasion, Japanese targeted overseas Chinese for their anti-Japanese activities, particularly their economic assistance to China through overseas remittances. Even though the Japanese attempted to conciliate Chinese goodwill in the hopes that overseas Chinese would help revive the shattered economy of Southeast Asia, the bloody "*sook ching*" 肃清 massacres of overseas Chinese in Singapore resulted in widespread passive resistance. After several months, those *qiaopiju* firms that refused to work with the Japanese by remitting their funds through the Bank of Taiwan began either smuggling their remittances to Haiphong and then to Mongcay or telegraphically transferring the remittances to the Guangdong Provincial Bank's branch in Dongxing 东兴, across the border from Moncay, which first opened in 1939 (*Nanyang Siang Pau* 1939b). For the next several years, the Working Office of the Postal Remittance and the Savings Bank in Dongxing, established in August 1942, also played an essential role in the so-called *Dongxing huilu*

东兴汇路 (Dongxing remittance route) by cooperating with the *qiaopiju* in Southeast Asia to help them smuggle remittances and family letters through its Distribution Centre network, a method that worked effectively until the Japanese replaced the Vichy authorities in Indochina in March 1944 (Chen 1991).

Although the Postal Bank's Dongxing Office worked for several years to help *qiaopiju* firms smuggle their remittances into occupied areas, the latter years of the war saw the bulk of international remittances come from Canada, the United States, Great Britain, Australia, and Cuba, through branches of the Bank of China in those countries. The various branches of the Bank of China usually transferred the remittances by cable to the Chongqing branch, which handed over the remittances to the Postal Remittance and Savings Bank for delivery through the Distribution Centers (SHAC 1942a). Between April and October 1942, for example, the Post Office delivered a total of ninety million in national currency from overseas Chinese in Canada and the United States (SHAC 1942b). The problem, however, was that ninety million represented a serious decline in the total amount remitted by overseas Chinese, given the extent of wartime inflation.

In 1942, the Nationalist Government's currency began a long inflationary spiral that would not end until the early 1950s. In terms of overseas remittances, the gradual and then quickening pace of inflation meant that most remitters began shifting their remittances away from the state-run remittance network and once again started patronizing the *qiaopiju*, which could offer much better black market exchange rates and lower remittance charges. By June 1945, the black market rate was CN$1,705 to US$1 while remittances sent through the state-run overseas remittance financial network were still converted at the official exchange rate of 20: 1 (Chang 1958, 382–383). With little hesitation, overseas Chinese made the obvious choice to shift the bulk of their business back to the *qiaopiju*, which undermined the effectiveness of the overseas Chinese remittance financial network.

Conclusion

There are severe limitations to the image of the Chinese state and its economy as exclusively national and domestic; and severe limitations to our conceptions of the sovereign state as territorially bound. Prasenjit Duara has outlined the efforts of the Chinese state in the early twentieth century to discursively "nationalize transnationals" in the overseas Chinese diaspora (Duara 1997). This chapter, by contrast, has outlined some of the ways in which the wartime Chinese state engaged in practices that transnationalized the national. In the early twentieth century, international law, the conventions of the Universal Postal Union, and the accepted practices of international relations all understood the sovereignty of the territorial state as bounded, but the exigencies of war and the Chinese state's economic dependence on overseas Chinese remittances led it to construct an albeit short-lived transnational network that represented a re-conception of the state as a deterritorialized entity providing services to a global Chinese population.

The rhizomatic and acephalous nature of the *qiaopiju* networks made it exceptionally difficult for the Post Office to replicate their business model. We might, in hindsight, say that the state's efforts to supplant the *qiaopiju* by building a state-run transnational network was doomed from the start, but taking such an ahistorical view overlooks the significance of a national state literally crossing its own borders to interfere in the transnational space occupied by overseas Chinese and the considerable success of the Post Office's network in capturing overseas Chinese remittances. Under peacetime conditions, the Chinese Post Office could not supplant the *qiaopiju*. It tried to do so many times, but the Japanese invasion so disrupted *qiaopiju* networks that it created enough space for the opportunistic Post Office to move into the overseas remittance market, a move that proved successful and profitable in the years prior to the outbreak of the wider Pacific War.

Whatever the performance of the "overseas Chinese remittance financial network", the Post Office and the larger Chinese state had created physical links between the overseas Chinese diaspora and the mainland. Although primarily designed to attract overseas remittances to bolster the wartime economy, these practices reveal the creativity and flexibility of the state in its efforts to influence the culture, loyalty, and, most importantly, finances of overseas Chinese communities.

Notes

1 During the war years, the postage rate on clubbed packages was set in accordance with the destination. *Qiaopiju* firms sending clubbed packages to the Philippines, Indochina, and the Dutch East Indies paid 20 cents per 20 grams, those sent to the Federated Malay States, Singapore, North Borneo, and Thailand paid 10 cents per 20 grams, and those sent to Hong Kong only paid 5 cents per 20 grams.
2 These figures describe the Post Office in 1941. That year, the Directorate General of Posts had 70,999 post offices, 40,988 employees, and 597,639 kilometres or 371,355 miles of post roads (Jiaotongbu youzheng zongju 1956, 3).
3 The Shanghai *Banshichu*, the first of its kind, opened on 1 March 1939 under the control of Shanghai Postal Director A. M. Chapelain (SHAC 1939c).
4 For the duties of the remittance couriers, see "Qiaohui paochai choucha qiaopiao gongzuo dagang" 侨汇跑差抽查侨票工作大纲 [Work outline for overseas Chinese remittance couriers when checking remittance stamps] (1941) in Yuan *et al.* 2014: Appendix 4).

References

Archival sources

Note: All citations of archival material from the Second Historical Archives of China should be read: catalogue number, file number, sub-file number.

Second Historical Archives of China, Nanjing (SHAC). 1930. "Zanxing Minju guahao lingzhao banfa" 暂行民局挂号领照办法 [Provisional regulations for Minju registered licences] as attachment to Circular Memo No. 520, Director General Wei Yifu, 29 September in SHAC-137.6272–5.

Second Historical Archives of China, Nanjing (SHAC). 1935. "Jiaotongbu youzheng zongju tongchi di 1486 hao, juzhang Guo Xinsong" 交通部邮政总局通饬第1486号，局长郭心嵩 [Ministry of Communications, Director General of Posts, circular memo no. 1486], 21 January in SHAC-137.6284–1.

Second Historical Archives of China, Nanjing (SHAC). 1936a. Directorate General of Posts, *Postal Compendium*. Shanghai: Supply Department of the Directorate General of Posts. In SHAC-127.6223.

Second Historical Archives of China, Nanjing (SHAC). 1936b. "Remittances from Overseas Chinese, Inspector Chang Chi-hsi", 4 December in SHAC-127(2)123.

Second Historical Archives of China, Nanjing (SHAC). 1937a. "Summary of Pixinju Mails Despatched to and Received from Foreign Ports", January 1937–November 1938 in SHAC-127.321.

Second Historical Archives of China, Nanjing (SHAC). 1937b. "S/O No. 254, Guangdong Postal Commissioner Molland to Director General of the Postal Remittance and Savings Bank S. K. Shen", 11 October in SHAC-127(2).123.

Second Historical Archives of China, Nanjing (SHAC). 1937c. "Letter from Chew Hock Leong, Head Office Manager in Charge of Branches, Overseas Chinese Banking Corporation to de Sercy, Deputy Commissioner, Guangdong Head Post Office", 14 September in SHAC-127(2).123.

Second Historical Archives of China, Nanjing (SHAC). 1938a. "Postage on Pixinju Mails Despatched, January–November 1938", in SHAC-127.321.

Second Historical Archives of China, Nanjing (SHAC). 1938b. "Xiamen youju pixin tongji biao, Minguo ershiliu nian zhi ershiqi nian" 厦门邮局批 信统计表，民国二十六年至二十七年 [Statistical table of *pixin* handled by the Xiamen post office] in SHAC-137.2287.

Second Historical Archives of China, Nanjing (SHAC). 1938c. "Report by S. K. Fong, Remittances from Overseas Chinese: An Outline Concerning the Causes of the Inauguration of the Service and Its Present Condition", 14 March in SHAC-127(2).123.

Second Historical Archives of China, Nanjing (SHAC). 1938d. "Letter from Overseas Chinese Banking Corporation to W. H. Chu, United China Syndicate", 26 May in SHAC-127.5233.

Second Historical Archives of China, Nanjing (SHAC). 1938e. "Mail Telegram, No. 580, Director General Guo Xinsong to Guangzhou Head Office", December 28, 1938 in SHAC-137.5033.

Second Historical Archives of China, Nanjing (SHAC). 1939a. "Overseas Remittances, 1939 (petty only)" in SHAC-127(2).114.

Second Historical Archives of China, Nanjing (SHAC). 1939b. "Li he yue ren Zhongyang yinhang Zhongguo yinhang ji Youzheng chujin huiye ju" 立合约人中央银行中国银行及邮政储金汇业局 [Contract between the Central Bank, the Bank of China, and the D.G. of P.R. & S.B.], 23 March in SHAC-127.5233.

Second Historical Archives of China, Nanjing (SHAC). 1939c. "Shanghai banshichu micheng di yi hao, Shanghai banshichu chuzhang Zhapeilin" 上海办事处密呈第一号，上海办事处处长乍配林 [Confidential petition no. 1, Shanghai Working Office, Office Manager Chapelain], 16 May in SHAC-137.5705.

Second Historical Archives of China, Nanjing (SHAC). 1939d. "I.M.O's from Malaya, 1938–1939" in SHAC-127.321.

Second Historical Archives of China, Nanjing (SHAC). 1940a. "The Activities of Our Competitors by Zhang Jixi to Director General of Postal Remittance and Savings Bank", 4 June in SHAC-127(2).121.

Second Historical Archives of China, Nanjing (SHAC). 1940b. "Report by Zhou Yundong" 周云东, 18 March in SHAC-127(2).123.

Second Historical Archives of China, Nanjing (SHAC). 1940c. Youzheng chujin huiye ju 邮政储金汇业局, *Huaqiao huipiao fenfaqu diming biao* 华侨汇票分发区地名表 [Table of place names in the overseas Chinese remittance stamp distribution areas]. N.p.: Youzheng chujin huiye ju in SHAC-127(2).150.

Second Historical Archives of China, Nanjing (SHAC). 1941a. "Letter from C. Y. Yeh to C. H. Liu", 16 January in SHAC-127.1181–2.

Second Historical Archives of China, Nanjing (SHAC). 1941b. "Minguo sanshi niandu qiaohui yewu jihua" 民国三十年度侨汇业务计划 [Plan for the development of the overseas remittances business for 1941], 8 February in SHAC-127(2)3.91.

Second Historical Archives of China, Nanjing (SHAC). 1941c. "Report No. 5, Director General of Postal Remittance and Savings Bank, HK, Inspector Y. F. Humann Loh", 23 August in SHAC-127.1181–2.

Second Historical Archives of China, Nanjing (SHAC). 1941d. "Overseas Petty Remittances Reports", in SHAC-127(2).114.

Second Historical Archives of China, Nanjing (SHAC). 1941e. "Zhaolu bangonghan di 53 hao, juzhang Guo Xinsong, youzheng chujin huiye ju juzhang Liu Gongyun", 照录半公函第53号，局长郭心嵩致邮政储金汇业局局长刘攻芸 [Semi-official no. 53, Director General Guo Xinsong to Director General of Postal Remittance and Savings Bank Liu Gongyun], 3 November in SHAC-127.2748.

Second Historical Archives of China, Nanjing (SHAC). 1941f. "Overseas Remittances Received by the Postal Remittance and Savings Bank since the Inauguration of the Overseas Remittance Service", in SHAC-127(2).114.

Second Historical Archives of China, Nanjing (SHAC). 1942a. "Letter No. 14321 from Foreign Department, Chongqing Head Office, Bank of China, to Director General of Postal Remittance and Savings Bank", 15 August in SHAC-127.2638–1.

Second Historical Archives of China, Nanjing (SHAC). 1942b. "Letter No. 13878 from D. G. Xu Jizhuang to Foreign Department, Chongqing Head Office, Bank of China, to Director General of Postal Remittance and Savings Bank", 2 November in SHAC-127.2638–1.

Second Historical Archives of China, Nanjing (SHAC). Undated(a). *Youju banli huaqiao huikuan yewu xuzhi* 邮局办理华侨汇款业务须知 [Handbook for handling overseas remittances by the Post Office], in SHAC-127(2).123.

Second Historical Archives of China, Nanjing (SHAC). Undated(b). "Nanyang qiaomin huikuan" 南洋侨民汇款 [South Seas overseas Chinese remittances], in SHAC-127(2).442.

Second Historical Archives of China, Nanjing (SHAC). Undated(c). "Notes signed by Kan Wen-sheng, for the International Secretary", in SHAC-137(5).2635.

Second Historical Archives of China, Nanjing (SHAC). Undated(d). "Documents to and from Jean Jouvelet, Haiphong Transmission Office", in SHAC-137.9445.

Second Historical Archives of China, Nanjing (SHAC). Undated(e). "Qiaohui yewuyuan daiyu zanxing banfa" 侨汇业务员待遇暂行办法 [Provisional method for the treatment of overseas remittance workers], in SHAC-137.75–1.

Second Historical Archives of China, Nanjing (SHAC). Undated(f). "Qiaohui xunyuan shicha qiaohui baogao shu" 侨汇巡员视察侨汇报告书 [Reports on overseas remittances by overseas remittance inspectors], in SHAC-127.1808–1.

Second Historical Archives of China, Nanjing (SHAC). Undated(g). "Qiaohui xunyuan xingcheng baogao biao" 华侨巡员行程报告表 [Reports on the routes of overseas remittance inspectors], in SHAC-127.1808–2.

Other sources

Akashi, Yoji. 1970. *The Nanyang Chinese National Salvation Movement, 1937–1941*. Lawrence: Center for East Asian Studies, University of Kansas.

Caizheng pinglun she 财政评论社. 1940. *Zhanshi caizheng jinrong fagui huibian* 战时财政金融法规汇编 [Compilation of wartime financial regulations]. Hong Kong: Caizheng pinglun she.

Cao Qian 曹潜. 1979. *Youzheng chuhui fazhan shi* 邮政储汇发展史 [History of the expansion of postal service remittances and savings]. Taipei: Youzheng chujiu huiye ju.

Chang, Kia-Ngau. 1958. *The Inflationary Spiral: The Experience in China, 1939–1950*. Cambridge: Technology Press of MIT.

Chen Liyuan 陈丽园. 2006. "Huanan yu Dongnanya Huaren shehui de hudong guanxi – Yi Chaoren qiaopi wangluo wei zhongxin (1911–1949)" 华南与东南亚华人社会的互动关系-以潮人侨批网络为中心 [Interactions between south China and the Chinese communities in Southeast Asia: A study of the Teochew remittance networks, 1911–1949]. PhD diss., National University of Singapore.

Chen Liyuan 陈丽园. 2014. "Lun kuaguo qiaopi hudong de shuangchongxing: Yi Chao-Shan qiaopi wei zhongxin" 论跨国侨批互动的双重性：以潮汕侨批为中心 [On the dualistic interactions of transnational *qiaopi*: Using *qiaopi* from Chaozhou-Shantou as an example]. *Shantou daxue xuebao (renwen shehui kexue ban)* 汕头大学学报（人文社会科学版）[Shantou University journal (Humanities and social sciences edition)] 30(3): 12–17.

Chen Shuren 陈树人. 1940. "Kangzhan qizhong de qiaowu gongzuo" 抗战期中的侨务工作 [Overseas Chinese work during the War of Resistance]. *Xiandai huaqiao* 现代华侨 [Contemporary overseas Chinese] 2(5) (May): 4–6.

Chen Zhifang 陈植芳. 1991. "Chao-Shan qiaojuan de shengmingxian – Ji kangzhan houqi kaipi de Dongxing huilu" 潮汕侨眷的生命线 – 记抗战后期开辟的东兴汇路 [A lifeline for overseas Chinese relatives in Chao-Shan: Remembering the opening of the Dongxing remittance route in the later years of the war]. *Shantou wenshi* 汕头文史 (Shantou historical materials) 10: 140–153.

The China Press. 1937a. 11 and 28 August, 13 and 18 September.

The China Press. 1937b. 22 July.

The China Press. 1938a. 27 December.

The China Press. 1938b. 15 April.

Choate, Mark I. 2007. "Sending States' Transnational Interventions in Politics, Culture, and Economics: The Historical Example of Italy". *International Migration Review* 41:3 (August): 728–768.

Council of International Affairs. 1941. *The Chinese Year Book, 1940–1941*. Chungking: Commercial Press.

Council of International Affairs. 1943. *The Chinese Year Book, 1943*. London: Thacker & Co.

Dongnan ribao 东南日报 (Jinhua 金华). 1939. 19 September.

Duara, Prasenjit. 1997. "Transnationalism and the Predicament of Sovereignty: China, 1900–1945". *American Historical Review* 102(4) (October): 1030–1051.

Federal Reserve Bulletin. 1941. December.

Harris, Lane J. 2012. "The Post Office and State Formation in Modern China, 1896–1949". PhD diss., University of Illinois, Urbana-Champaign.

Harris, Lane J. 2015. "Overseas Chinese Remittance Firms, the Limits of State Sovereignty, and Transnational Capitalism in East and Southeast Asia, 1850s–1930s". *Journal of Asian Studies* 74(1) (February): 129–151.

Huang Yuanbin 黄元彬. 1989. "Huaqiao huikuan zongdongyuan yundong yijian" 华侨汇款总 动员运动意见 [A recommendation for a movement to mobilize overseas Chinese remittances]. In Fujian sheng dang'anguan 福建省档案馆, ed. *Fujian Huaqiao dang'anguan shiliao* 福建华侨档案馆史料 [Archival materials on overseas Chinese from Fujian], Volume 1, 412–414. Beijing: Dang'an chubanshe.

Huaqiao xiehui zonghui, ed. 1999. *Huaqiao yu kangri zhanzheng lunwenji* 华侨与抗日战争论文集 [Collected writings on overseas Chinese and the War of Resistance against Japan]. 2 vols. Taipei: Huaqiao xiehui zonghui.

Jiao Jianhua 焦建华. 2006. "Jin bainian lai Zhongguo qiaopi ye yanjiu zongshu" 近百年来中国侨批业研究综述 [A historiographical review of the *qiaopi* industry over the last hundred years]. *Huaqiao Huaren lishi yanjiu* 华侨华人历史研究 "Overseas Chinese History Studies" 2: 49–58.

Jiao Jianhua 焦建华. 2014. "Taipingyang zhanzheng qian Chao-Shan lunxianqu qiaohuiye yanjiu (1939.7–1941.12) 太平洋战争前潮汕沦陷区侨汇业研究 [Research on the overseas Chinese remittance industry in occupied Chaozhou-Shantou prior to the Pacific War]. *Nanyang wenti yanjiu* 南洋问题研究 [Southeast asian affairs] 1: 69–77.

Jiaotongbu youzheng zongju 交通部邮政总局. 1956. *Zhongguo youzheng tongji huiji* 中国邮政统计汇集 [Collection of Chinese postal service statistics]. Taipei: Jiaotongbu youzheng zongju.

Jingji huibao 经济汇报 [Economic report]. 1941. 4:8: 91–93.

Jinrong zhoubao 金融周报 [Financial weekly]. 1937. 4:18: 8.

Koh, Ernest. 2013. *Diaspora at War: The Chinese of Singapore between Empire and Nation, 1937–1945*. Leiden: Brill.

Kong Xiangxi 孔祥熙. 1994. "Caizhengbu di'er qi zhanshi xingzheng jihua shishi fang'an (xu)" 财政部第二期战时行政计划实施方案（续） [Program for the implementation of the second phase of the Ministry of Finance's wartime administrative plan (continued)]. *Minguo dang'an* 民国档案 [Republican archives] 1: 29–39.

Kong Xiangxi 孔祥熙. 2006. "Kong Xiangxi zai Guomindang wu jie wu zhong quanhui shang de caizheng baogao" 孔祥熙在国民党五届五中全会上的财政报告 [Kong Xiangxi's financial report to the fifth plenary session of the fifth congress of the Chinese Nationalist Party]. *Minguo dang'an* 民国档案 [Republican archives] 1: 3–15.

Leong, Stephen. 1979. "The Malayan Overseas Chinese and the Sino-Japanese War, 1937–1941". *Journal of Southeast Asian Studies* 10(2) (September): 293–320.

Lin Zhongyou 林忠友. 1995. "Fujian youzheng wushi nian" 福建邮政五十年 [Fifty years in the Fujian post office]. In *Fujian wenshi ziliao* 福建文史资料 [Historical sources from Fujian] 17 (1987). Reprinted in Zhang Zhihe and Hu Zhongyuan 张志和, 胡仲元 eds. *Quanguo geji zhengxie wenshi ziliao: Youdian shiliao* 全国各级政协文史资料 [Literary and historical materials from all levels of the national Chinese People's Political Consultative Conference]. Beijing: Beijing Yanshan chubanshe, pp. 593–681.

Lu, Yan. 2014. "Together with the Homeland: Civil Activism for National Salvation in British Hong Kong". *Modern China* 40(6): 639–674.

Maoyi yuekan 贸易月刊 [Trade monthly]. 1941. 3: 2.

Mar, Lisa Rose. 2010. *Brokering Belonging: Chinese in Canada's Exclusion Era, 1885–1945*. New York: Oxford University Press.

Nanyang Siang Pau 南洋商报. 1938a. 16 May.

Nanyang Siang Pau 南洋商报. 1938b. 11 June.

Nanyang Siang Pau 南洋商报. 1938c. 24 February.

Nanyang Siang Pau 南洋商报. 1938d. 24 October.

Nanyang Siang Pau 南洋商报. 1939a. 4 July.

Nanyang Siang Pau 南洋商报. 1939b. 28 August.

Qiaowu ershiwunian bianji weiyuanhui 侨务二十五年编辑委员会. 1957. *Qiaowu ershiwunian* 侨务二十五年 [Twenty-five years of overseas Chinese affairs]. Taipei: Haiwai chubanshe.

Remer, C. F. 1933. *Foreign Investments in China*. New York: Macmillan.

Shao, Dan. 2009. "Chinese by Definition: Nationality Law, Jus Sanguinis, and State Succession, 1909–1980". *Twentieth-Century China* 35(1) (November): 4–28.

Sheng hang tongxun [Fujian] 省行通讯 [Provincial bank communications]. 1938. 1: 3.

Singapore Free Press and Mercantile Advertiser. 1937. 24 August.

Singapore Free Press and Mercantile Advertiser. 1940a. 6 July.

Singapore Free Press and Mercantile Advertiser. 1940b. 6 September.

Straits Times. 1937. 7 October.

Straits Times. 1939. 28 August.

Straits Times. 1940a. 19 August.

Straits Times. 1940b. 30 August.

Tan, Kah Kee. 1994. *The Memoirs of Tan Kah-Kee*. Edited and translated with notes by A. H. C. Ward, Raymond W. Chu, and Janet Salaff. Singapore: Singapore University Press.

Treasury Department. 1943. *Administration of the Wartime Financial and Property Controls of the United States Government.* Washington: US Treasury Department, Foreign Funds Control.

Tung, Liu. 1939. "The Fate of the Over-Sea Chinese in Burma". *The China Critic* (16 February).

Universal Postal Union. 1907. *Convention of Rome* (26 May 1906). London: Eyre and Spottiswoode.

Wu, Chun-hsi. 1967. *Dollars, Dependents and Dogma: Overseas Chinese Remittances to Communist China*. Stanford: The Hoover Institute.

Xingdao ribao 星岛日报 (Hong Kong). 1940. 9 September.

Xinhua ribao 新华日报 (Chongqing). 1940. 25 September.

Young, Arthur N. 1965. *China's Wartime Finance and Inflation, 1937–1945*. Cambridge, MA: Harvard University Press.

Yuan Ding, Chen Liyuan, and Zhong Yunrong 袁丁, 陈丽园, 钟运荣. 2014. *Guomin zhengfu dui qiaohui de guanzhi* 国民政府对侨汇的管制 [National government controls on overseas Chinese remittances]. Guangzhou: Guangdong renmin chubanshe.

Zhang Saiqun 张赛群. 2008. Nanjing guomin zhengfu qiaowu zhengce yanjiu 南京国民政府侨务政策研究 [Research on the policies towards overseas Chinese by the Nanjing national government]. Beijing: Zhongguo yanshi chubanshe.

Zhongguo yinhang hangshi bianji weiyuanhui 中国银行行史编辑委员会. 1991. *Zhongguo yinhang hangshi, 1912–1949* 中国银行行史, 1912–1949 [A history of the Bank of China, 1912–1949]. Beijing: Dang'an chubanshe.

5 The evolution of the *qiaopi* trade

A case study of the Tianyi firm

Junying Jia[1]

In the fifteenth century, Chinese businessmen brought rice, sugar, cotton, and other foodstuffs and raw materials to China and took Chinese products, including handicrafts and tea, to Southeast Asia. Immigration from Guangdong and Fujiian to Southeast Asia led to the creation of a circular trade between South China and that region. *Shuike* (couriers) took migrants' letters and remittances back to the migrants' towns and villages. In the course of the continuous expansion of this circular trade, the *shuike* evolved into *qiaopiju* (remittance houses) in the latter half of the nineteenth century, and the *qiaopiju* gradually became one of the trade's central points of reference (Hamashita 2006, 152). The *qiaopiju* were private institutions specializing in letters-cum-remittances, and thus functioned simultaneously as a sort of post office and an exchange bank. There has been much research in China on the *qiaopi* trade (Zheng Linkuan 1940; Yang Jiancheng 1984; Hamashita 1999; Shen Xianyang 1998; Wang Zhuchun *et al.* 2006; Dai Yifeng 2003, 70; Jiao Jianhua 2005, 64), but few scholars have focused specifically on the role of trust (Long Denggao 2003; Liu Jiansheng *et al.* 2008, Yan Hongzhong 2009, 15) and the associated local features of the migrants' sending areas and places of settlement and the networks that ran between them.

The *qiaopiju* as an institution embodied the transition from traditional trust to modern trust. With the development of a circular trade between South China and Southeast Asia, the *qiaopi* network's traditional form of trust, based on personalized relations, gradually developed into systemic trust based on material considerations and contracts, and subsequently came to take the form of organizational trust based on regulations and government behaviour based on mechanisms designed to protect the interests of overseas Chinese and to maintain regional stability. The Overseas Chinese Bureau 侨务局 was deeply rooted in a particular regional culture. Although different forms of trust evolved over time, their traditional and modern variants cannot be completely separated from one another. Instead, they combined symbiotically, both in normal times and in times of crisis. Tianyi, which survived for forty-nine years after its founding in 1880, epitomized the development of *the qiaopi* system in southern Fujian and Southeast Asia, from its initial emergence, through its further development, and ending frequently in failure (Guo Boling 1999; Lin Nanzhong 2009). This chapter analyses that process on the basis of oral and archival data and newspapers.

Traditional trust as a basis for the *qiaopi* trade

Traditional trust lay at the heart of the *qiaopiju* as an institution. In traditional society, geosanguineous relations linked people together. Everyone stood at the centre of a circle of social influences. However, each circle had its own characteristics, even though different circles coincided in terms of place and time (Fei Xiaotong 1998, 27–31). The social order was hierarchical, and within it trust relations were established and maintained on the basis of traditional morality and collective rewards and punishments.

The role played by traditional trust in the rise of the qiaopi *trade*

Chinese migrated to Southeast Asia from Fujian and Guangdong along chains, starting in the fifteenth century, leading to a constant flow of new arrivals as migrants joined their relatives, friends, and fellow-villagers overseas (Dai Yifeng 2002, 82–90). A respondent in Manila told me: "Our parents' and our own generation arrived in the Philippines with the help of relatives and associates. After arrival, food, shelter, and work were provided with their help."[2] As a consequence of chain migration, Chinese formed dense settlements in Southeast Asia based on geosanguineity. Chain migration and centralized settlement were the foundations for the emergence of the *qiaopi* trade. *Shuike*, *ketou* (migrants' escorts), and the hostels they frequented and the stores with which many became linked played a major role in trafficking cash, goods, and new immigrants, and in founding the *qiaopi* trade. Most *shuike* carried a visiting card with a photo and a message along the lines of "I have the pleasure of introducing [his name], who has been registered in [such-and-such a place], to do business with you" (Ta Kung Pao 2009).

Tianyi was established by Guo Youpin, born in 1853 in Longxi. Aged seventeen, he went to the Philippines, where in 1870 he began working as a *shuike* carrying *qiaopi* back to Xiamen with the help of his cousin Guo Youde. In 1880,[3] he founded Tianyi. In the early days, he took personal charge of the business. On one occasion, the ship in which he was travelling sank in a typhoon, along with the *qiaopi*, so he sold his land and house to compensate his clients. After that, his fame spread across the region.[4]

Subsequently, Guo Youpin turned personal trust and credit into capital, and thus laid the foundations for the creation and development of Tianyi. Initially, in the absence of a systemic guarantee, migrants entrusted their *qiaopi*, including the letters that accompanied the remittances, to people or organizations with which they shared a relationship of blood or geography. According to Shi Wenzhi, a well-known Philippine-Chinese author, "the *qiaopiju* was strongly rural in character. Everyone knew each other, so no one was afraid the firm's owner would go bankrupt or run off."[5]

Kinship and geography were not only the basis for the formation of traditional credit institutions but also the driving force behind their further development. Information was in short supply, so ties of blood and geography were important in facilitating its flow between migrants' sending places in China and their receiving places in Southeast Asia. Good and bad trust or credit spread rapidly along the network of relations, and the ensuing system of collective rewards and punishment formed a strong invisible sanction. Moral turpitude was frowned on in popular morality. According to Wu Guofan, a Metrobank official who worked in the *qiaopi* trade from 1949 to 1960, "There are lots of local legends about people suffering immediate retribution if they engaged in embezzlement. So almost everyone in the *qiaopiju* behaved responsibly." Wu Guofan also explained that a customer's money was refunded if a cheque was returned within five years. Trust lay at the heart of the *qiaopiju* system, and personal trust relations enabled companies like Tianyi to establish subsidiaries throughout South China and Southeast Asia and to develop transnational business networks.

The role of traditional trust in the family business model of the **qiaopi** *industry*

The family is the basic cell of life and production in traditional society, fanning out vertically and laterally into clan or lineage and the various levels of local community. Workers of the same lineage and provenance had common economic interests that were more easily twisted into a common sinew with which to confront the unstable external environment of earlier times, before the birth and consolidation of forms of legal protection. This was certainly the case with Tianyi, and explains the coherence of its management and the strength of its customer base.

Guo Youpin set up a general administration for Tianyi in Longxi and a subsidiary in Manila in 1880, followed by subsidiaries in Xiamen and Jinjiang in 1892, when the Xiamen customs were established. He applied for a licence from the Qing Post Office in Xiamen in 1896, in the name of Tianyi ju. The available data show that Tianyi had its head office in Liuchuan and an additional thirty-four branches, nine in China and twenty-five overseas (principally in Southeast Asia) (see Table 5.1 and Table 5.2). The Taiwan bank survey carried out by the Japanese in 1914 confirmed that "Tianyi and Yueren are the largest *qiaopiju*, with more than thirty offices in Saigon, and that both of them are the largest *qiaopiju* in Rangoon" (Yang Jiancheng 1984, 109).

Guo Youpin had three sons, Yongzhong, Hezhong, and Chengzhong, and a daughter, Helian. Guo Yongzhong (1884–1947) was the first headmaster of Liuchuan's private elementary school (Si li Liuchuan Liang deng xiao xue tang), founded by his father in 1905 (Huang Jianlan 1993, 829), He had eight sons and one daughter. When his father died in 1901, he became leader of Tianyi and took responsibility for the family, at the age of seventeen, with the support of his cousin Guo Xingduan.

Table 5.1 (Tianyi's foreign subsidiaries) and Table 5.2 (Tianyi's domestic subsidiaries)[6] show that of the twenty-three domestic and foreign bureaus of Tianyi for which we have appropriate data, twenty were managed by a member of the Guo family and the most important ones in Xiamen, Shanghai, and Hong Kong were under Guo Youpin's sons. Table 5.3 shows that the Guo family was closely linked by marriage with the Cai and Huang families (Guo Boling 2010) – no fewer than nine marriages took place between a Guo and a Cai or a Huang in the years 1905–1963. The Huang lineage had settled in Jiaomei and Shimei, close to

Table 5.1 Tianyi's foreign subsidiaries

Bureau name	*Country*	*Address*	*Manager (relation)*
Luzon	Philippines	Wangbin Street in Chinatown, Manila	Zheng Shuiren (Guo Youpin's friend), Zheng Shangben
Cebu	Philippines	–	Huang Yayan, Guo Shanglian (Guo Yongzhong's oldest son), Cai Zhaoqing
Iloilo	Philippines	–	Cai Zhaoqing, Huang Yaqiu
Zamboanga	Philippines	–	GuoShangzhong (Guo Youpin's grandson)
Sulu	Philippines	–	–
Ilagan	Philippines	–	Guo Jinglan
Calbayog	Philippines	–	–
Batavia	Indonesia	–	Guo Yuanzhong (Guo Youpin's nephew)
Cirebon	Indonesia	–	–
Semarang	Indonesia	–	–
Surabaya	Indonesia	–	Guo Qinsheng
Palembang	Indonesia	–	Guo Shangbian (Guo Youpin's grandson)
Bandung	Indonesia	–	–
Medan	Indonesia	–	–
Penang	Malaya	–	Guo Chengzhong (Guo Youpin's second son)
Perak	Malaya	–	Guo Shangwei (Guo Youpin's grandson)
Malacca	Malaya	Jiling Street	–
Siam	Thailand	–	–
Song Khla	Thailand	–	–
Hue	Vietnam	Shunhua Street	–
Batri	Vietnam	Pleiku	Guo Shanglian
Saigon	Vietnam	–	–
Singapore	Singapore	Shunyuan Street	Huang Qiongyao
Rangoon	Burma	–	–
Phnom Penh	Cambodia	–	–

Table 5.2 Tianyi's domestic subsidiaries

Bureau name	*Address*	*Manager (relation)*
Tianyi Zong Ju	Liuchuan Street in Longxi Country in Zhangzhou	Guo Yongzhong (Guo Youpin's oldest son)
Xiamen	Shuixiangong in Zhenbang Road Gangkouzai Street	Guo Hezhong (Guo Youpin's third son), Yang Xianfu
Anhai	Shicheng Street in Anhai Jinjiang	Guo Bingkun
Hong Kong	–	Guo Xuankui, Guo Chengzhong (Guo Youpin's second son), Guo Shangben (Guo Youpin's grandson)
Maluan	Tongan	Guo Xuankui
Zhangzhou	–	Guo Shu'er
Quanzhou	–	Guo Yuanzhu
Fugong		Ding Bigong
Shanghai	–	Guo Anfu
Gangwei	–	Cai Ciqing, Guo Zhigan

Table 5.3 Inter-marriage between the Guo family and the Huang and Cai families

Member of Guo	*Status in family*	*Date of birth*	*Marriage*
Guo Shanghang	Guo Hezhong's eldest son	1905	Wife Cai Lihua
Guo Suxin	Guo Hezhong's second daughter	1922	Husband Cai Ziren
Guo Wenyan	Guo Shanghang's third daughter	1942	Husband Cai Shuiyuan
Guo Wenshu	Guo Shanghang's fifth daughter	1949	Husband Cai Yabo
Guo Sijing	Guo Guosong's eldest son	1969	Wife Cai Huirong
Guo Shangxi	Guo Hezhong's fourth son	1902	Wife Huang Liqing
Guo Shangjian	Guo Hezhong's sixth son	1925	Husband Huang Yaqin
Guo Wennuan	Guo Shanghang's fourth daughter	1943	Husband Huang Youcai
Guo Yishan	Guo Shangyan's third daughter	1963	Huang Hepei

Tianyi's location, in the Ming Dynasty, so the tie was presumably long-standing (Lin Diange 2007, 431–432). The Huang and Cai families formed a majority of both the membership and the leadership of the Longtonghai (Longxi Tongan Haicheng) Association in Philippines (Longtonghai lianxiang zonghui 2011), That is to say, the Huang and Cai families were also influential in Longhai (which had jurisdiction over Liuchuan). According to Guo Youpin's grandson Guo Shangbiao,

Tianyi staff were all members of local families.[7] Tianyi's management system was therefore entirely family-based (other *qiaopiju*, for example the Jiangnan huidui xinju, were also family-based).[8]

Relationship-based trust reduces transaction costs and makes *qiaopiju* management more competitive. This was especially so in the early years. However, the system was not without serious drawbacks, which gradually emerged in the course of Tianyi's development. In family firms, internal supervision is crucial. If a manager lacks ability and there are no clear lines of responsibility, a company is bound for trouble. This trouble proved to be insoluble, when Tianyi managers in the Philippines and Hong Kong speculated recklessly on exchange deals, in a situation in which mutual help was unavailable. Customers were unable to cash their cheques, and Tianyi went out of business. Guo Shangbiao believes that the main reason for the collapse was the lack of a regulatory system, typical of family management. He said: "Had there been a more advanced form of management, Tianyi might have survived" (Lu Xianxiang 2004, 163).

Systemic trust in the *qiaopi* trade

Economists assert that "as long as the income gained by breaking rules seems to exceed the cost of violation, individuals and businesses are free to do so, within the informal system. On the other hand, the formal system can reduce costs and uncertainty in transactions."[9] Tianyi gradually progressed in the direction of a systemic form of trust.

After this system emerged, the oral agreement between company and customer was printed on the envelope in the form of a credit seal, visible to everyone. Tianyi use different credit seals in different periods and regions, all of which carried Tianyi's name and address and promised measures against counterfeiting and other forms of malpractice. For example, one bore the following information: "Guo Youpin's Tianyi remittance house, in association with Tongan's remittance office, located in Anhai Shicheng Street. No tips will be demanded." In 1905, another Tianyi credit seal stated: "Our *qiaopi* can be exchanged on the spot, without need for any form of tip. Otherwise, you can tell us or write to us, and we will put things right. We will keep our word and never break this promise." In 1908: "If there is any discrepancy in the amount of money, the customer can get twice the amount compensation. Tianyi will never break its promise."[10] In 1918:

> Tianyi does not write replies [on behalf of recipients of remittances, a measure designed to prevent fraud or extortion]. Any courier who helps [a customer] to write a reply will be in breach of our rules. If any employee offers to write a reply on behalf of a customer, please feel free to tell us. We will deal with him in the office. This is because someone who constantly helps write replies will know customers' private business.
>
> (Chen Zhanqi 2006, 2191)

Tianyi's unique mode of transmitting "silver and letters" (i.e. *qiaopi*) was divided into four parts: receipt of the remittance, cash transfer, delivery, and payment.

In this process, accuracy and speed were of the essence. The "ship number" was a key feature of the registration of a *qiaopi* and ensured its safe delivery. The *qiaopiju* encoded each envelope with the number of the ship that carried it and the location of the custom house. These two features were indispensable links in the transmission process, in a system designed to prevent errors at every point in the delivery. Tianyi's account books between 1917 and 1918 listed 108 ships and 13,264 *qiaopi*.[11] When the customer initially handed over the *qiaopi*, the *qiaopiju* registered it in accordance with the so-called "Suzhou code", stamped or written on the envelope and registered on a stub. The *qiaopiju* kept the original stub for checking later and sent a copy to the *qiaopiju* in Xiamen, which, once the *qiaopi* had arrived in Xiamen, sent a further copy to the *qiaopiju* in the migrant's hometown or village. Because of this system of registration, each *qiaopiju* at each stage in the delivery could quickly and accurately ascertain the recipient's address. Each *qiaopiju* in turn cancelled the registration number on receipt of the recipient's reply, to ensure that every *qiaopi* arrived safely at its intended destination.

This process required a large amount of human and material resources, but it guaranteed that little if anything was ever lost. The official Post Office admired and spoke highly of this technique: "We have tried hard to get into this business, but so far with only partial success" (Fujian Province Archives).

According to the 1914 Japanese survey from Taiwan,

> only Tianyi and Yueren had their head offices in Xiamen. Most other *qiaopiju* had their head offices in Southeast Asia and set up agencies in Xiamen. Tianyi was the only one with an office in a remote mountainous area, while others delivered the *qiaopi* by way of a *pijiao* [foot delivery man] not attached to any office, and whose job was to deliver the *qiaopi* directly to the [recipient's] door.
>
> (Yang Jiancheng 1984, 110)

Tianyi also set up its own route into the migrants' sending areas.

> In 1920, Tianyi purchased 3 steamboats – the Nantaiwu, the Zhengtaiwu, and the Hongjiang – to develop shipping ties, initially between Zhuoqi and Xiamen and Shimei and Xiamen and subsequently between Shima and Xiamen, Shima and Jinmen, Zhangzhou, Shima, and Xiamen, and Zhangzhou and Shimei. These continued to operate until the 1950s.
>
> (Zhangzhou City Local Records Compilation Committee 2003, 366)

The transfer of "silver", i.e. money in its various forms, was the most important and the riskiest task of the *qiaopi* trade, and was carried out by way of the money transfer company. The *qiaopiju* in Southeast Asia sent "silver" and "letters" separately, so they arrived at different times. The *qiaopiju* used the "silver" to profit from the exchange transaction or to engage in trading, and did their best to exploit market fluctuations. Only after having earned their profit did they actually set about delivering the remittance. When the *qiaopiju* overseas issued a remittance, usually without transmitting actual money, it incurred a debt in Xiamen, which was eventually squared on the foreign exchange market (usually in Shanghai or Hong Kong). Given that exchange rates fluctuated constantly, this procedure was akin to gambling.

Between 1917 and 1918, Tianyi transferred 153,671 yuan, the equivalent of 426.86 yuan a day during the months January to December (*Minnan Ribao* 2011), In Hongkong, the Youxin *yinzhuang* (native bank) made daily inquiries about the state of the financial market (Chen Da 1938, 84). Tianyi was unique in that it had its own primary, secondary, and tertiary *qiaopiju* and its own money transfer company in Shanghai and Hong Kong, which on the one hand made transactions easy but on the other hand meant that there was a lack of supervision. Tianyi collapsed in 1928 because of reckless risk-taking on the financial market by some of its managers. A witness described it thus:

> This activity is similar to stock market operations, it is very easy to fail if the practitioner's skill and luck fall short. I recall that Tianyi in Xiamen purchased remittances in advance, and lost more than one million yuan when the price of the quotation fell.
>
> (Huang Lugu 1984, 143–144)

Issuing so-called credit tickets was one way of maintaining credit flows in troubled times. To reduce the risk associated with carrying cash, the tertiary *qiaopiju* in the migrant-sending area issued their own bills, which could be used as cash and circulated on the market. These credit tickets were known as *shanpiao* (mountain tickets) or credit bills. These bills were usually low in value. The date, amount, order, anti-fake seal, and *anma* 暗码 (test key) were printed on the *shanpiao*. The *anma* usually consisted of several rare Chinese characters, alluding to the date and amount of the *shanpiao*, in order to prevent forgeries. Every issuer of *shanpiao* had a test key book representing the numbers 0–9, and changed it frequently.

Issuing *shanpiao* reduced the risks associated with the delivery of cash and temporarily eased shortages of funds. The customer could choose either to cash in the bill at the *qiaopiju* or to use it to buy goods in the local store in the village. The store could then use it to trade with other companies, which in turn could trade it on the market or exchange it for cash in the *qiaopiju*. However, the issue of "mountain tickets" required a sufficient amount of cash to back it. If the amount of "mountain tickets" issued exceeded the reserve fund, the *qiaopiju* would experience a credit crisis and would, eventually, be forced to close down. According to a report, "there were up to 50 million yuan's worth of mountain tickets that could not be cashed when Tianyi closed down. … At least 24 *qiaopiju* went bankrupt or were reorganized between 1920 and 1936" (Lin Chunsen 1996, 40).

The unique mode of transmission of "silver" and "letters", a combination of tradition and modernity, resulted in the formation of a huge, complex network of *qiaopiju* carrying a steady flow of *qiaopi*. This process involved three elements: the mode of transfer of the "silver" and letters, the transnational network between the hometown and Southeast Asia, and the traditional system of family management. Taken together, these three elements explain why the *qiaopiju* could not be superseded by the Post Office or the modern banking system, and also why Tianyi started its decline and eventually closed down.

Organizational trust and government supervision in the *qiaopi* trade

The *qiaopi* trade depended for its development on the support of traditional trust mechanisms and systemic trust, but it also required the constraint of organizational trust at the popular level and government supervision at the official level, in order to ensure the orderly operation of the market in a free-market environment. Although relationship-based trust and the legal system could regulate credit, organization was also essential for strengthening and promoting the development of a credit system, especially in the chaos of the late-nineteenth and early-twentieth centuries in China, when law was often inoperable. Under such circumstances, constraints operated by members of the same trade organization were more effective than individual constraints. They helped to promote the long-term interests of member organizations by aiming for honest management and were an important part of the market system (Zheng Chenglin 2007, 59). One example is the Xiamen Yinxinju Association, set up in 1920 by Yang Shuisheng, the manager of Tianyi in Xiamen and the association's chairman. Yang Shuisheng was succeeded in his post by Chen Tianfang and Su Qichang, and the association was restructured and renamed the Xiamen Yinxin Guild by Yang Xianfu in 1930 (Xiamen General Chamber of Commerce 1940). Organizational trust at the popular level and government supervision at the official level were particularly important in dealing with the crisis caused by the sinking of the Fengmao in 1921 and that occasioned by Tianyi's bankruptcy in 1928.

Individual and organizational constraints at the time of the sinking of the **Fengmao**

The *Fengmao* belonged to Lin Bingxiang, a millionaire Peranakan in Singapore prominent in the shipping industry. Lin Bingxiang owned the Hefeng shipping company, whose ships sailed between Hong Kong, Shantou, Singapore, and Burma. He also owned the Hefeng Bank, the Hefeng insurance company, the Hefeng cement manufacturing plant, rice mills, and a coconut-oil factory, among other things. The sinking of the *Fengmao* in Shantou and of the *Yuanfeng* in Xiamen, both in 1921, affected his other business, and lost him tens of millions of yuan (Liang Shaowen 1924, 96–97). The *Fengmao* sank while en route from Singapore by way of Hong Kong to Xiamen, with many passengers on board and a large consignment of *qiaopi*, perhaps as many as several thousand (*Lat Pau* 1921c).

The Singapore Chinese Chamber of Commerce discussed the sinking of the *Fengmao* at a meeting on 9 March, and wired the Chambers of Commerce in Shantou and Xiamen to publish the news in the press and to tell the *qiaopiju* and other related companies that the draft from Singapore dated between 1 June and 16 June should be carefully checked in Shantou and Xiamen to prevent fraud. At the same time, plans were laid for a meeting with relevant companies of the Singapore Chinese Chamber of Commerce, on 10 March, to discuss solutions and ensure the safety of customers' money, including *qiaopi* and bills of exchange (Singapore Chinese Chamber of Commerce 1986, 102). Representatives of Tianyi, Xinlong, and other *huiduiju* (remittance offices) from Fujian and Chaozhou were invited to discuss how to deal with the aftermath of the sinking, including the loss of both lives and property. Lin Yishun, president of the Singapore Chinese Chamber of Commerce in the 1920s, said that the problem could be solved only if members of the trade stood together, and that the Chamber of Commerce would do its best to help (*Lat Pau* 1921a). Huang Qiongyao from Tianyi and Gao Cang from Yingfeng reported in detail to the meeting. Finally, they resolved that copies of all drafts sent between 1 March and 16 March should be sent to the Singapore Chinese Chamber of Commerce and then forwarded to the Chambers of Commerce in Xiamen and Shantou, which should tick off whether or not they had been received and check carefully those submitted for encashment. Recipients should be asked to collect drafts addressed to them, if no one turned up to do so after a given length of time (*Lat Pau* 1921a). Various difficulties were noted and different views put forward at the meeting on 11 March. Some companies argued that there was no need to re-record the information concerning the *qiaopi*, since the necessary details were sent to the *qiaopiju* in Xiamen or Shantou for them to retain and, if necessary, consult. Others argued that the information was not needed, since it was essential not to slow down the shipments and the *qiaopi* were too many in number to do so easily (*Lat Pau* 1921c). Representatives of the Singapore Chinese Chamber of Commerce argued that most passengers had drowned with their remittances, and that all the *qiaopiju* should recompense customers' relatives in order to preserve their own reputation, by whatever means necessary (*Lat Pau* 1921b). Those attending the meeting in Singapore agreed that the Chamber of Commerce would take general charge. The Chamber of Commerce asked each company to provide copies of the lost *qiaopi* and to publish them in the newspaper *Lat Pau* for public scrutiny (*Lat Pau* 1921b). As soon as responses to the *qiaopi* arrived in Singapore, they were to be sent to the Chamber of Commerce, which would deal with relevant companies and the Chambers of Commerce in Xiamen and Shantou in cases where no response was received from China (*Lat Pau* 1921b). Tianyi sent the Chamber of Commerce seventy-eight responses for checking (*Lat Pau* 1921d). The Chamber of Commerce published a list of *qiaopi* sent by the *qiaopiju* to the *Lat Pau* newspaper on 12 March and 20 March (see Table 5.4; *Lat Pau* 1921b and 1921d).

Table 5.4 Piju funds on 12 March and 20 March 1921

Name of company	*Items on 12 March*	*Total fund on 12 March (Yinyuan)*	*Additional items on 20 March*	*Total fund on 12 March (Yinyuan)*
Tianyi	272	105,279	849	13,548
Hefeng Bank	13	13,460		
Yuyuan Hao	21	14,140	97	1,705
Wuzu Huizhuang	17	8,205		
Xiangli Hao	14	2,113		
Wanyicheng Hao	17	15,634		
Yongxing Company	–	215,760		
Ruifeng Hao	12	6,250		
Shunde Hao	7	1,965	161	4,159
XinLong Hao	24	14,425		
Yingfeng Hao	33	25,080		
Wan xingyuan	20	11,675	44	590
Guo fucheng	1	100		
Guo hecheng	24	7,811.27		
Wan yicheng	17	15,603.4		
Cao runyuan	13	6,088.83		
Wan shunchang	33	156,412.17		
Zhicheng Hao	8	4,666		
Senfeng Zhan	6	4,009		
Gonghecheng	36	33,423.6		
Guangrongchang	36	47,599.37		
Wande Zhuang	4	8,700		
Yeweixing Hao	34	73,420		
Zengguangyuan	11	3,625		
Sihaitong Bank	8	1,800		
Jinji Company	7	1,070	22	609
Quanlongfa	4	700		
Dongchang Zhan	30	10,650		
Qingshunxiang	14	15,030		
Zhenyuxing	7	1,280		
Nanhe Hao	7	2,630		
Xinhecheng	–	–	175	3,620.5
Xianghe	–	–	91	2,016.6
Yuanmei	–	–	68	820
Quanhe	–	–	33	633

The Singapore Chamber of Commerce promised to check the accounts of relevant companies, in the interests of fairness, and to help solve problems on a voluntary basis (*Lat Pau* 1921d). The companies also promised to do nothing to damage their customers' interests and not to steal their money (*Lat Pau* 1921c). In actual fact, the Chamber of Commerce in Singapore clearly played a supervisory role, and acted jointly with the Chambers of Commerce in Xiamen and Shantou to deal with the crisis, maintain the reputation of the *qiaopi* trade, and protect the interests of overseas Chinese and their relatives.

The role played by (a) individual and civil and (b) organizational and official constraints on the occasion of Tianyi's bankruptcy

Tianyi had to close down because of cash flow problems on 18 January 1928, at a time of the year when its Chinese customers needed cash to fund celebrating the Spring Festival. In January 1928, Chiang Kai-shek had ordered Zhang Zhen and his troops to return to Zhangzhou (Fujian Province Local Records Compilation Committee 2003, 402) previously governed by Zhang Yi (Zhangzhou Xiangcheng's Committee of the Chinese People's Political Consultative Conference 1992, 734–735). In July 1926, at the start of the Northern Expedition, Zhang Zhen's forces had clashed with Zhang yi's troops, and seized most of Fujian. During the fighting, most of the old officials and businessmen in Zhangzhou supported Zhang Yi, and feared Zhang Zhen. The Communists were strong at the time, and led strikes in various sectors, including the postal and telecommunications industry, while at the same time leading campaigns to overthrow the "local tyrants and evil gentry". In short, the region was in serious chaos (Zhangzhou Xiangcheng's Committee of the Chinese People's Political Consultative Conference 1992, 735–741). Tianyi claimed, in its debt statement, that the postal and telecommunications strike affected its finances and was a main trigger of its collapse (*Shun Pao* 1928e).

At such a time, Tianyi's closure brought huge economic losses to its customers' relatives, damaged public confidence in the *qiaopi* trade, and caused a brief financial crisis in Southeast Asia and South China. Civil organizations such as the Chamber of Commerce, the Chinese Native Banks' Association (*Qianzhuang gonghui*), the Banks' Association (*Yinhang gonghui*), and official organizations like the Overseas Chinese Affairs Commission and the Fourth Independent Division of the National Revolutionary Army (under Zhang Zhen) took joint measures to resolve the debt crisis caused by the collapse of Tianyi, in order to maintain financial order and reduce the loss to remitters, investors, and recipients of remittances.

Tianyi held meetings with its big creditors to discuss the debt at Xiamen Chamber of Commerce, and finally the two sides agreed on a compensation scheme. The indemnity amounted to 20 per cent of the total debt, to be paid in two instalments. In March, Hong Wengan (a Singaporean creditor who had participated in the Chamber of Commerce meeting) asked to see Tianyi's books, but failed to get permission. At the same time, some large private creditors stood by Tianyi. Hong Wengan then denounced the compensation scheme in a newspaper article, sued Tianyi in the Xiamen courts, and asked Fujian's Overseas Chinese Affairs Committee and Zhang Zhen's Fourth Division to help the Singapore creditors (*Nanyang Siang Pau* 1928b). Guo Beixing (Tianyi's manager and partner in Palembang, Indonesia), Huang Qiongyao (Tianyi's manager and partner in Singapore), and Huang Xieyu (a well-known Chinese businessman in Iloilo in the Philippines) also asked Zhang Zhen to arrest Guo Yongzhong, Tianyi's general manager (*Shun Pao* 1928e).

Guo Yongzhong was arrested by the Independent Fourth Army in Zhangzhou on 23 April 1928, together with his younger brother Guo Hezhong. The next day, Xiamen's *Minguo ribao* published an article about these events. On 1 May, Zhang Zhen published a letter accusing Tianyi of secretly hiding large sums of money belonging to branches in China and overseas, and paying only the larger creditors, while ignoring the smaller ones (*Shun Pao* 1928e). Zhang Zhen's declaration caused an even greater panic. After that, three native banks closed down in Xiamen on 6 May 1928, eight native banks closed down until mid-May, and three native banks went out of business on 2 June (*Shun Pao* 1928a).

Lin Guogeng, the head of Xiamen Garrison Headquarters (Xiamen jingbei silingbu), summoned representatives of the Chamber of Commerce, the Chinese Native Banks' Association, and the banks to a meeting in the Garrison Headquarters on 3 June. Xiamen's General Chamber of Commerce met on the morning of 4 June to establish rules for bankrupt firms: the Chamber of Commerce and government offices was to make a provisional inventory of a firm's archive, buildings, implements, and accounts; creditors should set up a group to sort out the debt with the Chamber of Commerce; lawyers should not take over responsibility from owners; owners should report to the police station should they want to transfer property and funds (*Shun Pao* 1928c). The Xiamen Financial Maintenance Group (*Xiamen jinrong weichihui*) was set up by Xiamen's Chamber of Commerce, the Chinese Native Banks' Association, and the Banks' Association on the afternoon of 4 June (*Shun Pao* 1928b). The presidents of the Bank of Zhongnan, the Bank of China, and the Oversea-Chinese Banking Corporation and delegates of the military command, the Public Security Bureau, the Chamber of Commerce, and the Chinese Native Banks' Association agreed as follows: banks would continue to lend to bankrupt firms as usual, regulated by the Chamber of Commerce; firms would be able to borrow by pledging buildings and securities and other collatera; if a firm failed to repay a loan, the Financial Maintenance Group would be able to auction its assets after obtaining approval from the regional government (*Shun Pao* 1928c).

Xiamen's Chamber of Commerce also developed a set of "detailed rules governing mortgages and loans". However, these measures were of little use in the event, and existed more in name than in reality (Shanghai archives 1928). The Banks' Association expressed reservations about the proposals of the Financial Maintenance Group and Xiamen's Chamber of Commerce. However, these proposals meant that firms received cash to deal with the emergency. As a result, "the panic diminished and none of firms collapsed in the course of those two days" (*Shun Pao* 1928c).

Zhang Zhen ordered the Overseas Chinese Affairs Commission in Fujian to investigate Guo's assets and asked relevant institutions and departments at home and abroad to support him (*Shun Pao* 1928d; *Fuzhou Qiaowu Gongbao*, 1928, 57). The deadline for registration was 30 July 1928, and Zhang Zhen decided to discontinue the extensions, although many creditors asked for extensions (*Nanyang Siang Pau* 1928b). The Overseas Chinese Affairs Commission was responsible for registering claims, collecting property and account books, seizing property as collateral, communicating with the Independent Fourth commander in Zhangzhou, the Chinese Chamber of Commerce overseas, and the Chinese

Consulate overseas, and assisting in the establishment of a Creditors' Rights Committee (*Fuzhou Qiaowu Gongbao*, 1928, 57–58).

After Guo Yongzhong and Guo Hezhong's arrest, the Guo family campaigned for their release, which Zhang Zhen repeatedly refused (*Nanyang Siang Pau* 1928b). Tianyi published a statement of debt in *Shun Pao* on 7 September, 1928, in the name of Guo Yongzhong and Guo Hezhong's wives. The statement refuted Zhang Zhen's fraud allegation and mentioned various actions Tianyi had undertaken after its closure, in an attempt to secure the Guos' release.

Creditors met on 25 September and adopted various organizational rules proposed by Tianyi's Creditors' Rights Group, and elected Guo Longshu and Guo Beixing (members of the Guo family) and others as their representatives. The Creditors' Rights Group said that around 600 creditors were registered and that the total debt amounted to half a million yuan (*Jiangsheng bao* 1928). Tianyi took some steps to pay off its creditors, but some of the funds were embezzled. Zhang Zhen threatened to have Guo Longshu and Guo Beixing arrested otherwise. But still they failed to pay back all the money owed (*Nanyang Siang Pau* 1929c and 1929e).

Guo Yongzhong and Guo Hezhong, prominent among the arrested Tianyi managers, turned in the company's accounts in October 1928. Guo Hezhong later applied for medical parole. Zhang Zhen released Guo Hezhong in the hope that he would quickly solve the problem, particularly since the *qiaopi* affected people's livelihood (*Nanyang Siang Pau* 1929c).

Zhang Zhen also ordered the Chamber of Commerce in Longxi and the Overseas Chinese Affairs Commission in Fujian to set up a Liquidation Committee with delegates from Tianyi's Creditors' Rights Group, and appointed Wei Zhao (one of his military adjutants) to keep an eye on things (*Nanyang Siang Pau* 1929c).

Qiu Jinjing (deputy director of Xiamen's *Minguo ribao*), Wei Zhao, Xue Yizhen, and Shi Zhishuang (delegates of the Overseas Chinese Affairs Commission), and Lin Chunyuan, Huang Qishan, and Sun Shaowu (delegates of Zhangzhou's Chamber of Commerce) joined together to check Tianyi's books. However, they got access only to the daily accounts book and general headquarters records from Xiamen in 1927 and lacked access to documents relating to transactions concerning banks and native banks and to documents from Tianyi's offices in Liuchuan and Anhai. They noted the following:

First, the Guo family transferred property together with Zheng Dayi (a businessman) in order to escape repaying debts, mortgaging assets in Zhangzhou and Shima and forging contracts (*Nanyang Siang Pau* 1929b). Second, Tianyi transferred 7,000 yuan to Jianyi (a native bank in Xiamen, and one of Tianyi's associates) after its closure to pay off large customers and thus to get their support, and thereby damaged the interests of the Creditors' Rights Group. Third, Tianyi failed to record bonds of $3,000 in its bookkeeping, retrieved at the time of the closure of the Sino-French Bank. Fourth, various fixed assets (buildings) had been under-recorded. Fifth, Tianyi asked the Xiezhen Company in Iloilo in the Philippines to subscribe 20,000 yuan even after its own closing down (*Fuzhou Qiaowu Gongbao*, 1928, 23–24).

The team of investigators asked relevant people to look into the above questions, and at the same time asked Tianyi to surrender all relevant bookkeeping and documentation covering the previous decade. Guo Hezhong was then re-arrested, together with Zheng Dayi and Guo Bingkun (the Tianyi manager in Qianan) (*Fuzhou Qiaowu Gongbao*, 1928, 59–60; *Nanyang Siang Pau*, 1929d). Tianyi later submitted 124 bookkeeping ledgers. Tianyi's chief managers and their relatives were very nervous and asked a group of their close friends in various fields (including writers, a county magistrate, a military ruler, a doctor, and a member of Xiamen's Chamber of Commerce) to negotiate with representatives of the Creditor Group to resolve the problem. But the Creditor Group was unable to agree on anything. All of this was reported to Zhangzhen (*Nanyang Siang Pau* 1929b). Regarding repayment of debts incurred, the investigation team proposed that the *qiaopi* should be honoured in order to protect the interests of Overseas Chinese and their dependants (*Fuzhou Qiaowu Gongbao* 1928, 23–24). The dispute continued until 1930, when the Overseas Chinese Affairs Commission assisted Tianyi's Creditors' Rights Group to draw up a compensation scheme, which made the following stipulations: First, compensation should be set at 25 per cent of the total debt, to be paid in four stages. Tianyi should make repayments by way of a local traditional mediator. Hong Xiaochun, Ma Jueyou, and Cai Yucun would transfer them to the Overseas Chinese Affairs Commission and delegates of the Creditors' Rights Group for distribution to all creditors. Second, Hong, Ma, and Cai would coordinate and act as guarantors of the compensation scheme. If Tianyi broke the agreement, Hong, Ma, and Cai would be allowed to auction off Tianyi's property in order to repay its debts (*Minzhong Ribao* 1930a). The coordinators were all famous and influential people. Hong was chairman of Xiamen's General Chamber of Commerce; Ma was a Chinese businessman from Semarang, founder of Semarang's Chinese General Chamber of Commerce and a member of Fujian's Provincial Council in 1912 (Xiamen General Chamber of Commerce 1940, 1–3); Cai was vice-chairman of Xiamen's General Chamber of Commerce. But despite the passing of resolutions, their implementation was far from guaranteed. For example, one letter to the coordinators demanded an answer to an earlier question about unpaid debt, and its authors were advised to wait (*Minzhong Ribao* 1930b; Hung clan council for welcoming the first ancestor in Dengshan Xiang' an 2008, 61). Clearly, the coordinators were unable, in this case and in others, to provide an explicit solution and to implement deadlines. Civil and government organizations also sought to resolve issues, but creditors were unable to gain satisfaction. This suggests that in resolving debt matters personal and relational trust played an important role. Tianyi was also expected to provide information for and to solve problems flagged up by Chinese Chambers of Commerce in Southeast Asia (Chen Zhanqi 2006, 2191). For example, the Chinese Chamber of Commerce in Deli in Indonesia wired Xiamen's Chamber of Commerce to ask them to help resolve Tianyi's debt problems.

Conclusion

Tianyi rose and developed on the basis of regional culture and migratory networks and of personal and relational trust, and used a family-management model to establish branches and a transnational commercial network both in China and in Southeast Asia. The relationship between blood, geography, and kinship created the possibility of forms of trust that mediated traditional morality and the associated collective rewards and punishment. Tianyi's development embodied the evolution from traditional trust to modern forms of credit. Systemic trust and credit grew up with the expansion of networks and an increasing division of labour in the *qiaopi* trade, based on material interests and contracts. The "credit steal" turned verbal agreements into contracts and the "ship number system" ensured the accurate and swift arrival of *qiaopi.* The unique mode of *qiaopi* transmission, combining tradition and modernity, depended on a vast, complex network of *qiaopiju.* The *shanpiao* or "credit ticket" system, on the other hand, led to the collapse of some *qiaopiju* and, because of the lack of constraints on it, harmed the interests of customers. The *qiaopi* trade required organizational trust at the popular level and government intervention at the official level to ensure the orderly operation of the market in a free-market environment. Civil organizations such as the Xiamen Yinxinju Association, the Singapore Chinese Chamber of Commerce, Xiamen's and Shantou's Chambers of Commerce, and Chambers of Commerce in Southeast Asia, as well as official organizations such as Fujian's Overseas Chinese Affairs Committee, the Consulate General, and agencies of the military government acted together to deal with the crisis, by formulating or improving the rules of the *qiaopi* trade. The importance to this trade of the symbiotic evolution of tradition and modernity in this process is the main finding of this chapter. Only when modern credit is rooted in Chinese culture and tradition could traders on the *qiaopi* market act with confidence and awareness.

Notes

1 Project supported by the National Social Science Foundation of China (Grant No. 12&ZD148) and the National Higher Education Institution, General Research and Development (Grant No. CCNU14Z2003). The author would like to thank Gregor Benton for his careful editing.

2 Amy Yao, whose husband is the Chinese Chamber of Commerce in Philippines, and interviewed by author in Manila on 26 November 2011.

3 Its creation time is controversial. The author thinks that the date of 1880 is credible. The creation time was proved by Guo Boling in "the day summarize the bank and credit bureau Historiette". "Advertisement of Tianyi in 1918" collected by the author also showed that the company had been in business for more than 30 years at that time. "Jinan Zazhi", *Minguo zhenxi duankan duankan-Fujian,* Quanguo wenxian suowei fuyinzhongxin, no. 5 (2006).

4 Guo Shangbiao, who was Guo Youpin's grandson, Guo Chengzhong's nineteenth son, and born in 1919, was interviewed by the author in Manila on 7 December 2011.

5 Shi Wenzhi, who was interviewed by author at Wang Bin Street in Manila on 7 December 2011, was a writer in the Philippines and won the highest literary award in the Philippines in 2011.

6 According to the mirror sent by branches jointly in 1911, which was engraved with names of all the branches; the letter of Tianyi; Guo Boling. 2010. "*Liu yang guoshi tianyi jiacheng*" [Guo's Genealogy], published internally; Yang Jiancheng. 1984. "*Qiaohui liutong zhi yanjiu*" [The study of flow of remittances]. Chinese Academy of Nanyang Research, 85–87, 95–130.
7 Guo Shangbiao, who was Guo Youpin's grandson, Guo Chengzhong's nineteenth son, and born in 1919, was interviewed by the author in Manila on 7 December 2011.
8 Zheng Yuanyuan was interviewed by the author on 12 December 2011, at 410 Santo Cristo St Binondo, Manila, which was the old address of Jiangnan Xinju, who was Zheng Guangde's son and born in 1926. Zheng Guangde established Jiangnan Xinju, which was located in Santa Elena Street until 1939.
9 Guo Shangbiao's interview.
10 The letter of Tianyi was provided by Guo Boling, who was the descendant of Tianyi, and Liu Bozi, who worked in Quanzhou Overseas Chinese History Museum.
11 The bookkeeping of Tianyi was collected by Su Tonghai, which were daily records. The author copied it in his house in January 2012.

References

Chen Da 陈达. 1938. *Nanyang huaqiao yu min yue shehui* 南洋华侨与闽粤社会 [Overseas Chinese in Southeast Asia and the Society in Minyue]. Shangwuyin shuguan.

Chen Zhanqi 陈湛绮. 2006. "Guoyoupin tianyi huidui yinxinju jinyao guanggao 1918" 郭有品天一汇兑银信局紧要广告 [Advertisement of Tianyi]. *Jinan Zazhi* 暨南杂志 [The Journals of Chin'an]. *Minguo zhenxi duankan duankan-Fujian* 民国珍稀短刊断刊-福建卷 [Rare Journals of the Republic of China – Volume of Fujian]. Quanguo tushu guan wenxian suowei fuzhi zhongxin, 5: 2191.

Dai Yifeng 戴一峰. 2002. "Nan zhongguo haiyu jindai dongnanya diqu shehui jingji bianqian – yi minnan diqu wei zhongxin" 南中国海与近代东南亚地区社会经济变迁 – 以闽南地区为中心 [The social and economic changes in the South China Sea and the Southeast Asia region – Taking the centre of the southern Fujian region as an example]. *Shi Lin* 史林 [Historical Review] 1: 82–90.

Dai Yifeng 戴一峰. 2003. "Wangluohua qiye yu qianruxing: jindai qiaopiju de zhidu jiangou (1850–1940)" 网络化企业与嵌入性：近代侨批局的制度建构 (1850–1940) [The network of enterprise and embedding: The system construction of modern *qiaopiju* (1850–1940)]. *Zhongguo shehui jingjishi yanjiu* 中国社会经济史研究 [The Journal of Chinese Social and Economic History] 1: 70–78.

Fei Xiaotong 费孝通. 1998. *Xiangtu zhongguo* 乡土中国 [From the Soil]. Beijing: Beijing daxue chuban she.

Fujian Province Archives. "Fujiansheng youzhengju dangan" 福建省邮政局档案 [Archives of Fujian Province postal]. Fonds No. 56, catalogue No. 1, volume No. 21.

Fujian Province Local Records Compilation Committee 福建省地方志编纂委员会. 2003. "Zhonghua renmin gongheguo difang zhi fujiansheng zhi renwu zhi" 中华人民共和国地方志. 福建省志. 人物志 [Biography of Personage, Fujian volume of the people's Republic of China] 1: 402. Beijing: Zhongguo shehui kexue chuban she.

Fuzhou Qiaowu Gongbao 福州侨务公报 [Fuchow Overseas Chinese Affairs Bulletin]. 1928. "Tianyi huiduiju daobi an: fujian qiaowu weiyuanhui han zhi tianyiju zhaiquan weiyuan hui daibiao baogao chahe qingxing qing chazhao han" 天一汇兑局倒闭案:福建侨务委员会函知天一局债权委员会代表报告查核情形请查照函 [The bankrupt of Tianyi: Official letter from The Overseas Chinese Affairs Commission in Fujian to Creditor's Rights Group of Tianyi].

Guo Boling 郭伯龄. 1999. “Tianyi huidui yinxinju shihua” 天一汇兑银信局史话 [Tianyi *Qiaopi* history]. *Zhangzhou Jingu* 漳州今古 [The Journal of Zhangzhou History] 1.

Guo Boling 郭伯龄. 2010. “*Liu yang guoshi tianyi jiacheng*” 榴阳郭氏天一家乘 [Guo’s Genealogy]. Internal issue.

Hamashita Takeshi. 1999. *Jindai zhongguo de guoji maoyi qiji–Chaogong maoyi yu jindai yazhou jingjiquan* 近代中国的国际贸易契机 – 朝贡贸易与近代亚洲经济圈 [The tribute trade system and modern Asia]. Beijing: zhongguo shehui kexue chubanshe.

Hamashita Takeshi . 2006. *Zhongguo jindai jingjishi yanjiu: Qingmo haiguan caizheng yu tongshang kou an shichangquan* 中国近代经济史研究：清末海关财政与通商口岸市场圈 [The Chinese modern economic history research: At the end of the Qing Dynasty customs fiscal and trade port market circle]. Nanjing: Jiangsu renmin chuban she.

Huang Jianlan 黄剑岚. 1993. “*Longhai xian zhi*” 龙海县志 [Annals of Longhai Country]. Beijing: Dongfang chubanshe.

Huang Lugu 黄鹿谷. 1984. “Chong yang qiaohui hua dangnian” 重洋侨汇话当年 [The year of remittance overseas. Fuzhou industrial and commercial history]. *Fuzhou gongshang shiliao* 福州工商史料 [Industrial and Commercial Historical Records of Fuzhou] 1. Fuzhoushi gongshangye lianhehui chuban.

Hung clan council for welcoming the first ancestor in Dengshan Xiang’ an 翔安区嶝山洪氏宗亲恭迎六桂始祖理事会. 2008. “Hong Xiaochun zhuanlue” 洪晓春传略 [Biography of Hong Xiaochun]. Internal publication. 61.

Jiangsheng bao 江声报 [Jiang Sheng News]. 1928. 30 October. “Tianyi zhaiquan shi” 天一债权事 [Creditors of Tianyi].

Jiao Jianhua 焦建华. 2005. “Zhidu chuangxin yu wenhua chuantong: shixi jindai pixinju de jingying zhidu” 制度创新与文化传统：试析近代批信局的经营制度 [Institutional innovation and cultural tradition: An analysis of the Management System of modern *qiaopiju*]. *Zhongguo shehui jingjishi yanjiu* 中国社会经济史研究 [The Journal of Chinese Social and Economic History] 3: 64–70.

Lat Pau 叻报. 1921a. 11 March. “Huiduiju zhi kaicheng bugong” 汇兑局之开诚布公 [The frank and sincere statement of Huiduiju]. 7.

Lat Pau 叻报. 1921b. 12 March. “Xinjiapo zhonghua zongshanghui zhengji yuandan qi zhi shiliu ri zhi huipiao zhi zongdan” 新加坡中华总商会征集元旦起至十六日止汇票之总单 [Singapore Chinese Chamber of Commerce collects the total bills of draft from 1 January to 16 January]. 7.

Lat Pau 叻报. 1921c. 12 March. “Huiduiju yijue fengmaochuan linxing shi jieshou geke jihui yinxin zhi banfa” 汇兑局议决丰茂船临行时接收各客寄回银信之办法 [The resolution of receiving Yinxin from customers by Huiduiju]. 7.

Lat Pau 叻报. 1921d. 20 March. “Ge xinju chao bao zongdan cunan zhi jianshu” 各信局抄报总单存案之件数 [The total bills of every Xinju]. 2.

Liang Shaowen 梁绍文. 1924. *Nanyang lvxing manji* 南洋旅行漫记 [Nanyang Travel Journey]. Shanghai: Shanghai Zhonghua shuju.

Lin Chunsen 林春森. 1996. “Xiamen qiaopi ye jianshi” 厦门侨批业简史 [Xiamen *qiaopi* trade history]. In Huang Qinghai 黄清海, ed., *Minnan Qiaopi shi jishu* 闽南侨批史记述 [The history of Minnan *qiaopi*]. Xiamen: Xiamen daxue chubanshe.

Lin Diange 林殿阁. 2007. *Zhangzhou xingshi* 漳州姓氏 [Zhangzhou surname]. Beijing: Zhongguo wenshichubanshe.

Lin Nanzhong 林南中. 2009. “Pindu tianyi qiaopi” 品读”天一”侨批 [Read Tianyi *Qiaopi*]. *Huiwang minnan qiaopi: Shoujie minnan qiaopi yantao hui* 回望闽南侨批: 首届闽南侨批研讨会 [The first Minnan *Qiaopi* Symposium]. Beijing: Huayi chubanshe.

Liu Jiansheng 刘建生, *et al*. 2008. *Jinshang xinyong zhidu jiqi bianqian yanjiu* 晋商信用制度及其变迁研究 [Study on the credit system and its changes of Shanxi Merchants]. Taiyuan: Shanxi jingji Chuban she.

Long Denggao 龙登高. 2003. *Haiwai huashang jingying guanli tanwei* 海外华商经营管理探微 [Overseas Chinese management]. Xianggang: Xianggang shehui kexue chubanshe.

Longtonghai lianxiang zonghui 龙同海联乡总会. 2011. *Longtonghai lianxiang zonghui tongxunlu* 龙同海联乡总会通讯录 [Long Tonghai, the township association address book]. Manila.

Lu Xianxiang 卢现祥. 2004. *Xin zhidu jingji xue* 新制度经济学 [New institutional economics]. Wuhan: Wuhan daxue chubanshe.

Minnan Ribao 闽南日报 [Minnan Daily]. 2011. 11 January. Su Tonghai 苏通海. "Nianzhong jiezhang – jiedu tianyiju fugong fenju yiben liushuizhang" 年终结帐 – 解读天 – 局浮宫分局 – 本流水帐 [Checkout at the end of the year – Interpretation of the bookkeeping of Tianyi].

Minzhong Ribao 民钟日报 [Minzhong Daily]. 1930a. 8 July. "Guoyoupin tianyiju zhaiquantuan weiyuanhui qishi" 郭有品天一局债权团委员会启事 [The organization of Guo Youpin Tianyi's Creditor's Rights Group]. 3.

Minzhong Ribao 民钟日报 [Minzhong Daily]. 1930b. 5 August.

Nanyang Siang Pau 南洋商报. 1928a. 3 August. "Qing biaofeng tianyi ju chanye qiaoweihui liangzhi disishi han" 请标封天一局产业侨委会两致第四师函 [The second letter to Fourth Independent Division for sealing up Tianyi's property]. 10.

Nanyang Siang Pau 南洋商报. 1928b. 17 October. "Tianyiju zhaiquantuan dahui bing zhaiquan weiyuan jiuzhi dianli" 天一局债权团大会并债权委员就职典礼 [General meeting of creditors of Tianyi]. 10.

Nanyang Siang Pau 南洋商报. 1929a. 5 January. "Tianyi zhaiwu tiaoting yi pie" 天一债务调停一瞥 [Mediate between the creditors and debtors]. 10.

Nanyang Siang Pau 南洋商报.1929b. 5 January. "Longxi zhengdayi juya shibu yi yu guohezhong you chuantong xianyi" 龙溪郑大益拘押师部疑与郭和中有串通嫌疑 [Longxi Zheng Dayi was arrested, because he was suspected of complicity with Guo Hezhong]. 10.

Nanyang Siang Pau 南洋商报. 1929c. 19 January. "Longxi tianyi zhai an shimo" 龙溪天一债案始末 [The whole story of the Longxi Tianyi debt case]. 10.

Nanyang Siang Pau 南洋商报. 1929d. 2 February. "Tianyi zhai an nei zhi guobingkun beidai xuanji yao zhun baoshi" 天一债案内之郭炳坤被逮旋即要准保释 [Guo Bingkun involved in Tianyi debt case was arrested, but soon released]. 10.

Nanyang Siang Pau 南洋商报. 1929e. 26 April. "Jinggao jugang sishui qiaobao juanshu shu" 敬告巨港泗水侨胞眷属书 [Announcement to the Chinese Overseas in Palembang and Surabaya]. 7.

Shanghai Archives. "Shanghai zhongnan yinhang 1928 nian youguan guxi ji tianyi ju daobi xiamen ge qianzhuang geqian deng yu xiamen zhongnan yinhang de wanglai hanjian" 上海中南银行1928年有关股息及天一局倒闭厦门各钱庄搁浅等与厦门中南银行的往来函件 [Correspondence between China and South Sea Bank Limited in Shanghai and Xiamen about the bankrupt of Tianyi and Xiamen financial agitation in 1928]. Fonds No. 265, catalogue No. 1, volume No. 153.

Shen Xianyang 申显扬. 1998. *Lun jindai minnan qiaopiye* 论近代闽南侨批业 [Overseas remittance trade in modern Minnan]. MA diss., Xiamen University.

Shun Pao 申报. 1928a. 4 June. "Xiamen jinrong fengchao" 厦门金融风潮 [Xiamen financial agitation]. 8.

Shun Pao 申报. 1928b. 6 June. "Xiamen jinrong weichihui chengli" 厦门金融维持会成立 [The fount of Xiamen financial maintenance]. 8.

Shun Pao 申报. 1928c. 11 June. "Xiamen jinrong konghuang yi you jiuji banfa" 厦门金融恐慌已有救济办法 [Relief measures of Xiamen financial agitation]. 9.

Shun Pao 申报. 1928d. 15 June. "Minshi jiyao" 闽事纪要 [Important things in Fujian]. 7.

Shun Pao 申报. 1928e. 7 September. Ding (Guo Yongzhong's wife) and Lin (Guo Hezhong's wife) 郭用中的妻子林氏与郭和中的妻子丁氏. "Fujian xiamen tianyi huidui yinxinju zhaiwu xuanyan" 福建厦门天一汇兑银信局债务宣言 [For Tianyi's debt statement]. 3.

Singapore Chinese Chamber of Commerce compiled. 1986. *80th Anniversary of Singapore Chinese Chamber of Commerce*. Singapore: Singapore Chinese Chamber of Commerce Press.

Ta Kung Pao 大公报. 2009. 22 July. "Shuike shenfen zheng" 水客身份证 [Shuike's identity card].

Wang Zhuchun 王朱唇, *et al*. 2006. *Minnan qiaopi shihua* 闽南侨批史话 [Minnan remittance history]. Beijing: Zhongguo guangbo dianshi chubanshe.

Xiamen General Chamber of Commerce. 1940. *Xiamen shanghui tekan* 厦门商会特刊 [Special issue of the Xiamen General Chamber of Commerce]. Xiamen zongshanghui chuban.

Yan Hongzhong, Hanyun 燕红忠、韩芸 2009. "Jinshang xingshuai de xinyong jiexi–jiyu lishi zhidu fenxi fangfa de shijiao" 晋商兴衰的信用解析 – 基于历史制度分析方法的视角 [The rise and fall of the Shanxi Merchants credit analysis – Based on the perspective of the historical institutional analysis method]. *Jingji wenti* [On economic problems] 3: 15–29.

Yang jiancheng 杨建成. 1984. *Qiaohui liutong zhi yanjiu* 侨汇流通之研究 [The flow of remittances]. Zhonghua xueshuyuan nanyang yanjiusuo.

Zhangzhou City Local Records Compilation Committee. 漳州市地方志编纂委员会. 2003. "Zhangzhou shi zhi" 漳州市志 [Annals of Zhangzhou City]. Beijing: Zhongguo shehui kexue chuban she.

Zhangzhou Xiangcheng's Committee of the Chinese People's Political Consultative Conference 中国人民政治协商会议漳州市芗城区委员会. 1992. *Zhangzhou xiangcheng wenshi ziliao* 漳州芗城文史资料 [Zhangzhou Xiangcheng historical materials] 2. Zhangzhou: Hua'an yinshua.

Zheng Cheng Lin 郑成林. 2007. "Shanghai yinhang gonghui yu jindai zhongguo yinhang xinyong zhidu de yanjin" 上海银行公会与近代中国银行信用制度的演进 [The credit system evolution of Bank of China with the Shanghai bank association]. *Zhejiang xuekan* 浙江学刊 [Zhejiang Academic Journal] 4: 59–65.

Zheng Linkuan 郑林宽. 1940. *Fujian huaqiao huikuan* 福建华侨汇款 [The Foukien Overseas Chinese remittance]. Fuzhou: Fujiansheng mishuchu tongjishi.

6 The operating modes of the *qiaopi* trade and impact on the *qiaopiju*

A case study of the Oversea-Chinese Banking Corporation (OCBC)[1]

Bozi Liu

As a result of the colonization of Southeast Asia by Western countries and the expansion of immigration from Southeast China to Southeast Asia, overseas Chinese communities emerged in places like Manila, Batavia, Palembang, Singapore, and Penang, whence they expanded into other areas. The immigrants from Fujian stayed in close touch with their hometowns with the help of the *qiaopi* trade, and an international market therefore came into being, linking overseas communities with the *qiaoxiang* and facilitating the remittance process. *Shuike* (couriers) played an important role in the early years of this international trade. As the market for *qiaopi* expanded and matured, informal economic organizations like the *qiaopiju* (Liang Yingming 1999, 182) emerged, combining both banking and postal functions. They spread throughout the *qiaoxiang* of Fujian, Guangdong, Guangxi, and Hainan and in Southeast Asia in the middle and late nineteenth century.

The economic contribution of the *qiaopi* trade not only helped support the homeland economy but in some respects fostered financial development, both at home and abroad. Some individuals who started out as *qiaopi* traders later became bank managers overseas. Informal financial institutions like exchange shops and money houses sprang up in the hometowns as a result of the development of the *qiaopi* trade and the need for a turnover of capital, leading to an overlapping network of international finance and exchange between overseas Chinese communities in Southeast Asia and their sending or ancestral places. The reverse also happened – bank managers became *qiaopiju* operators.

The operating network comprised offices and branches of the *qiaopiju* and the banks. The OCBC was established mainly on the basis of Chinese capital. The OCBC in Singapore was an international bank, typical of a number of different Chinese banks.

This chapter explores the operating network of the *qiaopi* trade between overseas Chinese *xinju* 信局 (postal agencies) and Chinese banks, including their cooperation in the *qiaopi* trade and the differences between the management styles of the two institutions, on the basis of a study of the OCBC and the Cheng Tye Xinju 正大信局. Through an examination of recently found material objects of the *qiaopi* trade and bills of exchange issued by the OCBC, it explains their operation and features, and shows how the OCBC set a precedent through its conduct of the *qiaopi* trade and by promoting the cash flow between Southeast Asia and China and the transfer of financial resources by way of the *qiaopiju*.

Summary of operations of the OCBC

The Oversea-Chinese Bank was established in Singapore in 1912 by Lim Boon Keng, Lim Nee Soon, Oei Tiong Ham, and others, with a paid-in capital of 5 million Straits dollars. Lim Boon Keng became chairman of the first Board of Directors and Xie Zhongyi was General Manager. In the 1920s, the bank had branches in Penang, Rangoon, Kuala Lumpur, Malacca, Kelantan, Jambi, and Xiamen. As a result of the world economic crisis of 1929, the bank went into recession, and during the crisis it joined together with the Chinese Commercial Bank and the Ho Hong Bank to form the OCBC, with a total capital of 40 million Straits dollars and a paid-in capital of 10 million Straits dollars (Liang Yingming 1999, 182).

Lee Kong Chian became Vice-Chairman of the Board of Directors, and later became Chairman, from 1937 to 1954 (Lin Xiaosheng 1987, 3–20). The evidence shows that the OCBC had agents in Singapore, Kuala Lumpur, Teluk Anson, Batupahat, Klang, Penang, Seremban, Segamai, Muar, Malacca, Johor Bahru, Ipoh, Batavia, Surabaya, Jambi, Medan, Palembang, Rangoon, Haiphong, and Bangkok, and branches in Hong Kong, Shanghai, and Xiamen. These agents and branches in China and Southeast Asia constituted its operating network.

The OCBC, which officially opened in January 1933, adopted a Western management style. It employed professional managers to run its main departments, but at the same time it emphasized the corporation's cultural background in China and the overseas Chinese milieu. The OCBC was, according to its regulations, an incorporated body in the charge of a Board of Directors that authorized the management, which, in turn, was authorized to set up departments and branches where necessary, in order to manage procedures. Service personnel at all levels were in charge of the head office and the branches (Yang Yan 2012, 55–82). So the OCBC had adopted a system of management whereby administrative authority was separate from proprietorship. The administration was in the hands of four managers, Zhou Fulong 周福隆, Ke Shouzhi 柯守智, Wang Bingding 王丙丁, and Lin Wuji 林戊己 and an assistant manager Tan Chin Tuan 陈振传 and a general affairs clerk Ye Pingyu 叶平玉 (Yang Yan 2012, 55–82). Zhou managed, inspected, and supervised the branches, Ke looked after foreign exchange, and Wang and Lin were in charge of loans. Chen had charge of property and real estate and Ye supervised clerical work. The middle and senior managers had, on average, more than ten years' banking experience and were fully qualified for their work (Yang Yan 2012, 55–82). The operating modes of the *qiaopi* trade adopted by the OCBC.

In conducting financial transfers on behalf of the *qiaopiju*, the OCBC knew that the *qiaopi* trade required a wide range of specialized competencies. Thus, it set up a mail department to send individual remittances to China on behalf of overseas Chinese remitters. This marked the start of its engagement in the *qiaopi* trade. In the same year, in cooperation with the Postal Savings and Remittance Bureau, run by the Ministry of Transportation and Communications, the

OCBC delivered mail, on behalf of the Bureau, to areas accessible by the Post Office, and it also delivered remittances and return correspondence (the so-called *huipi*) entrusted to it by the *qiaopiju*. The OCBC advertised the existence of its postal department, and announced that its scope extended throughout Guangdong, Fujian, and Guangxi (Fujian Province Archives 2013, 80). The OCBC's *qiaopi* trade came to a standstill during the Pacific War, but afterwards the bank resumed trading and came into its heyday. In 1946, it converted 10 thousand yuan at the rate of 15.8 Straits dollars, and charged 0.4 Straits dollars for postage. The exchange rate followed by the *qiaopiju* was, on average, lower than that of the banks, at between 14 and 15 Straits dollars (Kua Bak Lim 2007, 167).

Cooperation in the *qiaopi* trade between the OCBC and overseas Chinese *xinju*

Figure 6.1 shows a *qiaopi* sent from Malacca in Malaya to Zengcuo Village in Maxiang, Tong'an, in 1945. It notes on the envelope that "Chen Manshui received the amount of 18 thousand Yuan sent by Chen Enwen in Malacca".

The envelope was endorsed with a purple seal affixed by Malacca's Guan Joo Hin Xinju 源裕兴信局 with the words "No. 101 of the first Bill of the Yuan List" and another purple seal affixed by the OCBC in Malacca, with the serial number AA37. This envelope shows that the OCBC was directly involved in the *qiaopi* trade in Malacca.

The envelope is also evidence of the cooperation between the OCBC and the *xinju*. The letters and remittances were received by the Guan Joo Hin Xinju in Malacca, which transferred them to the local office of the OCBC, which then

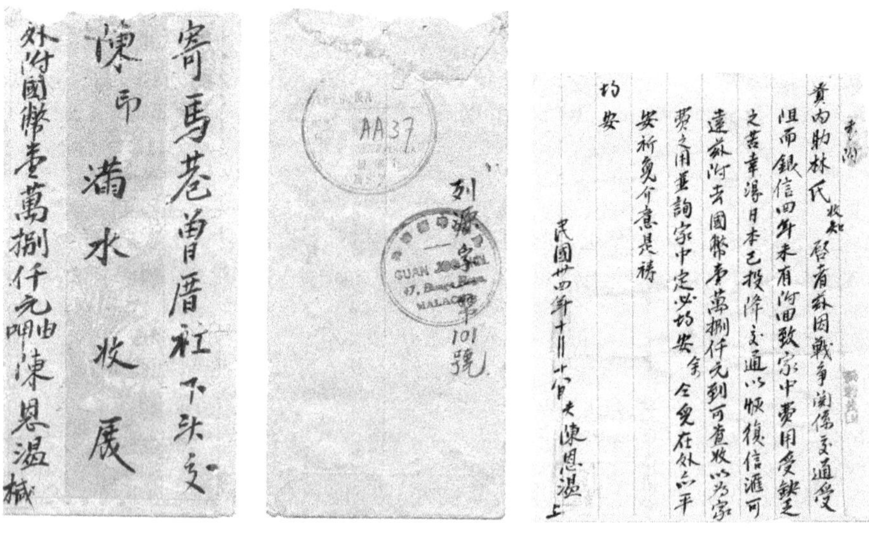

Figure 6.1 *Qiaopi* handled by the OCBC in Malacca.

sent them on to Xiamen. The envelope does not show how the *qiaopi* were eventually distributed in Tong'an.

This item was sent on 22 November 1945, more than three months after the Japanese surrender. The letter confirms that "since the Japanese surrender, letters and remittances have been able to reach to you, given the resumption of traffic".

There were also examples of the OCBC's direct involvement in the *qiaopi* trade in Rangoon and Haiphong (Xu Maochun 2008, 212). Fujian was the receiving point for most of these *qiaopi* The OCBC's branches in Singapore (Xu Maochun 2008, 212), Surabaya (Xu Maochun 2008, 332), Batavia (Xu Maochun 2008, 332), and Penang (Xu Maochun 2008, 249) forwarded *qiaopi* to Shantou and Jiangmen in Guangdong. So the OCBC's direct involvement in the *qiaopi* trade covered both Fujian and Guangdong, unlike individual *qiaopiju*, whose scale and network operation was far more restricted.

The OCBC made slow progress with its *qiaopi* trade, and its usual operating mode was to cooperate with overseas Chinese *xinju*.

The above *qiaopi* show that the OCBC, in conducting the *qiaopi* trade, cooperated with *qiaopiju* overseas, which had customers and delivery networks in China. In its practical operations, the OCBC cooperated with these overseas *xinju* and carried out standard procedures, including the collection of remittances and letters, financial transfers, and the dispatch and payment of remittances.

Figure 6.2 shows a bill remitted by the OCBC's Postal Department on 8 July 1947. It contains the words "second bill of the *fu* 福 serial", and comprised eight

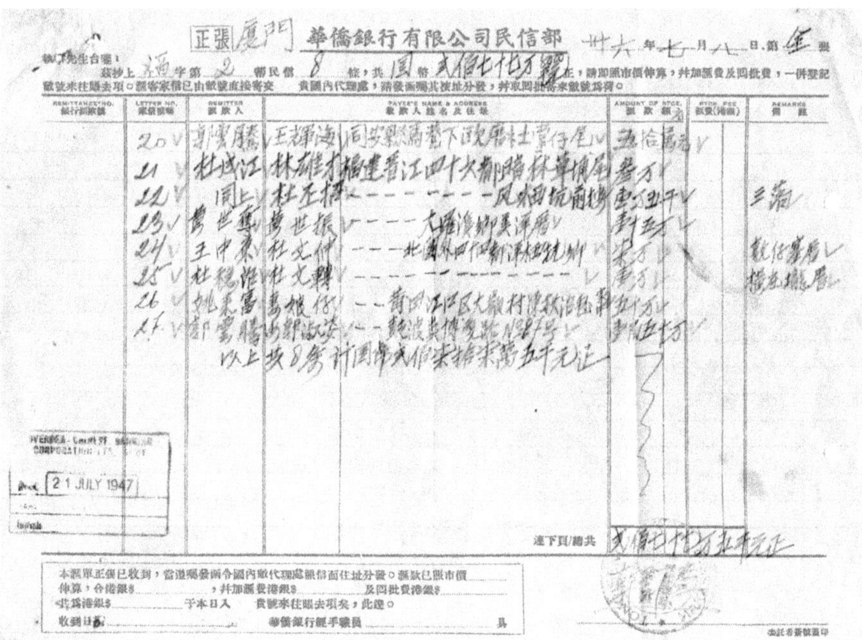

Figure 6.2 A bill of remittance issued by the OCBC's postal department.

items totalling 2,275,000 yuan, sent from Indonesia to Tong'an, Jinjiang, Nan'an, Putian, and Gulangyu. A seal of the Tong Seng Hien xinju 同成兴信局 of the OCBC's Trust and Banking Department in Makasar, Indonesia, was affixed to the lower right corner. Clearly, the procedures adopted by the OCBC were similar to those adopted by the *qiaopiju* in conducting the *qiaopi* trade. The transaction was recorded in the same way as it would have been recorded by the *qiaopiju*, using a Chinese character to denote the bill's general category and numbers to denote the bill's *fu* category.

The bill stated:

> To Whom It May Concern: this is to notify you that there are eight items on this second bill of the *fu* serial with a total remittance of 2,275,000 Yuan. Please exchange it at market value, taking account of the remittance fee and postage, and record it among our financial transactions. The reply envelopes sent from Indonesia to China, together with the addresses of recipients, have been sent to your domestic agencies, which should be notified so that they can distribute them as planned. It would be appreciated if the *huipi* could be sent to us as soon as possible.

According to the lower left-hand corner of the envelope, the transaction was completed on 21 July 1947, so turn-around took fourteen days.

Two of the procedures, the collection of the remittances and letters and the financial transfers, were managed by the OCBC, while the Tong Seng Hien xinju 同成兴信局 of the OCBC's Trust and Banking Department in Makasar, Indonesia, was responsible for the other two procedures, (1) acceptance for conveyance and dispatch and (2) payment of the remittances, including collecting the *huipi* and sending them back to the OCBC.

The complementary role of the OCBC and the *qiaopiju* in the running of the *qiaopi* trade

The *qiaopi* trade was a cross-regional affair, each historical stage of which had its characteristic network, run by *shuike*, *qiaopiju*, banks, and the Postal Remittances and Savings Bank.

A relatively dense network connected China and the trade's overseas destinations. This network collected the remittances and letters; arranged the financial transfers; accepted the *qiaopi* for conveyance and dispatch; and paid the remittances and returned the *huipi*. Normally, a Nanyang general office and its attendant branches or agencies was set up overseas, where it took charge of collecting letters and remittances and distributing the *huipi*. In the main domestic ports such as Xiamen, a head office (a directly managed branch or a company associated with the Nanyang General Office) and a secondary office (which collected mail and commissions on behalf of the Nanyang *qiaopiju*) were set up and given responsibility for transferring letters and remittances. Tertiary offices (payment bureaus) were set up in the *qiaoxiang*, where they were responsible for distributing *qiaopi* and collecting the *huipi* on behalf of the head office and the secondary office, which then sent them on to their destinations overseas.

At the end of the nineteenth century, the *qiaopiju* began to grow in number and extent, and started setting up operating networks between Southeast Asia and China.

The main personnel or institutions of the *qiaopi* trade in its successive historical stages were *shuike*, *qiaopiju*, and the OCBC. From the last half of the nineteenth century through to the first half of the twentieth century, the *qiaopiju* were concentrated in places with large concentrations of overseas Chinese, mainly from Fujian. They included Manila, Cebu, Batavia (modern-day Jakarta), Surabaya, Bandung, Singapore, Malacca, Penang, Rangoon, and Bangkok. The growth in the *qiaopi* trade in this period fostered the rise of a number of trade organizations. These included the Nanyang Chinese Exchange Remittance Association in Singapore and the Trade Organization of Overseas Chinese Exchange and *Huidui xinju* 汇兑信局 (Letter Agencies) in the Philippines. Their fundamental purpose was to strengthen ties among *qiaopi* traders, to safeguard the interests of the trade by negotiating with governments, and to coordinate ties among the *qiaopiju*.

There were two kinds of *qiaopiju* – specialized agencies and general agencies. The former concentrated on a single country or area in Southeast Asia. For example, the Ong Sun Heng xinju 王顺兴信局 in Quanzhou in Fujian focused principally on the Philippines. The latter, on the other hand, were active in two or more countries or areas in Southeast Asia.

The connection between the OCBC and the Cheng Tye xinju 正大信局

Figure 6.3 shows a bill of exchange sent by the OCBC in Singapore to the bank's branch in Gulangyu 鼓浪屿 in Xiamen in 1934, naming the Cheng Tye Xinju as beneficiary and endorsed with the OCBC's stamp and the personal seal of Manager Zhou. The bill was dispatched on 6 April and received in Xiamen on 16 April, a difference of eleven days, which was relatively fast for transnational banking at the time. This exchange bill was issued by the Oversea-Chinese Bank Ltd, the OCBC's predecessor. The Cheng Tye Xinju focused on the Philippines, where it ran a large number of different sorts of outlets. As a representative of the *qiaopi* trade in southern Fujian, the Cheng Tye Xinju had business networks both at home and abroad, which together formed an organic and integrated whole. The Cheng Tye Xinju, founded by Guo Yizhou 郭奕周 from Liuchuan village in Jiaomei, Zhangzhou, was a general agency that covered Southeast Asia and the principal *qiaoxiang* in southern Fujian (see Table 6.1).

The Cheng Tye Xinju was active not only in Southeast Asia's major cities, like Manila, Singapore, Batavia, Surabaya, Kuala Lumpur, and Rangoon, but in smaller places like Taiping (Malaya) and Surakarta and Makassar (Indonesia), where few Chinese banks operated, thus handing the *qiaopiju* an advantage. The domestic directly managed branches of the Cheng Tye Xinju covered almost all

Figure 6.3 A bill of exchange of the OCBC in Singapore in 1934.

Table 6.1 Offices and agencies run by the Cheng Tye Xinju in China and overseas

No.	*Name of overseas Chinese Xinju*	*Date of origin*	*Place of operation*	*Manager*
1	CHENG TYE 正大	1930	Gulangyu	Guo Shanglin
2	CHENG TYE 正大	1930	Anhai	Lin Haiteng
3	CHENG TYE 正大	1930	Jinjiang	Liao Jiezhi
4	CHENG TYE 正大	1930	Youxi	Hong Shicai
5	CHENG TYE 正大	1930	Shima	Yao Qiming
6	CHENG TYE 正大	1930	Liuchuan	Guo She'er
7	CHENG TYE 正大	1930	Baishuiying	Guo Zizai
8	CHENG TYE 正大	1930	Fugong	Xu Donghai
9	CHENG TYE 正大	1930	Shimei	Huang Xiecheng
10	CHENG TYE 正大	1930	Haichang	Lin Lianjing
11	CHENG TYE 正大	1930	Maluan	Chen Lianxing
12	CHENG TYE 正大	1930	Tong'an	Guo Ruilin
13	CHENG TYE 正大	1930	Jinmen	Zeng Yutian
14	CHENG TYE 正大	1930	Anxi	Bai Tiehan
15	CHENG TYE 正大	1930	Hui'an	Luo Ruicheng
16	CHENG TYE 正大	1930	Yongchun	Zheng Xianshi
17	CHENG TYE 正大	1930	Minhou	Shi Gengtang
18	CHENG TYE 正大	1930	Yongjia	Yang Dashan
19	CHENG TYE 正大	1930	Putian	Chen Guohua

No.	*Name of overseas Chinese Xinju*	*Date of origin*	*Place of operation*	*Manager*
20	CHENG TYE 正大	1930	Hanjiang	Tang Boyao
21	CHENG TYE 正大	November, 1934	Maxiang	Wu Diju
22	CHENG TYE 正大	November, 1934	Jimei	Huang Jiangyuan
23	CHENG TYE 正大	November, 1934	Xin'an	
24	CHENG TYE 正大	November, 1934	Gangwei	
25	CHENG TYE 正大	November, 1934	Shuitou	
26	CHENG TYE 正大	November, 1934	Luoyang	Yang Jiushi
27	CHENG TYE 正大	November, 1934	Zhao'an	Shen Zhongyuan
28	CHENG TYE 正大	November, 1934	Fotan	Yang Yuxiang
29	CHENG TYE 正大	November, 1934	Gaopu	Zheng Wencheng
30	CHENG TYE 正大	November, 1934	Jiaowei	Chen Dayou
31	CHENG TYE 正大	November, 1934	Dongshan	Wang Kecheng
32	DA FU 大福	November, 1934	Minhou	Shi Shengmei
33	XIN TONG 信通	August, 1930	Yunxiao	Wang Wentao
34	XIN TONG 信通	August, 1930	Singapore	Zhang Yisheng
35	ZHEN YUAN 振源	August, 1930	Singapore	Cai Yufu
36	SHAO CHANG 紹昌	August, 1930	Singapore	Hong Shaoshi
37	FENG LONG 丰隆	August, 1930	Singapore	Huang Tianfu
38	TIAN MEI 天美	August, 1930	Kedah	Huang Zan Bo
39	SHUN MEI 顺美	August, 1930	Kedah	Huang Hengcang
40	YUAN Co. 源公司	August, 1930	Kangsar	Cai Changshu
41	GAO LONG XING 高隆兴	August, 1930	Palembang	Gao Yanzhi
42	WU MEI 五美	August, 1930	Medan	Li Bingwen
43	SHUN AN 顺安	August, 1930	Singkawang	Xie Junban
44	YUAN CHENG XING 源成兴	August, 1930	Batavia	Huang Jianghan
45	ZHANG HE XING 漳合兴	August, 1930	Surabaya	Guo Zhihan
46	YUAN HE 源和	August, 1930	Semarang	Zhang Tianxiang
47	HONG YI XIANG 洪怡祥	August, 1930	Pekalongan	Hong Yixiang
48	LI MIN 利民	August, 1930	Chelibin 彻里宾	Huang Bilan
49	ZHENG TONG 正通	November, 1936	Penang	Chen Qichang
50	DA ZHONG 大中	November, 1936	Manila	Guo Shangshen
51	XIE MAO 协茂	August, 1939	Singapore	Huang Yudai
52	SHUN MAO 顺茂	August, 1939	Singapore	He Qingwan
53	New QUAN HE 新泉和	August, 1939	Singapore	He Fumin
54	LIAN QING 联庆	August, 1939	Sarawak	CaiRongjie
55	YUAN Co. 源公司	August, 1939	Tai Binh	Cai Changjie
56	ZHEN CHANG 振昌	August, 1939	Sarawak	Huang Wuhan
57	NAN SHENG 南生	August, 1939	Palembang	Liu Qiaoshan
58	JIAN YU 建裕	August, 1939	Jambi	Li Huolu
59	ZHANG HE XING 漳合兴	August, 1939	Surakarta	Chen Yushui
60	New HE XING 新和兴	August, 1939	Bandung	Chen Tianxing
61	New FU SHUN 新福顺	November, 1939	Gangsar	Chen Fushun
62	NAN SHUN 南顺	November, 1939	Pontian of Johore	Li Zhiyan
63	MIN NAN 闽南	November, 1939	Batavia	Chen Wucai
64	TONG CHENG XING 同成兴	November, 1939	Makassar	Guo Yunteng
65	TIAN AN 天安	November, 1940	Manila	Cai Cimin
66	FA AN 福安	August, 1941	Singapore	Gao Shuiyuan
67	YUAN CHONG MEI 源崇美	October, 1941	Singapore	Yan Huiyun
68	YUAN AN HE 源安和	May, 1941	Pontian of Johore	Yu Shaoze
69	JIN YU 锦裕	September, 1941	Miuaer (缪阿尔)	Zheng Jinyuan
70	YING CHANG 永昌	August, 1941	Batavia	Chen Zhuan

of southern Fujian's main *qiaoxiang*, except for Minhou and Yunxiao. The branches of the Cheng Tye Xinju in places like Singapore, Indonesia, and Malaysia consisted of agencies of other *qiaopiju*.

The areas where the Cheng Tye Xinju and the OCBC opened branches, including Xiamen, Singapore, Batavia, Surabaya, Penang, and Palembang, made it easy for these two units to conduct business in a complementary fashion.

Figure 6.4 shows a financial transfer by the Cheng Tye Xinju of 500 silver dollars to Xiamen by way of the OCBC in Batavia in 1935, a demonstration of the complementary relationship between the two institutions.

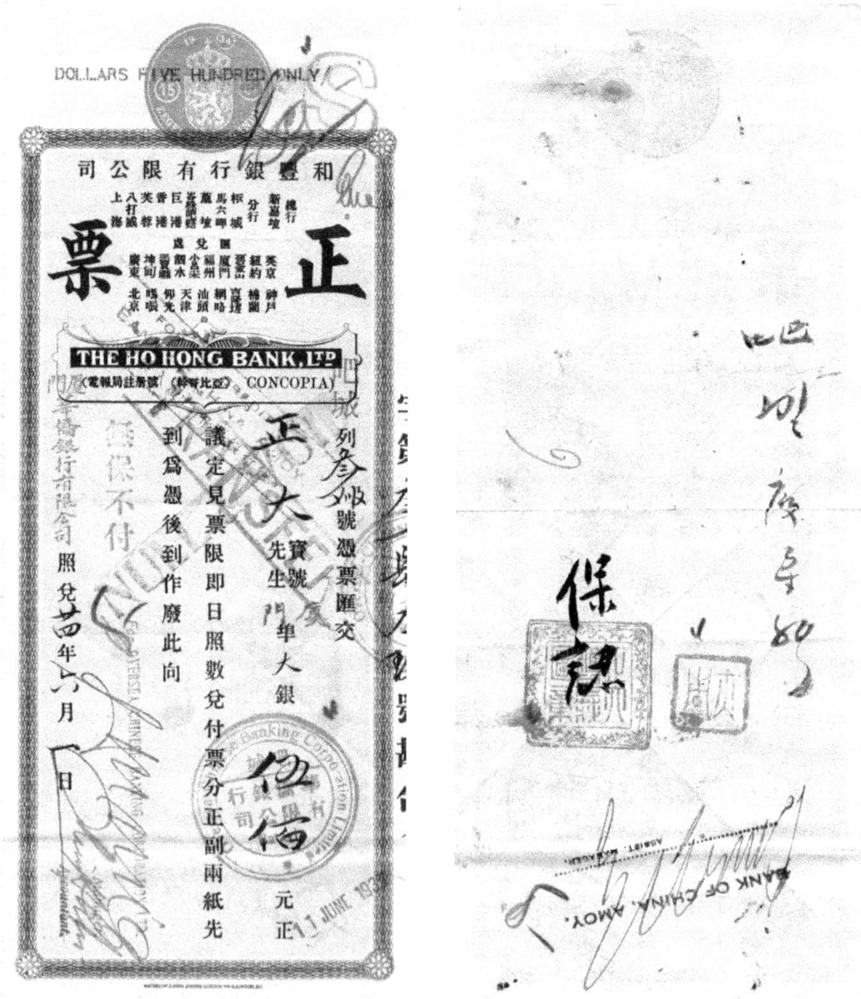

Figure 6.4 The Cheng Tye Xinju's financial transfers to Xiamen by way of the OCBC in Batavia in 1935.

The impact of the OCBC on the modernization of *qiaopiju*

The early *qiaopiju* usually delivered actual money to places of business in China, which then distributed it to recipients by means of deliverers. A disadvantage of this practice was that it took too long as a result of poor communications. As a result, some *qiaopiju* took advantage of the OCBC's wider operating network in China and abroad to conduct their financial transfers. Figure 6.5 is an example of a financial transfer made on behalf of a *qiaopiju* Chiat Hin Xinju by the OCBC.

Figure 6.5 shows a bill of exchange sent by the OCBC in Kuala Lumpur to the OCBC in Xiamen in 1929. The bill specifies the Chiat Hin Xinju as beneficiary, and is endorsed with the Chiat Hin Xinju's stamp and the personal seal of Manager Li Chengtian 李成田, the business seal of Son Sin Co. 顺成公司汇兑信局, and the business seal of the OCBC. The bill was for 1,000 Xiamen dollars, the silver dollar circulating in Xiamen at that time. It was sent on 20 December 1929, and paid out by the OCBC in Xiamen on 16 January 1930, so it

Figure 6.5 A bill of exchange issued by the OCBC in Kuala Lumpur in 1929.

took twenty-seven days, a relatively slow transaction, caused by inefficiencies in transportation and the exchange of information at the time. The bill of exchange had no receiving date and only a payment date. This shows that the Oversea-Chinese Bank Ltd, the predecessor of the OCBC, provided financial transfers on behalf of the *qiaopiju*.

The Chiat Hin Xinju, founded by Li Yingui 李引贵 from Furong, Nan'an, focused its business on Singapore, Malaya, and the Philippines, and was closed down in 1927 due to poor management. In the same year, however, Li Yingui's sons, Li Chengtian 李成田 and Li Chengpu 李成埔, revived the original firm and renamed it Yuan Xing Xinju 源兴信局. This firm was also mainly active in Singapore, Malaya, and the Philippines. Note that the old name, Chiat Hin, had been retained on this bill of exchange.

Figure 6.6 shows a bill of exchange sent by the OCBC in Kuala Lumpur to the OCBC in Xiamen in 1936, intended for the Chiat Hin Xinju and endorsed with the stamp of the Chiat Hin Xinju and the personal seal of Manager Li

Figure 6.6 Bill of exchange of the OCBC in Kuala Lumpur in 1936.

Chengtian. It was sent on 18 September 1936, and was paid out by the OCBC in Xiamen on 28 September, so it took only ten days to deliver, a relatively fast time. The bill was in the form of an old-style bill of exchange of the sort issued by the Oversea-Chinese Bank Ltd with a black line containing the words Oversea Chinese Banking Corporation Ltd on the front, reflecting the fact that the OCBC, after the merger, had continued to provide business in the form of financial transfers for *qiaopiju*.

These examples show that it was a common practice for the *qiaopiju* to transfer overseas remittances to Xiamen through the OCBC, whereupon the remittances were paid out by its branch in Xiamen. This method was faster and safer, and also cheaper, than the earlier practice of directly delivering actual cash to agencies in China.

Conclusion

Broadly speaking, the *qiaopiju* set up an operating network between Southeast Asia and the main *qiaoxiang* in southern Fujian. This network was built on the basis of the southern Fujian dialect group and catered to a steady flow of customers thanks to the social capital represented by ties of geography and blood. The *qiaopiju* business network aimed at individuals, which were based on mutual trust and cultural commonality.

For a while, the *qiaopiju* had an advantage over the Chinese banks in the sense that they had access to a customer base in remote areas of the *qiaoxiang*, as a result of the personal trust and business standing created by their ties of geo-consanguinity. Another of their advantages over the OCBC was that they were able to deliver letters and remittances to the doors of their kinsfolk and neighbours in the *qiaoxiang*.

Modern enterprises like the Chinese banks commonly expanded the scale of their network by operating directly managed branches and agencies. The appearance on the scene of Chinese banks, notably the OCBC, created a situation in which the *qiaopiju* had a good partner with which to cooperate in making financial transfers. This was because the Chinese banks operated networks that covered the distributing centres of *qiaopiju* in Southeast Asia, including cities such as Singapore, Kuala Lumpur, Batavia, Rangoon, and Xiamen. This greatly facilitated the *qiaopi* trade. Thus, the OCBC entered the *qiaopi* trade in an indirect way, but ended up trading directly in *qiaopi* in places such as Singapore, Malaya, Myanmar, and Vietnam.

To secure their business position, the *qiaopiju* had to strive to expand and improve their operating networks. As a well-capitalized general agency, the Cheng Tye Xinju had built its operating network in overseas Chinese communities in Southeast Asia and the *qiaoxiang* in China. The OCBC set up agents in areas where it lacked branches, using *qiaopiju* or other business establishments.

These specialized, small-scale agencies had, unlike the general agencies, gone to great lengths to build operating networks between their overseas businesses and their business outlets in southern Fujian, in order to increase their share of the market. Where they themselves had fewer branches, they used other *qiaopiju* or business establishments in southern Fujian as their agents.

The *qiaopiju* built extensive business networks across the main areas of Southeast Asia in the first half of the twentieth century, while the OCBC set up branches in major cities of Southeast Asia and southeastern China, including Singapore, Penang, Rangoon, Hong Kong, Shanghai, Xiamen, and Shantou. During the period of gestation and development of the *qiaopi* trade, the business networks of the *qiaopiju* and the OCBC were closely linked, although both institutions also had their own specialized domains. With the expansion in volume of the *qiaopi* trade, the OCBC built business networks overlapping with those of the *qiaopiju* in the major trading ports of Southeast Asia. Its growing involvement in the *qiaopi* trade led to an increase in the trade's general efficiency.

In conclusion, there was a significant difference between the *qiaopiju* in Southeast Asia and the Chinese banks, notably the OCBC, in terms of the way in which each institution dealt with the *qiaopi* trade. The networks run by the *qiaopiju*, as non-governmental economic organizations, had the advantage of a cultural and regional affiliation based on social relations. However, the *qiaopiju* took advantage of the OCBC's operating network to conduct financial transfers. Because of its lack of strong cultural and regional ties and the limitations of its operating network, the OCBC was unable to engage directly in the business of collecting and delivering *qiaopi* on a large scale. However, in accordance with its modern business philosophy, it could, under the risk control principle, carry out financial transfers and get involved in other aspects of the *qiaopi* trade. Singapore, as a main centre of the OCBC's involvement in the *qiaopi* trade, was a regional financial hub of Southeast Asia.

Note

1 Many different names were used in English to denote the *qiaopiju*. They included Postal Agency, Private Mail Bureau, Postal Office, Overseas Chinese Letter Bureau, Credit Bureau, Remittance Banker, and so on. This chapter was initially written in Chinese and was translated and edited by Gregor Benton.

References

Fujian Province Archives. 1945. Serial No. of (1945) 56–5–2004.

Fujian Province Archives. 2013. *Bainian kuaguo liangdishu: Fujian qiaopi dang'an tuzhi* 百年跨国两地书：福建侨批档案图志 (Letters across the Border during the Last Century: Illustrated Guide to the *Qiaopi* File in Fujian). Xiamen Lujiang chuban she.

Kua Bak Lim 柯木林. 2007. *Xinjiapo qiaohui yu minxinye yanjiu (1945–1949)* 新加坡侨汇与民信业研究 (1945–1949) [The Study of Overseas Remittance and Private Postal Industry in Singapore (1945–1949)]. Singapore Youth Press.

Liang Yingming 梁英明, ed. 1999. *Huaqiao huaren baikequanshu: jingji juan* 华侨华人百科全书：经济卷 [Encyclopedia of Chinese Overseas: Volume of Economy]. Zhongguo huaqiao chuban she.

Lin Xiaosheng 林孝胜. 1987. "Li Guangqian de qiye wangguo (1927–1954)" 李光前的企业王国 (1927–1954) [Lee Kong Chian and his Southeast Asian Business Empire (1927–1954)]. *Yazhou wenhua*亚洲文化 [Asia Cultural Studies], 9: 3–20.

Liu Bozi 刘伯孳. 2013. "Li Guangqian shidai huaqiao yinhang de qiaopiye jingying" 李光前时代华侨银行的侨批业经营 [The *Qiaopi* Trade of the OCBC in the Era of Lee Kong Chian], in Quanzhou Historical Society of Overseas Chinese and Nan'an Furong Foundation, eds. *Li Guangqian ji'nian wenji* 李光前纪念文集 [Collected Works in Memory of Lee Kong Chian]. Xiamen Lujiang chuban she.

Xu Maochun 许茂春. 2008. *Dongnanya huaren yu qiaopi* 东南亚华人与侨批 [Overseas Chinese and *qiaopi* in Southeast Asia], n.p.

Yang Yan 杨妍. 2012. "1933 nian zhi biange: Lun Xinjiapo zaoqi huaren yinhang fazhan – yi huaqiao yinhang weili" 1933年之变革：论新加坡早期华人银行发展 – 以华侨银行为例 [The Reform of 1933: On the Development of Earlier Chinese Banks in Singapore – Taking the OCBC as an Example]. *The International Journal of Diasporic Chinese Studies* 4: 55–82.

7 Sex scandals, Gold Mountain Guests' Wives, and female roles in the Siyi *qiaoxiang*

A study of the family letters of overseas Chinese in the Republican era

Jin Liu

Introduction

In the Wuyi region of Jiangmen in Guangdong, which has jurisdiction over the five counties of Taishan, Xinhui, Kaiping, Enping, and Heshan, large numbers of *qiaopi/yinxin* are preserved in museums, while others continue to be held by families. They have become items of considerable value, and are sought by specialist collectors and auction houses or stored in universities, research institutions, libraries, official archives, and museums. Previously, overseas Chinese and their dependants preserved these family documents at home, but unfortunately unscrupulous antique dealers have split them up to sell them for profit, thus spoiling their integrity. Documents from the Qing Dynasty, the Republican era, and the period of the People's Republic of China today circulate in specific markets. Recently a friend of mine, an amateur collector, bought a chest of family documents, including letters, photos, papers, and land leases, from a Chinese American named Tse originally from Kaiping, and brought them back to China. These letters date from the 1900s to the 1910s, and include no fewer than sixty letters from the Qing Dynasty (see Figure 7.1 and Figure 7.2).

Many researchers have analysed the contents of *qiaopi* and demonstrated their academic value, including in the field of gender relations. Gender relations necessarily characterize all human societies, and provide an important perspective from which to explore different forms of civilization.

After the Opium War of 1840, in Guangdong's Siyi region (encompassing the four counties of Taishan, Xinhui, Kaiping, and Enping), large numbers of young males in their prime went overseas to make a living, so that their families and relatives could survive on the remittances they sent home. The tradition of "men ploughing and women weaving" was thus abandoned, leading to a pattern of long-term separation and, at best, short-term reunion for the affected couples. Chinese migrants in North America and Australia were generally known among people in the *qiaoxiang* (areas of Chinese emigration) as "Gold Mountain Guests". Correspondingly, their dependants were called "Gold Mountain Guests' Wives" and "Gold Mountain Guests' Sons". The

Figure 7.1 The chest of letters brought back from America by Mr Tse.

Figure 7.2 One of Mr Tse's letters.

name was meant to symbolize wealth and honour, and was an expression of the envy people in the *qiaoxiang* felt for those fortunate enough to go overseas (*Xinning zazhi* 1922, 36).

However, the real situation of Gold Mountain Guests' Wives, rich and honoured in the eyes of others, did not necessarily live up to perceptions. In 1947, a news report by a local person on social problems in Siyi posed a pointed question. The article, titled "The Dissolute and Flirtatious Women of the Siyi region", said:

> Whenever our hometown is mentioned, this serious social problem springs to mind. Unfortunately, nothing has been done about it for decades. Outsiders often doubt that it is as romantic as Europe and America. Some say, "Why do the Siyi newspapers always devote an entire section to sex scandals? Is this merely a gimmick got up by journalists?"
>
> (*Beikeng yuebao* 1947, 25)

Confronting doubts like this expressed by outsiders, the author wrote: "To be honest, if these were all gimmicks got up by journalists, the journalists would have been censured." Unfortunately, however, the accounts were true. "Siyi society indeed has such a problem." Moreover, such problems were far from new. An American Chinese magazine commented: "There are many 'dissolute and flirtatious women' in the *qiaoxiang*." The author declared himself highly insulted by such reports. He posed the following question: "In every town and village in Siyi, large numbers of women elope, and political representatives appeal for an end to this secret absconding. Readers are fed up with these sex scandals. But has anyone discussed their cause?" (*Beikeng yuebao* 1947, 25–26).

The *qiaokan*[1] of the late Qing Dynasty and the Republican era frequently reported sex scandals, including elopements and adultery. It is a well-known marketing strategy of the tabloid press to attract readers by publishing exotic and titivating stories. However, the readers of the *qiaokan* were local people and their relatives overseas. Groundless stories would hardly have stood the test of time, so we can assume that the sex scandals reported in the *qiaokan* were true. Yet the reports were quite rudimentary, and failed to explore the causes and effects of such incidents in any depth.

Compared with these news reports, family letters to and from overseas Chinese, which were written by the parties concerned, are more detailed and exact in their recounting of events. They can be taken as a truer reflection of what actually happened. This chapter therefore takes the example of a sex scandal that took place in Haiyan 海晏, Taishan台山, in 1939, together with news reports in *qiaokan*, to explore the real situation, social roles, and status of Gold Mountain Guests' Wives and the underlying causes of their actions.

The key issues in the Haiyan sex scandal

We know of more than one hundred family letters addressed to Chen Zhongbo, a Mexican Chinese from Haiyan. The senders of these letters were mostly members of Chen Zhongbo's clan in Taishan and Hong Kong. These letters were taken back to China by Chen Zhongbo sometime after victory in the Anti-Japanese War and were preserved by his family. The letters mostly concern the many problems that plagued the *qiaoxiang*, against the background of the family's transnational connections. However, by far the most interesting thing about them is that they contain a complete record of a sex scandal involving Chen Zhongbo's wife. Compared with other family letters, they cover the case in comprehensive detail. However, they are not entirely opaque, since different writers have their own agendas in recounting events. I have therefore done my best to elucidate the letters and clarify the key issues.

The incident takes place

The sex scandal occurred in Xikang, Chen Zhongbo's home village. His wife's family name was Zhang. Chen probably first read the bad news in a letter from his mother-in-law dated 22 March. She wrote:

> An injustice happened in your family at 10 a.m. on 19 February. Your nephew Yaobo falsely accused my daughter of committing adultery. ... As a matter of fact, my daughter and Zusheng's wife went to the home of Jinming to get a pattern [for a curtain]. Yaobo started causing trouble and tried to extort 300 yuan from my daughter. They went to the township office. My daughter was proved innocent, so no money was paid to [Yaobo]. Later, [Yaobo] wrote a letter and asked Fourth Great-Uncle to sign it. Fourth Great-Uncle refused. Thus, the accusation proved to be false.[2]

The letter was brief and to the point.

Clearly, a mother would never, on her own initiative, confess her daughter's "wrongdoing" to the party allegedly wronged. That would have been to "hang out one's dirty linen in public". Moreover, there was no evidence against the daughter. However, the mother-in-law must have known that "while good news never goes beyond the gate, bad news travels far and wide", and that "words have wings". Given that village people were in frequent contact with their relatives overseas, she cannot have doubted that someone would attempt to frame her daughter. So she took the initiative to clarify the matter pre-emptively.

The sex scandal recorded in Chen Zhongbo's correspondence was by no means a one-off. A year earlier, Chen Zhongbo's cousin Chen Hua'an informed him of a similar "curious case". One day, while out walking in Wen Village 汶村, he came across a man called Yiling

> who invited three men – Buhan, Tianyi, and Rimao – to enter his house and commit adultery with his wife, thus cuckolding himself. He charged them five yuan each. The next day, Yiling invited the three men back. During the adultery, Yiling made an excuse to leave the house. Later, he came back with Huiyao to catch the adulterers in the act. The three men wanted to hush up the scandal, so Buhan paid 50 yuan, Tianyi paid 40 yuan, and Rimao gave Huiyao a ring.

Even so, the scandal still spread among the villagers: "All these men are worthless. It's absurd that a man would willingly cuckold himself. Such a thing has never been heard of before." After that, the three adulterers "were never seen again in the village". However, Chen Hua'an had no evidence to prove the scandal, so he reminded Chen Zhongbo "not to spread the news among others", since the perpetrator's father was, at the time, making a living in Mexico. "If he got to know of it by accident, he would make further inquiries, and I would be held responsible."[3] Chen Hua'an commented on the incident: "Xi Kang villagers' morality is steadily decaying."

Who defended Chen Zhongbo's wife against the accusation?

It is easy to imagine Chen Zhongbo's anger at the news of his wife's involvement in the scandal. Naturally, he wanted to know whether the rumour about his wife's adultery was true. His mother-in-law's explanation was not enough to dispel his doubts. Perhaps he was reassured by the fact that all the letters reporting "the scandal" pleaded his wife's innocence. Their writers included Chen Zhongbo's uncles Chen Shuntong and Chen Caizhong, his brothers Chen Hua'an and Chen Jingtang, and his nephew Chen Zhengze.

Of these people, Chen Hua'an wrote most about the incident – a total of seven letters in all. After Chen Zhongbo's mother-in-law had sent her letter, Chen Hua'an also informed him of the matter: "On the 19th of this month, an obscene affair was exposed in our village, and your wife was involved in it."[4]

A comprehensive reading of all these letters shows that their description of the incident was generally consistent, save for a few details. All the writers believed that Chen's wife was innocent of adultery, and that she had been "wronged" by others. Their arguments were as follows.

First, Chen Zhongbo's wife had just happened to "call on" the woman who was the "real" adulterer in the case. Chen Hua'an wrote on 27 March to explain that Fuhou's wife and Botan's wife had invited Chen Yuzhen from Sandieshi Village 三叠石村 into Fuhou's wife's house, where they "hid in a room to talk and have fun". Fuchi, who lived in the same house, found out, and gathered a group of people to catch the adulterers. When the group swarmed into the house and blocked the way into the room, Chen Zhongbo's wife was also trapped inside, but the group believed her when she said she was only passing by, and released her on the spot.[5] Chen Zhongbo's uncle Chen Shuntong also said the two were innocent and chaste, though "not careful enough in their choice of friends".[6] Chen Zhongbo's nephew Chen Zhengze also defended the pair's innocence.[7]

Second, Chen Zhongbo's wife "was past her prime and had lost her charm, so she was too old to be involved in this affair". Even so, she was not sufficiently careful in her choice of friends. After learning of the affair, Chen Zhongbo wrote letters to other people to make further inquiries, and formed his judgment on the information they provided. After recounting what happened, Chen Hua'an said in his letter that after the affair had been finally settled, he would "call on Chen Zhongbo's wife and advise her to be more cautious in her behaviour and to stay away from these misbehaving women".[8] In a later letter, he said: "Your wife is already past forty. She should have known better than to disgrace herself in such scandals."[9] In a reply to Chen Zhongbo, Chen Jingtang was quite critical of his wife's connection with those "misbehaving women", and said that they had become "wild and flirtatious". However, he couldn't believe that Chen Zhongbo's wife "had committed adultery", mainly on the grounds that she was "too old to flirt and must have been misled by others".[10] Chen Jingtang's ambiguous comments left Chen Zhongbo confused.

Who framed Chen Zhongbo's wife?

Chen Zhongbo's wife had just been passing by, and had been released on the spot, and was therefore found "not guilty" of adultery. So why did she subsequently land in trouble? The letters suggest two main reasons.

First, someone was out to blackmail her for money. When the affair was reported at the township office, "the adulterer Chen Yuzhen was fined no less than 300–400 yuan [in the Hao currency that circulated in Guangdong during the early Republican era]. Fuhou's wife was fined more than 200 yuan."[11] Assisted by Chen Hua'an and Chen Shuntong, Chen Zhongbo's wife "spent 32 yuan" on officially settling the affair. Chen Hua'an and Chen Shuntong both got two yuan as a reward. The balance was paid to the township officers and other relatives concerned, who received sixteen yuan each. It seems that someone told Chen Zhongbo that the affair had "cost a fortune, up to hundreds", but Chen Hua'an refuted the rumours.[12]

Second, members of the younger generation in Chen Zhongbo's home did not get along well with each other, and were therefore manipulated by outsiders. One of his correspondents, Chen Zhongluan, who lived in Taishan, was probably his elder brother. Blind in one eye, he was known as "sick-eye brother" to Chen Hua'an. Chen Yaobo was Chen Zhongluan's son. The letters show that when the adultery took place, Chen Zhongluan was on a business trip to Hong Kong. Chen Yaobo's attitude towards the adultery was unusual. Chen Hua'an said in his letter: "As his father was not yet back, Yaobo was persuaded to lend a helping hand."[13] It seems that Chen Yaobo helped his aunt but only because he was forced to do so.

Chen Shuntong said: "The young people in our family are not loyal to each other. The internal conflicts result in insults from outside." Who did he have in mind? He didn't say so clearly, and merely talked about "somebody". Just when Chen Zhongbo's wife was relieved to feel that "the trouble was over", the sex scandal "came to the ears of 'somebody', who tried by every means to land the nephews' wives back into trouble in order to avenge himself". "This 'somebody' then had a secret talk with Yaozu. They summoned the township police to surround Fuhou's wife's house (with Tan's wife inside). Your wife's house was also surrounded, and she was not allowed to leave." Chen Shuntong "went out onto the street and found 'somebody' elated and overjoyed".[14]

Why was there such deep resentment among brothers, sons, and nephews? The letters imply that division of property may have been at the root of the problem. In 1935, Chen Zhongbo's uncles wrote to him inquiring about discord in the family, and advising him to "ensure that everyone is happy about how the money is used and distributed, in order to pre-empt criticism and dissatisfaction".[15]

Did the resentment among brothers, uncles, and nephews really arise because of a dispute about money? Chen Hua'an surmised in his letter that "some people resent others for not lending them money and take advantage of trivial incidents to provoke others, in order to get back lost property. They thus become enemies."[16] This suggests that Chen Zhongbo's brothers and nephews' attitude to his wife was motivated by disputes over the division of property.

How was the dispute settled?

In rural society, people can end up badly hurt by scandals, whether true or not. According to the letters, Chen Zhongbo's wife was wrongly implicated in the scandal, although they do not name the real protagonists.

The reason Chen Zhongbo's wife was able to extricate herself from the incident and prove her innocence was the strong support she gained from Great-Uncle Chen Shuntong and her brothers-in-law Chen Hua'an and Chen Caizhong. Chen Hua'an told Chen Zhongbo: "The affair was finally brought to an end to thanks to Uncle Shuntong's efforts. If you have time, write him a letter of thanks."[17] Thanks to all these people, combined with the help provided by "Fourth Uncle and Village Chief Zhongyang", the incident was resolved. At one point, when the Village Chief interrogated the adulterer, he wanted to call Chen Zhongbo's wife to the township office to interrogate her too. However, Chen Shuntong and Chen Hua'an strongly opposed this measure, and explained to the Village Chief:

> She is not guilty of the affair, so she does not fear any form of interrogation. But as a young woman, she will face great danger when walking out on the streets. Will you please condescend to come to Brother Zhongluan's place and hold the trial there?

The Village Chief did as asked, and Chen Zhongbo's wife was "acquitted".[18]

From this incident, it can be seen that Chen Shuntong and Chen Hua'an were quite powerful in their village. They were both businessmen. Chen Shuntong spent some time in Hong Kong, and kept in close touch with Chen Zhongbo, by exchanging *yinxin* with him. Chen Hua'an only conducted his business in Taishan, but he did quite well from it. The two men were unlikely to have been Chen Zhongbo's uncles and brothers in the real sense, but they maintained close contact and established a friendly relationship with him. They would therefore do all they could to save face for Chen Zhongbo, who held firmly to the traditional belief that it is "better to starve than to forfeit one's moral integrity". What's more, Chen Zhongbo's wife has earned their trust, so they were willing to give her their full support.

People's violent responses to the sex scandal

To judge from local records, adulterers and adulteresses were severely punished in the Siyi *qiaoxiang*. Sex scandals triggered feelings of excitement, anger, and revenge. Chen Hua'an described how the "adulterer and the adulteress" were bound by ropes and threatened, with the intention of blackmailing them. When the alleged adulterer tried to bargain, he was beaten to a pulp, while the villagers applauded. Finally, he was released in exchange for a bribe.[19]

In fact, the "adultery" mentioned in the letters was never proved. The male caught up in the incident also denied adultery, and claimed that he "merely came to collect debts from Fuhou's wife".[20] So it is rash to assume that the man and the women were engaged in adultery simply because they were sitting together in the same room, quite apart from the fact that there were others present. However, in a traditional village "men and women are supposed to keep at a distance from one another". For a strange man to be found within a woman's house was considered "wrongdoing". No one would be particularly concerned to dig out the actual truth of the matter. Apart from descriptions of violent behaviour, the letters are also full of verbal violence, including abusive and insulting names aimed at the women involved.

The serious consequences of getting involved in the sex scandal

The people involved in the scandal were severely persecuted. "Botan's wife fled for fear of conviction",[21] and the male protagonist was harshly beaten and insulted. However, the letter writers were not concerned about these people, but focused instead on what had happened to Chen Zhongbo's wife.

From the letters, it can be inferred that if Chen Zhongbo's wife had really "committed adultery" there would have been serious consequences. Chen Zhongbo repeatedly "blamed" his wife in his letters, and ordered that she should be "expelled, or allowed to kill herself". Zusheng too wrote letters blaming his own wife, and Chen Hua'an demonstrated his understanding for their reaction.[22]

The letters show that although Chen Shuntong and others tried to defend Chen Zhongbo's wife, their criticism of her "carelessness in choosing friends" filled his mind with doubts about her. Japanese aggression was impending, his village was in great peril, and prices were soaring. Even so, after the incident, he stopped sending his wife money. In December 1939, Chen Hua'an wrote to Chen Zhongbo telling him:

> I hope you can cast off your doubts and send *yinxin* as usual … If you still have doubts, send 180 yuan or so to me, and I will transfer the money to her on a regular basis. In this way, she can sustain herself and the family.[23]

It is unclear how Chen Zhongbo responded. However, his wife suffered so many blows that she was physically and mentally devastated, and lost her mind. In early 1940, Chen Hua'an wrote a letter detailing her mental state in vivid and pitiful language:

> Respected Brother Zhongbo,
> … Not long ago, I heard that your wife had gone crazy. I went to pay her a visit and told her that I would go to the market the next day and buy the

> things she needed. However, she said she didn't want to buy anything. She said: "Since I got caught up in the incident, I have had nowhere to vent my grievances. What's worse, my enemies made up endless stories about me. They incite rogues to land me in trouble. As for me, I don't want to live in humiliation, but nor do I want to forsake my life in vain before justice is done. I will wait until my husband is back and explain the whole thing to him. I will be at his disposal and willingly accept what he decides. Looked down upon as I am, I have also heard that my husband recently sent sponsorship letters for the people who framed me when I got caught up in this trouble. ... My husband is very considerate towards his neighbours, but he never shows concern for his family. I think there is no point in me preserving my life until his return. I have wanted to hang myself for a long time now, but I can't resign myself to my humiliation. I have lost my appetite. Wine and meat no longer have any taste for me." Upon saying that, your wife burst into tears and wept. I then explained to her that I have written to ask you for remittances.[24]

Chen Zhongbo's compassion for his wife and family seems finally to have conquered his apprehension and doubts, so he resumed sending remittances home. Following Chen Hua'an's advice, he channelled the money through Chen Hua'an. Chen Hua'an immediately reported to tell him that "but for your remittance, she would not have survived the crisis".[25]

The social background to the sex scandal

Sex scandals were common in *qiaoxiang* society at the time. This phenomenon can be analysed in terms of politics, cultural tradition, economy, social structure, and gender relations. Here, I touch briefly on the following issues.

The wealth gap and the loss of women's economic independence

Once overseas migration took off in Siyi, the inflow of remittances resulted in a big gap between rich and poor in the region. Chen Hua'an described the superior lifestyle enjoyed by families supported by overseas remittances during the Anti-Japanese War, when prices soared:

> In these hard times, poor families find it difficult to sustain themselves, while the Gold Mountain Guests' families enjoy prosperity. Hong Kong dollars are converted into 330 yuan in national currency, and 430 yuan [in local Hao currency]. At present, if there is any Gold Mountain Guest in the family, the whole family need no longer worry about money.[26]

This wealth gap had been growing wider and wider ever since the Qing Dynasty's Guangxu reign. The market in the Siyi *qiaoxiang* boomed, and inns and teahouses flourished. Taicheng, Taishan's central point, was as prosperous as a "little Guangzhou". Overseas Chinese and their dependants celebrated their weddings in style, and the brides wore copious gold adornments. Some women wore "as many as six gold rings on one hand, and gold bracelets on both wrists" (Lao Xiang 1947, 5–6). This wealth resulted from the overseas earnings of young adult men, who were considered an excellent catch on the marriage market. A Siyi ballad went as follows:

> Never marry your daughter to a scholar, for she will live alone in a cold chamber; never marry your daughter to a ploughman, for his feet are covered in ox manure and his head with dirt; do not hesitate to marry your daughter to a Gold Mountain Guest, for his gold piles up mountain-high.
>
> (Chen Yuanzhu 1929, 1)

Lacking education and economic independence, women became a form of merchandise as the wealth gap widened. Mercenary marriage was the norm, and marriages based on free love and courtship were rare exceptions. During the period of the Northern Expedition, the Kuomintang's Ministry of Home Affairs issued a circular describing the situation:

> The marriage system in our country continues to be inhumane. Women are still commodities in marriages, owned and sold by their fathers and brothers. … Guangdong and Fujian have a typically mercenary marriage system. Wealthy men can have several wives and concubines, while poor men remain unmarried even after the age of 34. These unmarried men can be found everywhere. Some are said to have become monks. Those who want to marry must first negotiate a price and pay for wedding gifts worth at least 300–400 yuan. This shows how costly it is to get married. Even overseas Chinese who have made a living far from home and saved for decades cannot fulfil their dream of marrying, let alone those poor men who stayed behind. You can imagine how many hardships and grudges they must bear.
>
> (*Xinning zazhi* 1928, 80–81)

In a society where the gap between rich and poor was wide, the pursuit of economic well-being was the top priority.

The abnormal family pattern created by overseas separation under the US Exclusion Act

During the period of Chinese Exclusion in the United States, Gold Mountain Guests showed in their letters home that their main aim was to save money and return home in glory, in order to enjoy their retirement and family life. In 1943, Chen Zhongze wrote to Chen Zhongbo as follows:

> At present, American wages are high, so you must be earning a lot of money. After the War against Japan is over, you must come home and set up a business in Guangzhou to earn money for your old age. Foreign lands are not a place for long-term stay.

Statements like this abounded in such correspondence. The overseas Chinese ideal was "to adorn one's house, delight one's parents, accumulate property, and dream of orchids".[27] Most of these aims speak for themselves, but "dreaming of orchids" had a special meaning: to make one's wife pregnant, so that she gives birth and perpetuates the family line.

"The husband sings and his wife responds" meant that the wife would follow and obey her husband, a requirement of women in Chinese society as it then was. In agricultural society, men ploughed and women wove; people went out to work at sunrise and returned at sunset. This lifestyle was not without its pleasures. However, during the period of Chinese Exclusion, couples were separated by the Pacific. In the absence of a normal family life, letters and remittances became the bond between them. Living in their husband's family, amidst relationships that were often highly complicated, to whom could these women pour out their hearts? Excessive material consumption was one way to fill the emotional void and banish loneliness. Not all overseas Chinese made money, and those who failed to do so dared not face up to their kinsmen, and were therefore unable to return home and become reunited with their families. Needless to say, this drove their wives to despair. Examples abound.

Gold Mountain Guests' Wives generally had fewer children than other women. Chen Zhongbo's wife was a typical example. It cannot be known for certain when she married. She was not without money, so she was able to employ a maid to take care of household chores. However, she still had no children even after reaching the age of forty. Like other Gold Mountain Guests' Wives, she very much wanted to buy a "bollworm son".

"Bollworm sons" had a bad reputation in the Siyi *qiaoxiang*. Alongside sex scandals, stories about "bollworm sons" eating, drinking, visiting prostitutes, and gambling appeared in almost all the local *qiaokan*. Some were described as "whoring and swindling in the name of doing business", "became adopted sons in multiple families at the same time", and "bringing trouble to the local area". Reports called for the "driving out of bollworm sons" (*Ziyang yuekan* 1930, 67–68).

It is interesting to note that Sun Yat-sen's first wife, Lu Muzhen, asked local officials in Taishan to help investigate the abduction of Zhang Jingqing's 5-year-old son from Macau to Taishan. She wrote:

> The practice of buying adopted sons is more common in our county than anywhere else in the province. Wherever the child may be from, he is abducted and brought to Taishan for sale. Cases of abduction are often heard about in town, and reports of them are increasing daily.
>
> (*Ziyang yuekan* 1930, 80–82)

The prevalence of abductions of children in Taishan was directly connected with the social problems caused by the large population of Gold Mountain Guests and their wives.

Chen Zhongbo's wife was aware of the dangers, but the dread of a lonely old age helped overcome her scruples. She was determined to seek out an adopted son, in her case an older one. She talked about this a lot with her husband. In early 1938, Chen Hua'an mentioned her wish for the first time, in a letter to Chen Zhongbo:

> Currently, your wife is seeking a child to adopt, but has not found a suitable one. Not long ago, Big Mouth Di at the North Gate had a four-year-old son, and wanted 130 yuan for him. I thought the price was acceptable. However, in the current situation it is not appropriate to adopt a child. As you know, the Japanese aggressors have not been defeated, and they continue to threaten Haiyan. If Haiyan were occupied, how would we cope? So I didn't approve of the adoption, and your wife couldn't make up her mind either. I persuaded her to postpone it, and she agreed. I will tell you more about this later.[28]

The letters show that Chen Zhongbo rejoined his wife around 1935, but failed to get her pregnant. When war broke out, the Japanese forces put the *qiaoxiang* under siege. When would her husband return in glory? She was already past forty, and the chances of getting pregnant were quickly fading. That is probably why she was so desperate to adopt a son. In a letter to her husband, she wrote: "It is no good adopting a baby boy. I am growing old, so a more grown-up boy would be better. For the moment, I can't find a suitable one. I will write to you when I do."[29] Later, she found what she wanted. Chen Yuanqing the magistrate of the district court in Kaiping county, wrote Chen Zhongbo a letter to tell him: "Your wife has adopted a son, who is 17 or 18 years old. Did you know that? The boy is strong and healthy, but he need stricter discipline, to become a good man of achievement." Chen Zhongbo was evidently unhappy with what his wife had done. In January 1947, she wrote to him explaining:

> Respected Husband Zhongbo,
> As for the matter of adopting a son, I hear that you "were heartbroken", which astonishes me greatly. I guessed you might be dissatisfied because he is older than you expected. But please forgive me. You should understand that it would take a long time to rear a baby boy to take care of affairs at home. Even if I raised him, I don't know whether he would grow up to be good man. The boy I have adopted is honest and upright. It's really hard to find someone for adoption now. Anyway, I will take care of affairs at home, and I promise never to do anything to dishonour you. Some envious people may be trying to drive a wedge between us and say bad things about me. Please don't believe their stories, don't be used by them. To drive away the adopted son would be like abandoning me, so that I lose my foothold in the family.[30]

In order to talk her husband round, Zhang asked the adopted son to write a touching letter to his foster father, sending him greetings and telling him that "he had been in the family for five to six months" and had attended Wen Village

Middle School, although he had "too little literacy". He asked his foster father whether he should continue his schooling or leave to get a job, and if so, what job. Unfortunately, however, the adopted son turned out to be a disappointment. Tianyi wrote to tell Chen Zhongbo:

> During the *jiao* period 醮期 [a Daoist religious ceremony], your adopted son went gambling at the East Gate, and lost more than 100 thousand yuan. He knew that he had acted wrongly, so he fled to Nanpeng 难朋 in Yangjiang 阳江 with someone from Shapu 沙浦 and caught pigeons there. I don't know what his future plans are.[31]

Chen Zhongbo was undoubtedly upset when he read the letter.

Women's rebellion and struggle against the patriarchal social tradition

In both *qiaokan* and family letters, men dominated the discourse, but instances of women's resistance and rebellious spirit still occasionally shine through.

During the late Qing Dynasty and in the early Republic, the patriarchal tradition continued to dominate the Siyi region. Although there was Western food, Western clothing, and Western-style apartments and villas, traditional values still played a powerful role in people's lives. These included family-centred values, notions such as "men are superior to women", and the injunction that "men and women should keep their distance from one another". News stories in the *qiaokan* often subjected remarried women to ridicule and contumely.

It is clear from press reports that Gold Mountain Guests' Wives in the Siyi *qiaoxiang* suffered physically and mentally as a result of the trans-Pacific separation from their husbands during the Exclusion Era. There was no shortage of stories about Gold Mountain Guests' Wives and other women killing themselves or eloping. Reporters unfamiliar with the inside story could only level groundless accusations and provide superficial accounts of such happenings. For example, a news item titled "A curious case of female suicide" reported that the 30-year-old wife of Songqin, a Chinese American from Xiudun Village 秀墩村 in Taishan, had killed herself by jumping down a well. She was educated and had received large amounts of money from her husband's annual remittances. Some explained her death as the result of an accident within the family, while others claimed she had been haunted. Her son had already graduated from high school, and was keen to discover the truth behind his mother's demise (*Taishan zhixiaoduqin yuekan* 1948, 45).

In many cases, female suicides and elopements were both, to some extent, a form of protest and rebellion, one passive, the other active. Some women, tortured by their husbands' long-term absence, ran off with other men. Needless to say, the *qiaokan* ridiculed and denounced them mercilessly.

Some educated women refused to allow their parents or matchmakers to arrange marriages on their behalf, and fought hard to make their own decisions.

One case involved a man called Chen Yanhua, whose parents had engaged him to be married even before his birth. Later, he migrated to America, while his fiancée Yueqin pursued her studies in Hong Kong. When Chen Yanhua returned home to prepare for the wedding, Yueqin began arguing in favour of "free marriage" and against "forced marriage". With the agreement of both sets of parents, Chen Yanhua borrowed 2000 HK dollars to pay for the wedding, but Yueqin found an excuse to flee and stayed away for a long time. When Chen Yanhua married another woman from another village, Yueqin prosecuted him for bigamy, and won her case (*Taishan zhixiaoduqin yuekan* 1948, 41).

The author of the report on the "dissolute and flirtatious women of the Siyi region" cited at the beginning of this chapter asked why the Siyi *qiaoxiang* was so plagued with sex scandals. His own explanation was that women in the Siyi region were pitiful, and their forced marriages and loss of freedom were likely to result in sex scandals, which marked the beginning of a "chronic death sentence" (*Beikeng yuebao* 1947, 25).

In seeking husbands for their daughters, overseas Chinese families took into account the prospective groom's economic status, and sought out well-off families with overseas or business connections. They also looked hard at the prospective groom's family's status and influence in the local area. In the Siyi region, different families, and different branches within the same lineage, were often in fierce competition with one another. Marrying someone from a large clan would help strengthen one's own family. For example, in the 1920s Chen Yilin's family in Kaiping included a large number of Chinese Americans. Chen Yilin's son Chen Hongzhuang suggested to him adhering to the following principles in marrying off the younger generation of the family:

> Senyuan and Senpei had better go back to the US to study, and should preferably learn both Chinese and English. Senpei should return to the US to pursue Manchu and Mongolian Studies for two more years. It will still not be too late for him to go back to get married after he graduates. Matches should be made with members of big families rather than small families. Girls from the Guan, Situ, Wu, and Fang families should be considered. No one would mind spending money on wedding gifts for good girls.[32]

We don't know from which family Senpei took his bride, but we do know from Chen Hongzhen's letter that "Senpei's wedding banquet was sumptuous, and cost thousands of yuan. It was so extraordinary that it won honour and admiration for the family."[33] Marriages of this kind were designed to consolidate and strengthen a family's domestic and overseas connections.

On the other hand, Chen Zhongbo's wife's experience shows that the disadvantaged wives of Gold Mountain Guests lived morbidly distorted lives under a system of institutional and ideological oppression, as well as the pain of separation from their husbands as a result of unjust immigration laws and policies (Shi Jianping 2011).

Notes

1 *Qiaokan* were local magazines produced by clans, communities, or other bodies in the Chinese immigrants' sending places. They were sponsored by the migrants and distributed among migrants and their families and communities.
2 Yuemu wushi gei nüxu Chen Zhongbo de xin" [Chen Zhongbo's mother-in-law to Chen Zhongbo] (22 March 1939). No. Luo 1.2–51, Luo Daquan Collection.
3 Chen Hua'an's letter to Chen Zhongbo (29 March 1938). No. Luo 1.2–116, Luo Daquan Collection.
4 "Chen Hua'an gei Chen Zhongbo de xin" [Chen Hua'an's letter to Chen Zhongbo] (seventh day of the second lunar month, 1939). No. Luo 1.2–81, Luo Daquan's Collection. The date was 27 March 1939, according to the solar calendar.
5 Ibid.
6 "Chen Shuntong gei Chen Zhongbo de xin" [Chen Shuntong's letter to Chen Zhongbo] (14 July, 1939). No. Luo 1.2–88, Luo Daquan Collection.
7 "Chen Zhengze gei Chen Zhongbo de xin" [Chen Zhengze's letter to Chen Zhongbo] (date unknown). No. Luo 1.2–83, Luo Daquan Collection.
8 "Chen Hua'an gei Chen Zhongbo de xin" [Chen Hua'an's letter to Chen Zhongbo] (seventh day of the second lunar month, 1939). No. Luo 1.2–81, Luo Daquan Collection.
9 "Chen Hua'an gei Chen Zhongbo de xin" [Chen Hua'an's letter to Chen Zhongbo] (fourth day of the sixth lunar month, 1939). No. Luo 1.2–50, Luo Daquan Collection.
10 "Chen Jingtang gei Chen Zhongbo de xin" [Chen Jingtang's letter to Chen Zhongbo] (22 June 1939). No. Luo 1.2–142, Luo Daquan Collection.
11 "Chen Hua'an gei Chen Zhongbo de xin" [Chen Hua'an's letter to Chen Zhongbo] (seventh day of the second lunar month, 1939). No. Luo 1.2–81, Luo Daquan Collection.
12 Ibid.
13 Ibid.
14 "Chen Shuntong gei Chen Zhongbo de xin" [Chen Shuntong's letter to Chen Zhongbo] (14 July 1939). No. Luo 1.2–88, Luo Daquan Collection.
15 "Wenzuan, Guodong, Jiongjian he Zhengbing gei Chen Zhongbo de xin" [Wenzuan, Guodong, Jiongjian, and Zhengbing's letter to Chen Zhongbo] (5 October 1935). No. Luo 1.2–114, Luo Daquan Collection.
16 "Chen Hua'an gei Chen Zhongbo de xin" [Chen Hua'an's letter to Chen Zhongbo] (fourth day of the sixth lunar month, 1939). No. Luo 1.2–50, Luo Daquan Collection.
17 "Chen Hua'an gei Chen Zhongbo de xin" [Chen Hua'an's letter to Chen Zhongbo] (seventh day of the second lunar month, 1939). No. Luo 1.2–81, Luo Daquan Collection.
18 Ibid.
19 "Chen Hua'an gei Chen Zhongbo de xin" [Chen Hua'an's letter to Chen Zhongbo] (seventh day of the second lunar month, 1939). No. Luo 1.2–81, Luo Daquan Collection.
20 Ibid.
21 "Chen Hua'an gei Chen Zhongbo de xin" [Chen Hua'an's letter to Chen Zhongbo] (seventh day of the second lunar month, 1939). No. Luo 1.2–81, Luo Daquan Collection.
22 "Chen Hua'an gei Chen Zhongbo de xin" [Chen Hua'an's letter to Chen Zhongbo] (fourth day of the sixth lunar month, 1939). No. Luo 1.2–50, Luo Daquan Collection.
23 "Chen Hua'an gei Chen Zhongbo de xin" [Chen Hua'an's letter to Chen Zhongbo] (fifth day of the twelfth lunar month, 1939). No. Luo 1.2–112, Luo Daquan Collection.
24 "Chen Hua'an gei Chen Jinming de xin" [Chen Hua'an's letter to Chen Jinming] (seventh day of the first lunar month, 1939). No. Luo 1.2–107, Luo Daquan Collection.
25 "Chen Hua'an gei Chen Zhongbo de xin" [Chen Hua'an's letter to Chen Zhongbo] (tenth day of the fifth lunar month, 1939). No. Luo 1.2–77, Luo Daquan Collection. The date was 26 June, according to the solar calendar.
26 "Chen Hua'an gei Chen Zhongbo de xin" [Chen Hua'an's letter to Chen Zhongbo] (sixth day of the eleventh lunar month). No. Luo 1.2–113, Luo Daquan Collection.
27 "Wenzuan, Guodong, Jiongjian he Zhengbing gei Chen Zhongbo de xin" [Wenzuan, Guodong, Jiongjian, and Zhengbing's letter to Chen Zhongbo] (5 October 1935). No. Luo 1.2–114, Luo Daquan Collection.

28 "Chen Zhang shi gei Chen Zhongbo de xin" [Ms Zhang's letter to Chen Zhongbo] (29 March 1938). No. Luo 1.2–116, Luo Daquan Collection.
29 "Chen Zhang shi gei Chen Zhongbo de xin" [Ms Zhang's letter to Chen Zhongbo] (fourteenth day of the fifth lunar month). No. Luo 1.2–150, Luo Daquan Collection.
30 "Chen Zhang shi gei Chen Zhongbo de xin" [Ms Zhang's letter to Chen Zhongbo] (8 January 1947). No. Luo 1.2–150, Luo Daquan Collection.
31 "Tianyi gei Chen Jinming de xin" [Tianyi's letter to Chen Jinming] (25 December 1946). No. Luo 1.2–70, Luo Daquan Collection.
32 "Chen Hongzhuang zhi Chen Yilin xin" [Chen Hongzhuang's letter to Chen Yilin] (third day of the twelfth month, 1921). Wuyi Overseas Chinese Museum, Jiangmen.
33 "Chen Hongzhen zhi Chen Yilin xin" [Chen Hongzhen's letter to Chen Yilin]. Wuyi Overseas Chinese Museum, Jiangmen.

References

Beikeng yuebao 北坑月报. 1947. August. "Siyi zai shizi jietou" 四邑在十字街头 [Siyi at the crossroads], 21: 25. 台山档案馆 Taishan Archives: 1–7–143.

Chen Yuanzhu 陈元柱. 1929. "*Taishan geyaoji*" 台山歌谣集 [Taishan ballads]. 台山档案馆 Taishan Archives: 1–7–238.

Lao Xiang 老乡. 1947. "Huangjin Waibi Zhuangshi xia de Taishan" 黄金外币装饰下的台山 [Taishan decorated by gold and foreign currency]. In Siyi Youth's Association, ed., *Siyi qingnian* 四邑青年 [Siyi's Youth], 1: 5–6.

Rusheng yuekan 溽声月刊. 1948. "Fuxu qiaowai sanshi nian bugui, jinshan po kuyi cheng chi" 夫婿侨外卅年不归，金山婆苦忆成痴 [Gold Mountain Guest away for thirty years, his wife mad for missing him too much], 8: 15. 台山档案馆 Taishan Archives: 1–2–14.

Shi Jianping 石坚平. 2011. "Guoji yimin yu hunyin jiya – yi zhanhou siyi Qiaoxiang weili de tantao" 国际移民与婚姻挤压 – 以战后四邑侨乡为例的探讨 [Marriage squeeze in overseas Chinese hometown of Siyi and remedies after WW II]. *Huaqiao-Huaren lishi yanjiu* 华侨华人历史研究 [Overseas Chinese History Studies], 4.

Taishan zhixiaoduqin yuekan 台山至孝笃亲月刊 [Taishan Filial Piety Monthly]. 1948: 45.

Taishan zhixiaoduqin yuekan 台山至孝笃亲月刊. 1948. "Chen Yanhua Chonghun an fayuan panxing liangnian, zhunyu liyi bu shenghuofei yiyuan" [Chen Yanhua sentenced to two years' imprisonment for bigamy, granted divorce with liability to pay 100 million yuan for his wife's living expenses], 41.

Xinning zazhi 新宁杂志. 1922. "Jinshan po kuochuo" 金山婆阔绰 [Gold Mountain guests' wives are wealthy], 25: 36.

Xinning zazhi 新宁杂志. 1928. "Jinzhi maimai hunyin" 禁止买卖婚姻 [Forbidding mercenary marriage], 20: 80–81.

Ziyang yuekan 紫阳月刊 [Ziyang monthly]. 1930. 10 December. 27: 67–68.

Ziyang yuekan 紫阳月刊. 1930. 10 December. "Sun Zongli yuanpei Lu furen han Wu Yinjiang qing shefa chaqi beiguai xiaotong, beiguai xiaotong xi lao tongzhi Zhang Jingqing zi" [Mr Sun Yat-sen's first wife's Letter to Wu Yinjiang appealing for an thorough investigation into the kidnap of Comrade Zhang Jingqing's son], 27: 80–82.

8 *Jinxin*

The remittance trade and enterprising Chinese Australians, 1850–1916

Mei-fen Kuo

In the last few decades, more than 160,000 remittance documents have been found and preserved in Guangdong and Fujian, as part of the *qiaopi* and *yinxin* project.[1] The recovery of these documents is important for empirical studies focusing attention on the historical development and social-economic impact of the Chinese remittance network. Remittances have been credited with helping to rectify China's international balance of payments, modernizing industry and commerce in Fujian and Guangdong, institutionalizing the remittance trade, and strengthening the transnational networks of Chinese families (Yao 1943; Lin 1987; Du 1995; Dai 2003; Chen 2008; Liu 2009; Chen 2010).

Most importantly, studies on Chinese remittances demonstrate that the Chinese approach to organising remittances was different from the remittance behaviour of English-speaking immigrants, who favoured the use of money orders and telegraphic transfers by individuals (Magee and Thompson 2006, 179–180). In Chinese remittance networks, local Chinese merchants, clan associations, mobile brokers, bankers, postmasters, and interpreters collaborated through various channels. Thus, a "social network" approach has been employed in *qiaopi* and *yinxin* studies to explain how economic behaviour was constructed and reconstructed locally and internationally by social associations (Chen 2000; Hsu 2000; Dai 2003; Chen 2008; Hamashita 2008; Liu and Li 2011; Benton and Liu 2015; Harris 2015). Rather than focus on self-interest and profit-seeking, the interrelationship between the growth of the remittance business and social associations is often implicit in the success of the former.

This chapter follows the same characterization of Chinese remittance network but asks how the world economy functionally influenced the Chinese approach to organizing the remittance business beyond social associations and cultural pursuits. It focuses on the Chinese Australian remittance trade in a world economy enhanced by gold output. Chinese Australian remittances have barely figured in *qiaopi* and *yinxin* studies, due to the limited amount of surviving remittance documents. By examining the remittance networks of Chinese Australians from the late nineteenth century through to 1916, this chapter argues that cultural pursuits and social-networks cannot adequately explain the Chinese Australian remittance trade, and that one must look beyond that to the emergence of Australian economic power in the Pacific region. It also discusses the impact of remittance networks and practices on enterprising Chinese Australians. *Jinxin* 金信 reflect the transformation of Chinese immigrants from gold diggers to trans-local capitalists at a time when the world economy was undergoing fundamental changes.

Jinxin and native-place networks starting in 1850

By analysing local Chinese newspapers, personal letters, company records, and Australian national archives, this chapter revives the name *jinxin*, which Chinese Australians used to describe their remittances. (*Jin* 金 means gold or gold sovereign, *xin* 信 means letter.) From 1850 up until the First World War, Chinese Australians usually transmitted gold sovereigns and gold dust together with their letters with the help of Chinese shippers, brokers, and merchants in the local towns and cities of Australia. Chinese merchants placed *jinxin* in the *jinxiang* 金箱 remittance boxes) together with other goods exported to Hong Kong and South China by British and Japanese steamers.[2] Non-commercial remittances were often first sent to Hong Kong, where the gold was exchanged for money, or used to purchase specified goods, which were then sent on to places in South China.

Although the name *jinxin* seems not to have appeared in documents before the late nineteenth century, sending sovereigns can be traced back to the Australian gold-rush period. Australia was a central motor of the worldwide gold boom in the second half of the nineteenth century (Bryan 2010, 27). After 1850, most Chinese first went to Australia's gold fields, where their numbers peaked at around 40,000. Wells Williams (1856, 162) stated that considerable amounts of gold were received in Guangzhou from Chinese in Australia and California.[3] Available records suggest that Chinese in Australia remitted 3,500,000 sovereigns in the period 1854–1870 (Chang 2008, 455).

Starting in the 1850s, Louis Ah Mouy (1826–1918) and Lowe Kong Meng (1831–1888) were the two main Chinese labour brokers as well as the two main gold exporters from Victoria to Asia (Macgregor 2012). They also dominated the early Chinese Australian remittance trade,[4] which was linked to Chinese native-place associations (Macgregor 2015, 73). Lowe Kong Meng established the Num Pon Soon Association 南番顺会馆 (the three counties of Sam Yup) while Ah Mouy helped to fund the Melbourne See Yup (Siyi) Association 四邑会馆. Starting in the mid-nineteenth century, the See Yup Association conducted the remittance trade, relieved poor and sick members, helped migrants save, bought them steamship tickets, and sent mail on their behalf.[5]

The link between Chinese gold export and native-place associations in the remittance business was a result of the credit-ticket system. Eighty per cent of Cantonese labourers on the Victorian goldfields in the 1850s were indebted labourers (Yong 1977, 1; Wang 1978, 90) who had purchased their steamship tickets in shops in China, with the support of family or friends. The tickets were issued under unwritten contracts supported by an arrangement between the migrants' local connections and international networks of Chinese firms in Hong

Kong and Australia. Native-place associations in Australia sent the initial remittance on behalf of miners to repay their debts to relatives and friends. Native-place associations also saved on behalf of their members up to the point where they had accumulated enough to transfer sums back to relatives and friends.[6]

After gold production declined in the 1860s, Chinese moved into market gardening and other occupations in the gold towns (Curthoys 2001, 115–116; Frost 2002, 117–119). A remittance ledger of Mew Chip Co. 刘妙捷记, a Chinese firm in the gold town of Tambaroora in New South Wales, confirms that Chinese Australians constantly remitted sovereigns and gold dust through personal channels in the 1860s and the 1870s, in association with relatives and friends.[7] The ledger indicates a growing remittance network in the 1880s among Chinese firms in local towns in Australia and between Sydney and Shekki in Guangdong. Mew Chip's main partners in Sydney in this remittance business were Tin War, On Yik Lee, and Gee Ick, from Zhongshan.

The emergence of remittance networks after the 1880s was rooted in commercial developments in Sydney. Between the 1870s and the 1890s, Australia reached a per capita income higher than that of any other country due to its adherence to the gold standard, its incorporated banking system, and its monetary technology (Butlin 1962; Maddison 1995; McLean 2007). In the last two decades of the nineteenth century Australia had begun to urbanize at a rapid rate, especially in Melbourne and Sydney (Powell 1988, 23). At the same time Sydney, already home to many Chinese in Australia, developed into a hub of the Chinese Australian remittance trade (Coghlan and Ewing 1903, 96; Yong 1977, 4; Wang 1978, 208–211; Fitzgerald 1997, 23).

On the eve of the 1880s On Chong 安昌号, Way Kee 维记号, On Yik Lee 安益利号, Tiy Loy 泰来, and Wah Hing 和兴 already engaged in the *jinxin* business in metropolitan Sydney. To aid their business, they helped establish native-place associations in the city. Interpersonal collaboration and kin-based ownership played an important role in the elaboration of an economic strategy for competing with European and British companies.

On Chong started out in the *jinxin* business in Sydney in 1865 (Chang 2008, 459). Between the late 1860s and the early twentieth century, On Chong operated a steamship that sailed between Sydney, Townsville, Hong Kong and China, and Butaritari in the Gilbert Islands, the only Chinese Australian firm to do so in the second half of the nineteenth century (Lydon 1999, 86; Willmott 2007, 9–20). Thomas Yee Hing (1860–1921) became On Chong's manager in the 1880s and maintained its prominence in Sydney. Yee Hing was described in an 1891 Royal Commission report as a straight, upright, and honest man, who was at the fore in every worthy cause and social movement at the time (New South Wales Royal Commission Report 1892, 479).

Another Chinese remittance firm was established in 1871 by Way Kee (1824–1892), who testified to the Royal Commission that his business had four branches in rural New South Wales (in Bega, Bourke, Stanthorpe, and Hillston) and that these expansions had happened on the basis of family and clan or native-place relationships. Way Kee said that he helped his fellow countrymen remit money back to China, and claimed to have remitted more than £10,000 in 1890 (New South Wales Royal Commission Report 1892, Q2125–2127). Way Kee helped to establish native-place societies such as the Koong Yee Tong in 1875 (it had 600 Chinese members from Dongguan) and Loong Yee Tong (a joint Association for migrants from Dongguan and Zhengcheng). Loong Yee Tong's main object was to collect money to "put coffins on board ships passing to and from China".[8] The success of his operation is a good illustration of the close link in the Chinese community between commercial transactions and clan or native-place activities.

Another association, the Hung Fook Tong, was established by two Chinese firms, Tiy Loy and Wah Hing, to support the Gaoyao Chinese. Its services included remittance and the dispatch of letters (Stephen 1997, 10). The On Yik Lee was founded by William Robert George Lee (1844–1911) in 1879, who had previously been a remittance broker. On Yik Lee ran a steamer ticketing agency, a boarding house, and a private bank. In late 1891, W. R. G. Lee and eight other Chinese merchants established the Lin Yik Tong 聯益堂 as a commercial agency that dealt initially with the Gibbs, Bright, and Co. shipping company.[9] Lin Yik Tong's structure was similar to that of a guild. In it, two representatives from each of the eight firms managed its business for a term of three months, and each representative received £10 a year (Kuo 2013, 37). One reason for establishing the Lin Yik Tong was so that its constituent firms could dominate the *jinxin* industry.

In 1897, the Lin Yik Tong became an agent for several steamships and eventually became the only Chinese immigrant agent in Sydney (Kuo 2013, 38). *Jinxin* was one of its services. Lin Yik Tong took 7.5 pence in commission on each remittance – Chinese firms in Australia received only 2.5 pence of this commission fee, while the Lin Yik Tong received the other 5 pence.[10] Its trading capital was between £600,000 and £800,000. The Lin Yik Tong claimed that, in line with its philanthropic functions, part of this sum went to charity.

1890s: *jinxin* beyond native-place associations

Before 1890, the Chinese Australian remittance trade had operated within native-place networks and associations. However, in the last decade of the nineteenth century, the *jinxin* trade was growing along with Australia's urbanization and healthy economy, Sydney's commercial developments, and the currency exchange market. By the end of the nineteenth century, Sydney had become the fourth largest seaport in the British Empire (Coghlan and Ewing 1903, 185 and 447). At the same time, Sydney's commercial development and social transformation in the 1890s gradually impelled Chinese immigrants to seek alternative forms of enterprise better suited to the new environment. The number of Chinese storekeepers and traders in metropolitan Sydney had reached 394 (799 in New South Wales in total, see Yong 1977, 264) by 1901. Many with only a small amount of capital began to work together and moved out of their earlier occupations, as miners and labourers, to emerge as traders, storekeepers, cabinet makers, laundry operators, and restaurant owners, usually in competition with other Australians (Wang 1978; Collins 2002, 115–116). An official report from the Chinese Consul-General in Singapore, who visited Australia in 1902, confirmed that the largest Chinese Australian communities were in Sydney and Melbourne. The report also noted that Sydney had the largest number of Chinese engaged in commerce and trade.[11]

More Chinese traders and storekeepers entered the remittance trade on the eve of the twentieth century. Transferring remittances in the form of sovereigns and gold dust through Chinese brokers and firms was still the primary channel. This did not mean that mail and telegram remittance was unavailable. However, such forms of remittance happened on a smaller scale.[12] A customer of On Yik Lee explained his remittance behaviour. He saved one thousand pounds in On Yik Lee because On Yik Lee was a trustworthy firm.[13] He stated that he trusted Chinese firms and traders more than he trusted Australian banking institutions and the Post Office, and that he appreciated the convenient and flexible service provided by Chinese firms.

Apart from remittance behaviour on the part of Chinese customers favouring Chinese firms, increased routes between Australia and Hong Kong also enhanced remittances in the form of gold exports. British owned vessels dominated Australia's overseas shipping routes in the nineteenth century. However, in 1896 the Japanese steamship company Nippon Yusen Kaisha set up an Australian route, and made its first voyage in October. Japanese and British vessels started competing in the Pacific region (Sawa 1943, 27). It could be argued that the Japanese vessels led to an increase in the Chinese remittance trade after 1897.

Chinese Australian remittance practices still favoured sending sovereigns and gold dust, also because more and more Chinese Australians became aware of the rise of the gold sovereign on the foreign-exchange market. Sydney's two new Chinese newspapers, the *Chinese Australian Herald* (*CAH*, 1894–1923) and the *Tung Wah News* (*TWN*, 1898–1937; changed to *Tung Wah Times* (*TWT*) in 1902), started to report regularly on the gold exchange rate in Hong Kong and the volume of gold exports to Hong Kong from Australia grew in the late 1890s. These newspapers reported that big profits could be made on Hong Kong's exchange market.[14] The exchange rate of gold to silver in the global market in the last decade of nineteenth century went from 19.75 in 1890 to 39.15 in 1902.[15] From 1898 through to the late 1910s, Chinese firms in Sydney, Melbourne, and Brisbane advertised the *jinxin* business (see Appendix 8.1). The scale and network of the Chinese Australian remittance trade included Chinese stores in Australian towns and cities as well as Chinese firms in New Zealand, Annam, Hong Kong, and San Francisco that carried out *jinxin* business.[16]

The increase in the remittance trade also led to new innovatory business practices. Sydney authorities had noticed the large volume of the Chinese remittance trade. In 1898, the Sydney authorities did away with Chinese deliverers and switched to using public transport to deliver *jinxiang* to the steamship companies.[17] The Sydney police claimed that public transportation would enable Chinese deliverers to avoid robbery. At the same time, Chinese remittance firms adopted new services to attract their customers as well as to ensure the safety and efficiency of the remittance process. For example, On Yik Lee started insuring remittances in order to enhance customer confidence.[18] It also sent remittance receipts back to remitters in Australia free of charge.[19]

Jinxin and gold output after the 1890s

The emergence of the *jinxin* phenomenon cannot be adequately explained in absence from the rise of Australian economic power in the 1890s. Australia's economic health, together with British imperial power, had benefited Chinese Australian remittances on the currency exchange market. Colonial Australia and the Commonwealth of Australia after 1901 had complied with London's adherence to the gold standard on the exchange market.

From 1896 to 1913, the world economy, including Britain, underwent a fundamental change due to the increase in global gold production, monetary expansion, and technological changes (Hobsbawm 2005, 168–171; Bryan 2010, 27). However, not every country benefited. From 1894 to 1911, the Chinese Haikwan tael lost in value in relation to the Chinese silver standard (Hsiao 1974, 189–192; Li 2010, 236–240). The declining value of silver was bad for those American traders that traded in silver. American Consulates in South China suggested that the declining value of silver starting in from 1894 was adversely affecting the US export trade in the Chinese Treaty Ports (*Los Angeles Herald*, 26 December 1908, 2). At the same time the idea of the gold standard as a modern, scientific system and its association with the status of a first-class nation influenced Japan's switch to the gold standard in the late 1890s (Bryan 2010, 153–159).

Takeshi Hamashita argues that the Chinese remittance network in Asia needs to be considered within a broad framework formed by financial systems and currency exchange markets. Because China's currency system was based on silver until 1935, Hong Kong bimetallism had benefited Chinese and foreign traders, who were able to sell gold for cash, and its high exchange rate allowed for an additional profit (Hamashita 2008; Chapter 3 of this book). Chinese Australian traders were also aware of the commercial opportunities in Hong Kong.

In 1892, gold was again discovered in Australia and caused another economic boom starting in 1894, at the same time as gold exports from San Francisco began to decline (Denzel 2010, 441). New South Wales alone sent £113,791 in gold to Hong Kong in 1894, rising to £179,476 in 1899 (NSW Statistical Register 1895, 1897, and 1900). During this period, Sydney Chinese newspapers recorded that Chinese sent gold to Hong Kong and China with a value of between £5,500 and £7,200 every month, although no precise statistics are available.

After the formation of the Australian Federation, the amount of gold exported to Hong Kong and China was as follows (see Table 8.1):

These statistics do not reveal the identity of the shippers, but Australian newspapers said the main exporters of gold to Hong Kong were Chinese, especially

Table 8.1 The amount of gold exported to Hong Kong and China

Year	*To Hong Kong*	*To China*	*Year*	*To Hong Kong*	*To China*
1903	279,923	15,289	1910	431,846	18,280
1904	336,484	15,870	1911	466,657	22,155
1905	329,250	54,000	1912	615,053	27,587
1906	360,616	6,100	1913	575,038	47,593
1907	397,522	11,940	1914–1915	380,729	13,000
1908	460,276	15,702	1915–1916	16,797	4,300
1909	385,056	30,402	Total	5,035,247	282,218

Sources: *Annual Statements of the Trade of the Commonwealth*, 1903, 1904, and 1905. *Trade and Customs and Excise Revenue of the Commonwealth of Australia*, 1906–1917.

Note
Value in gold sovereign (£1 in 1901 was worth $119 in 2007).

Sydney Chinese.[20] The amounts mentioned in the Sydney English newspapers were even higher than those recorded in official statistics. The report of the first Chinese Consul-General for Australia in 1909 on the commerce and industry of Chinese immigrants in Australia also confirmed that gold was the main article of export to Hong Kong and China in the first decade of the twentieth century.[21] As no information on remitters was given, it is impossible to separate commercial from non-commercial remittances. However, some capital was devoted to trade and investment, as discussed in the following section.

The Commonwealth Bank was inaugurated in January 1913, and became Australia's de facto central bank after the outbreak of the First World War. Chinese gold exports from Australia were targeted by the Australian Commonwealth Government in 1914. References to an unduly large amount of gold exports to Hong Kong and China were made in the Australian Parliament in late 1914.[22] In the three weeks up to 14 December, gold to the value of £48,562 was exported from Sydney.[23] Gold exports to Hong Kong and China were limited under the Customs Act to £50 per person in July 1915 – the prohibition took effect in 1916.[24] A lifting of the prohibition saw the amount allowed reduced to 20 sovereigns in the early 1920s (Cornish and Coleman 2014). This led to the transfer of remittances to mail and telegram after 1916.

Jinxin and the building of modern enterprise in the early twentieth century

The impact of gold exports on the Chinese Australian remittance trade in the period up to 1916 has not yet been analysed in the scholarly literature. Chinese Australian remittances of gold sovereigns and gold dust led to an increase in capital flows to new enterprises in Hong Kong, including the so-called gold mountain firms *jinshan zhuang* 金山庄 and modern department stores, which were said (anecdotally) to derive most of their finance from Chinese Australians (Yen 1998, 59). Lin and Zhuang (1985), Williams (2002, 87), and Pei (2013) show that Sincere Co. and Wing On Co. derived much of their capital from the remittance trade. Chinese Australians dominated investment in department stores in Shanghai too before 1919 (Lin 1982). The first managing director of the Wing On Department Store in Shanghai was George Bew 郭标 (1867–1932), who was also managing director and founder of Wing Sang in Sydney. Mainly as a result of Bew's efforts, the paid-up capital from Australia deposited in Shanghai's Wing On was HK$500,000.[25]

The remittance network enabled overseas Chinese merchants to circulate capital in order to expand their enterprises. Wing Sang Co. in Sydney was the most prominent Chinese Australian case. Wing Sang Co was founded by George Bew, Choy Hing 蔡兴, Ma Yin Piu 马应彪 (1868–1944), and Mar Young 马祖容.[26] Wing Sang's founders also founded Sincere Co., Wing On Co., and Sun Co. in Hong Kong and Shanghai in the first decades of the twentieth century. George Bew was managing director of Wing Sang Co. until late 1917, when he moved to Shanghai to manage the newly opened Wing On Department Store.

The Wing Sang Co. shows that Chinese Australian merchants did not establish remittance houses of the sort common in Southeast Asia. The Chinese Australian remittance trade was similar in many respects to California's *jinshan zhuang*. The *jinshan zhuang* model was strengthened by connections and partnerships with Chinese firms in the Pacific ports of Hong Kong and Guangdong (Williams 1856; Sinn 2013, 175–179; Lee 2015).

The remittance network formed by the *jinshshan zhuang* allowed for a flow of capital for investment in other enterprises. For example, it helped the Hong Kong entrepreneur Ma Tsui Chiu, a Taishanese who had returned to China from the US, to expand his business in Hong Kong and South China in the early twentieth century, including financial institutions like the Dahua Bank and Cheong Wah Co. Ltd (Lee 2015, 170–175). Lee also argued that Ma's international remittance network and capital enabled him to enhance his credit from foreign banks.

The *jinshan zhuang* model was also adopted by Chinese merchants in Sydney. For example, Ma Yin Piu, a founder of Wing Sang, opened the Wing Chong Tai 永昌泰 gold mountain firm in Hong Kong in 1894.[27] It was also a basis for the expansion of Wing Sang in Hong Kong. Another gold mountain firm in Hong Kong, War Hing 华信, was also engaged in a partnership with Wing Sang. (Its manager was George Bew's father-in-law.[28]) Both these gold mountain firms were active in the remittance trade. Their involvement helped Ma Yin Piu establish the Sincere Co., which was registered in Hong Kong in 1900. Six of its twelve shareholders were Chinese from Australia. When Sincere Co celebrated its twenty-fifth anniversary, Wing Sang was mentioned as an ideal business model.[29]

In Australia, the banana and fruit trade are seen as Wing Sang's cornerstone (Yen 1998, 50–51). Wing Sang was also sustained by remittance and investment by Chinese Australians in the first decades of the twentieth century. Wing Sang and other Zhongshan Chinese traders had established a network with Chinese firms in Shekki, a favoured zone for currency exchange (Lin and Zhuang 1985, 91). The Mew Chip ledger shows that Chinese firms in Shekki were already getting remittances from Australia as early as the 1880s. Another example of the network between Sydney and Shekki was Shekki's War Hing Cheong remittance house, which regularly published advertisements in Sydney to attract Chinese Australians customers. It also indicated that it had partner firms in Sydney and Hong Kong.[30] Appendix 8.1 shows that several remittance houses and firms in Shekki acted as remittance agents on behalf of Chinese Australians.

Chinese remittance traders benefited from currency exchange in Shekki, which was highly profitable. The profits from the exchange market led Chinese Australian merchants to establish currency exchange businesses in Hong Kong and Shekki after 1911 (see below). Remittance and currency exchange gave Chinese Australian merchants access to more working capital. Normally, Chinese Australian firms transferred money to the recipients within three months of receiving the remittance.[31] The time it took to transfer remittances made it possible for Chinese merchants to await better exchange rates and thus to enhance the flow of capital flow into their other businesses.

Lipton (2007, 829) argues that the high per capital income and wide distribution of wealth in Australian colonial society encouraged entrepreneurship and innovation. It also benefited incorporation among Chinese Australians. In 1902 Wing Sang, Wing On, and Wing Tiy amalgamated to form Sang On Tiy and Co. to cultivate and ship bananas from Fiji to Sydney at a rate of at least 2,000 bunches a week (Yong 1977, 50; Ali 2002). The chairman of the New South Wales Fruit Exchange, Thomas Jessep, confirmed that at the turn of the century control of the Queensland banana trade lay firmly in Chinese hands (Royal Commission on Customs and Excise 1906–1907, IV, 849). George Bew proclaimed that his business had increased to the value of £4,000 by 1903.[32] Entry into the Fiji banana trade was a milestone for Wing Sang and Wing On. The firm also became an agent for remittances by Chinese in Fiji. The increase in the remittance trade also improved the credit-worthiness of Chinese merchants when applying for bank loans (Gock 1949, 5).

The remittance network and the concomitant increase in investment and innovation enabled Wing Sang and Wing On to expand beyond fruit exporting. On 16 November 1902, in Wing On and Co.'s shop, a meeting was called to help Warley Chan Harr raise capital to build a department store, Warley and Co. 和利有限公司, in Hong Kong. This meeting succeeded in attracting thirty-eight Chinese shareholders (including Wing Sang) to the new company. Yong (1977, 55) flags this as the first attempt by Chinese Australians to start a new style of business in Hong Kong. In the early twentieth century the trade between Australia, Hong Kong, and China, for example, doubled between 1906 and 1907, from £222,790 to £416,441, and gold exports to Hong Kong and China grew from £366,716 to £409,462.

In 1908, Wing Sang established the Li Man Hing Kwok Weaving and Manufacturing Co. 利民兴国织造有限公司 in Hong Kong.[33] Wing Sang also became the agent for other investments in Hong Kong, South China, and Singapore, including the Commercial Press, Chinese and European Fire Marine and Life Insurance, the Bank of Mexico, the China Aviation Industry Corporation, the Xinghua noodle factory in Shanghai, the Chung Wah soft drinks company in Singapore, and the China-Australia Steamship Co.[34]

Wing On Company in Sydney also became an important investor in the Wing On Department Store in Shanghai. In 1908, one of Wing Sang's directors, Ma Joe Young, travelled back to Hong Kong (*Tung Wah Times*, 7 March 1908, 2) with seventeen boxes of gold worth £22,680, some of which was invested in Wing On in Hong Kong (Gock Chin 郭泉 1961, 29–33). When Wing On's department store was newly opened in Shanghai in 1917, about HK$500,000 was given from Australia and Fiji due to Wing Sang's efforts.[35]

Apart from the new enterprises in the form of manufacturing and department stores, Wing On and Wing Sang also established remittance bureaus in Shekki and Hong Kong after 1910 (Shanghai Academy of Social Science 1981, 8–9).[36] Chinese Australians' remittance bureaus controlled more than 80 per cent of the remittance trade in Zhongshan (Lin and Zhuang 1985, 91; Pei 2013). By 1914, Wing Sang's partners in Hong Kong had established Sincere Insurance Co. and Wing On Insurance Co., which dealt in remittances and investments (Gock 1949, 8–9; Yen 2013, 431). Investment in banking promised to be a sound proposition, since it supported the extension of the department store business (Gock 1949, 13–17; Norton 1970, 34; Yen 2013, 430–431). Starting in 1917, the Sincere and Wing On Department Stores began to deal in remittance in Shanghai on behalf of Chinese Australians.[37] In 1921 the Wing On Department Store set up a banking department to engage in remittance and currency exchange.

To extend and maintain its business in Hong Kong and China, Wing Sang in Hong Kong was registered as a limited liability company in 1919. Its directors were the former managers of Sydney Wing Sang.[38] In 1921, Hong Kong Wing Sang became the head office,[39] thus enabling Sydney Wing Sang to invest and expand its business in Hong Kong and Shanghai and even in Singapore. By 1924, Sydney Wing Sang's paid-up capital had increased to £75,000,[40] and by 1928 it had multiplied to £253,500.[41] The partnership between Sydney Wing Sang and Hong Kong Wing Sang was maintained until the 1980s.[42]

Conclusion

In the absence of an adequate cache of remittance documents, this chapter recovers the history of Chinese Australian remittances through an analysis of newspapers and private letters of the time and of Australian archives. Starting in the mid-nineteenth century, Chinese brokers and traders helped miners and labourers to send gold sovereigns and dust home with the help of native-place associations. Chinese Australian remittances were described as *jinxin* and in the early days the trade in many respects resembled California's *jinshan zhuang*.

By the 1860s, the Chinese Australian remittance trade had reformed itself in ways that transcended the *jinshan zhuang* model. From the late nineteenth century through to 1916, Chinese Australians continued to prefer to send wealth back to China in the form of gold sovereigns and gold dust, while gold exports from San Francisco were on the decline. At the same time, the world economy, including the Australian economy, underwent a fundamental change due to the increase in gold production, monetary expansion, and technological transformation.

As a central motor of the worldwide gold boom, Australia enjoyed the benefits of these developments. Its economic rise aided the flowering of the Sydney Chinese remittance trade between 1890 and 1916. At the same time, the increasing amount of working capital in Chinese Australian hands enabled the transformation of members of this group from gold mining labourers and market gardeners into trans-local capitalists. Their remittance business enhanced trade between Australia, Hong Kong, and China.

The *jinxin* trade from 1850 through to the early twentieth century mirrored the trajectory of Chinese diasporic enterprise in Australia, as influenced by gold output in the world economy. An important feature of this trade was its recycling of profits in the form of investment. Wing Sang was a remittance firm that eventually blossomed as an international investor and trader in Australia, Fiji, Hong Kong, and Shanghai between 1890 and the early twentieth century. Its experience shows how the accruement of capital led to innovation and to the strengthening of Chinese Australian enterprise in the early twentieth century.

Appendix 8.1

Appendix 8.1 Chinese Australian firms for remittance service, 1890s–1910s

City	*Names*	*Partner firms in HK/Sekki and Guangdoang*
Sydney	On Chong and Co. 安昌	N/A
	Way Kee and Co. 维记	N/A
	On Yik Lee and Co. 安益利	HK: Kong Shing Lee 江盛 Gudu: *Hui He Hao* 汇和号 Shekki: *Yuan Li Yinhao* 元利银号
	Hop War and Co. 合和号	Hong Kong: Hop Woo Chan 合和栈 Sekkei: *He Xing Chang* 和兴昌 Macau: Chung Woo 中和银铺
	S. G. S. Dockson 新昌盛	HK: Hook Wo Fong 福和昌, Yuet Cheung Cung 悦昌隆, Yue Kee Chan 裕记栈, *Bao Sheng Chang* 保生昌 Sekki: *Fu he cheng* 福和盛, *Sheng chang* 生昌 Gud: *Wushi xuzi lianhe yinhao* 乌石墟仔联合银号
	Kwong Tiy War and Co. 广泰和	HK: *Zhao he xiang* 肇和祥 Shekki: *Yong an chang* 永安昌
	Wing On and Co. 永安	HK: Wing Chong Tai 永昌泰, Wing On 永安 Sekkei: *Hui yuan* 汇源
	Wing Sang and Co. 永生	HK: Wing Chong Tai 永昌泰, Wing Sang 永生 Shekki: *Hui yuan* 汇源, Sincere Insurance Co. 先施燕梳公司, Win On Co. 永安歧局
	Wing Tiy and Co. 永泰	HK: Wing Sang 永生 Shekki: *Hui yuan* 汇源
	Lee Sang and Co. 利生	HK: Ching Li Sang 正利生号
	Kwong Wing Chong and Co. 广荣昌	HK: Kung Foon Chan 恭宽栈, Lin Sang Chan 连牲栈, *Xin yuan li* 新源利

Note
Text in italics indicates author's translation.

City	*Names*	*Partner firms in HK/Sekki and Guangdoang*
	Kwong War Chong 广和昌	HK: Lin Sang Chan 连牲栈, Kwong Man Loong 广万隆Shekki: *Guang wan an* 广万安
	King Young 荣记	HK: *Xin heng yu* 新恒裕
	Wing Loong and Co. 和隆	HK: *Xie ji zhan* 写记栈 Shekki: *Shui fu li jiu ba lan* 水福利九八栏
	Wing War Hing and Co 永和兴	HK: Wing Tung Hing 永同兴 Shekki: *Yong tai long* 永泰隆
	Goon Ping 公平	HK: *Ji an baoxian gongsi* 济安保险公司
	Sun Hing Jang and Co. 新兴栈	HK: Kwong Tai Yuen 广泰源
	Hop Lee and Co. 合记	HK: Hing Fat 兴记
	Sun Sam Choy 新三才	N/A
	Kwong Mow On and Co. 广茂安	N/A
	Hing Chong and Co. 庆祥	N/A
	Sun Quong Hing and Co. 新广兴	N/A
	Quong Hing Chong 广兴昌	N/A
	Gee Ick and Co. 义益	N/A
	Quong Yun Chong 广源昌	N/A
	Goon Lee Shing 公利盛	N/A
	Mow War 茂和	N/A
	Wing Fung and Co. 永丰	N/A
	War Hing and Co. 和兴号	N/A
	War Hing Tiy and Co. 和兴泰	N/A
	Wing Wah Hing and Co. 永和兴	N/A
	Yuen Tiy Tong Kee 源泰同记	N/A
	King Hing and Co. 经兴号	N/A
Brisbane	On War Tai and Co. 安和泰	HK: *Fang you long* 芳佑隆 Shekki: *Sheng chang long* 生昌隆
	See War and Co. 泗和号	HK: Po Yuen 宝源, Hop Wo Chan 合和栈, Wing Sang 永生, Kwog Mow On 广茂安 Shekki: *Si he long* 泗和隆, *He xing chang* 和兴昌
	Ah Day 郑帝号	HK: Wing Sang 永生
	Juy Sun Chan and Co. 彩新栈	N/A
	Kwong Sing Chong and Co. 广兴昌	N/A
	S. Jueyow and Sons 孙祖佑	N/A
	Sun On Lee 萧安利	N/A
Cairns	Lee On Kee and Co. 李安记	HK: Wing Tung Hing 永同兴 Shekki: *Yong sheng* 永升
Darwin	C. Yam Yan and Co	HK: *Xin tong chang* 新同昌
Melbourne	Mouey Kee 妹记	N/A
	Mee Ching 美珍	N/A
	Foon Kee 宽记	Foon Wo Cheung 宽和祥
	Quong Mee Loong 广美隆	HK: Kwong Tai Lung 广泰隆
	Sun Goon Shing and Co. 新源盛	HK: Shan Yuen Shing 新源盛
	Sing Lee Lung 胜利隆	HK: *Sheng li chang* 胜利昌
	Quan Hang Shing 均恒盛	HK: Wing Cheong 永祥, Fuk Wo Cheung 福和昌
	Wing Hing Loong 永兴隆	N/A
	Quong Hie Shing 广泰盛	N/A
	Sun Man Tai 新南泰	N/A
	Leong Lee 两利	N/A
	Gee Cheong 怡昌号	N/A

Various sources: *Tung Wah News*, *Tung Wah Times*, *Chinese Australian Herald*, *Chinese Times*, *Chinese Republic News*, Archives of Chinese Consul-general in Melbourne.

Notes

1 Research for this chapter was supported by the Australian Research Council (DP DE15010152 – Enterprising Chinese Australians and the diaspora network). *Qiaopi* are basically defined as documents of "letters, reports, account books and remittance receipts" resulting from communication between Chinese emigrants overseas and their families in China. In 2013, the *qiaopi* and *Yinxin* project was officially registered under UNESCO's Memory of the World Program.

2 See various articles and advertisements in *Chinese Australian Herald* (Sydney, hereafter *CAH*), *Tung Wah News* (Sydney, hereafter *TWN*), *Tung Wah Times* (Sydney, hereafter *TWT*), *Chinese Times* (Melbourne, hereafter *CT*) and *Chinese Republic News* (Sydney, hereafter *CRN*) from 1894 to the 1920s. Commercial records of Wing Sang reflect that the name of *jinxin* was still used after the 1920s, see annual balance of Wing Sang and Co., no: 42–71, box 3 at Archives of City of Sydney.

3 Chinese in California remitted gold from 1856 to 1890 (see Sinn 2013, 175–179).

4 An advertisement by Ah Mouy Co. in 1894 indicated that remittance was its main commercial service. See the Chinese almanac from 1894, Public Record of Victoria: VPRS 30 Unit 1005 case 32/1895.

5 *A History of See Yup Society of Victoria Australia (1854–2004)*, 2009. Also see records of See Yup Society, no. 526–001–015, 526–001–016 and 526–001–017 in Noel Butlin Archives Centre, Australian National University.

6 See minutes records of Kong Chow Society, dated 17 July 1897, no. 526–01–0015–097 in Noel Butlin Archives Centre, Australian National University.

7 The owner was Mew Chip (or New Chip, 1847?–1937) from Zhangshan district. See Hodge (1986). Further information of this ledger see the website of Chinese Australian historical Society at http://chineseaustralianhistory.org/bew-chips-ledger/. I wish to thank Dr Michael Williams for drawing attention to the record.

8 Tung Wah Hospital in the name of the Loong Yee Tong. See Tung Wah Hospital archives, no. 182.1 A87.v1 00163 (2/5), Tung Wah Museum, Hong Kong. Also see "Report of the Royal Commission on Alleged Chinese Gambling and Immorality", Q.2104; 2724.

9 *CAH*, 21 December 1901, 5; and 5 April 1902, 6.

10 *CAH*, 7 June 1902, 5.

11 Diplomatic Archives: 02–13–008–02–061, Institute of Modern History, Academia Sinica, Taiwan.

12 See various Post Office Reports from 1884, in Sessional Papers at Hong Kong Government Report Online 1842–1941, http://sunzi.lib.hku.hk/hkgro/index.jsp (25 August 2015).

13 *CAH*, 13 September 1902, 5.

14 See the report of *CAH*, on 16 August 1899, 3; *TWN*, 13 September 1899, 3.

15 Historical exchange rate data see: www.measuringworth.com/datasets/gold/result.php (accessed 7 August 2015).

16 An almanac produced by the Chinese merchant Wong Yeng Louey in 1894 in Melbourne, Public Record of Victoria: VPRS 30 Unit 1005 case 32/1895.

17 *TWN*, 10 November 1898, 2.

18 *CAH*, 9 August 1896,7.

19 *CAH*, 30 October 1896, 8.

20 *Daily Commercial News and Shipping List* in Sydney published the information of gold export regularly from 1890. Available via Trove http://trove.nla.gov.au/newspaper?q= National Library of Australia.

21 Report dated 18 April 1909, Record of Chinese Consul-General for Australia, no. 522–002, Kuo Min Tang Society of Melbourne.

22 *Sydney Morning Herald*, 29 December 1914, 9.

23 *Sydney Morning Herald*, 21 December 1914, 11.

24 See the *Register*, 19 December 1914, 18. See Australian Custom Notice to masters and crews of vessels No. A. 137 dated 19 October 1916 also *Ballarart Star*, 7 February 1916, 2, *TWT*, 27 May 1916, 7.
25 *CRN*, 20 January 1917, 4. Shanghai Academy of Social Science (1981, 10–12).
26 SRC19038, City of Sydney Archives.
27 See "Xianshi gongshi gongsi ershiwu nian jingguosh" (A history of the founding of the Sincere Company), in Zheng Tianjian (ed.), *Xianshi gongsi ershiwu zhounian jiniance* (The Sincere Company Limited: Twenty fifth anniversary 1900–1924) (Hong Kong, Shangwu yinshuguan, 'Jizai' column), pp. 1–5.
28 *Chinese Australian Herald*, 25 September 1896, 4. Wing Chong Tai was listed its address at 126 Des Voeux Road West in Hong Kong in *International Chinese Business Directory 1913*.
29 "Twenty fifth anniversary of the Sincere Co., Ltd", 3–4; also see George Bew's letter, Hoover Institute.
30 *TWN*, 4 July 1900, 3.
31 See a letter to NSW Chinese Chamber of Commerce dated 14 September 1917, no. 526–01–0001, Noel Butlin Archives Centre, Australian National University.
32 SP244/2, N1950/2/3885, National Archives of Australia. Wing Sang gained control of the fruit market in Queensland from 1894; see Testimony of George Bew to the Royal Commission on the Fruit Industry (1913, 1117). In 1899 George Bew visited Queensland to investigate chances to extend the banana trade (NAA, Attorney-General's Dept., Correspondence files, SP42/1, C1901/652 1/2). Because of his efforts, Wing Sang and Co. handled 7,000 bunches of bananas from northern Queensland a week in 1899 and gained entry to the Fiji trade in 1900 (Royal Commission on the Fruit Industry 1913, 1116–1117).
33 *TWT*, 24 October 1908, 8.
34 Miscellaneous records of Wing Sang Co., no: 42–71, Archives of City of Sydney. Private collections of Mr Gordon Mar (Sydney).
35 For example, Wing Sang was the agent in Sydney for selling shares of Wing On department store in Shanghai. See Shanghai Municipal Archives Q 225–4–1, Q225–4–3 and Q225–4–5.
36 Sydney Chinese newspapers indicated the transformation of a remittance office from Wing Chong Tai to Wing On in Hong Kong. *Tung Wah Times*, 7 January 1905, 1 (Wing Chong Tai) and 7 January 1911, (Wing On).
37 See Wing On records no. Q225–4–458, Q225–4–172 and Q225–3–1 in Shanghai Municipal Archives.
38 The directors of Hong Kong Wing Sang in 1919 were George Bew, James Choy Hing, Ma Yin Piu, Ma Joe Young, Ma Wing-Chan, and Choy Chong. See "Memorandum of Wing Sang Company Ltd. Hong Kong 1919", no. 42–7 box 3, Archive of City of Sydney.
39 A1, 1925/11716, National Archives of Australia.
40 Record of NSW Chinese Chamber of Commerce, no. 526-01-86.
41 Memorandum of Wing Sang Company Ltd. Hong Kong (1919) and Annual report of Wing Sang (1928), no. 42–7 box 3, Archive of City of Sydney.
42 Miscellaneous records of Wing Sang Co., no: 42–71, box 3, Archives of City of Sydney.

References

Publications

Ali, Bessie Ng Kumlin. 2002. *Chinese in Fiji*. Suva: Institute of Pacific Studies, University of the South Pacific.

Annual Statements of the Trade of the Commonwealth. Sydney: John Sands, 1903, 1904 and 1905.

Benton, Gregor and Liu Hong 2015. "Silver and letters: Chinese migrants write home, 1820–1970". Unpublished manuscript.

Bryan, Steven. 2010. *The Gold Standard at the Turn of the Twentieth Century: Rising Powers, Global Money, and the Age of Empire*. New York: Columbia University Press.

Butlin, N.G. 1962. *Australian Domestic Product, Investment and Foreign Borrowing 1861–1938/39*. Cambridge: Cambridge University Press.

Chang, Zengshu 常增书. 2008. "Aozhou taojin Huagong de 'yinxin'" 澳洲淘金华工的" 银信" [The Australian gold-miners' 'silver letters']. In Wang Weizhong 王炜中, ed., *Dierjie qiaopi wenhua yantao huilun wenxuan* 第二届侨批文化研讨会论文选 [Selected essays of the 2nd Conference on *qiaopi* culture]. Xianggang: Gong yuan chu ban you xian gong si, pp. 455–460.

Chen, Chunsheng 陈春声. 2000. "Jindai Huaqiao huikuan yu qiaopi ye de jingying: Yi Chaoshan diqu de yanjiu wei zhongxin" 近代华侨汇款与侨批业的经营：以潮汕地区的研究为中心 [Modern overseas-Chinese remittances and the administration of the *qiaopi* trade: With a focus on research on the Chaoshan region]. *Zhongguo shehui jingji shi yanjiu* 中国社会近代史研究 [The journal of Chinese social and economic history] 4: 57–66.

Chen, Liyuan 陈丽园 2008. "Qiaopi jingying wangluo de zuzhi xingtai yanjiu" 侨批经营网络的组织形态研究 [Research into the organizational form of the management of the *qiaopi* network]. In Wang Weizhong 王炜中, ed., *Dierjie qiaopi wenhua yantao huilun wenxuan* 第二届侨批文化研讨会论文选 [Selected essays of the 2nd Conference on *qiaopi* culture]. Xianggang: Gong yuan chu ban you xian gong si, pp. 185–194.

Chen, Liyuan 陈丽园 2010. "Qiaopi yu kuaguo Huaren shehui de jiangou" 侨批与跨国华人社会的建构 [*Qiaopi* and the construction of transnational ethnic-Chinese society]. In Wang Weizhong 王炜中, ed., *Disanjie qiaopi we hua yan taohui lunwenxuan* 第三届侨批文化研讨会论文选 [Selected essays of the 3rd Conference on *qiaopi* culture]. Xianggang: Tian ma chu ban you xian gong si, pp. 164–180.

Coghlan, T. A. and T. T. Ewing. 1903. *Progress of Australia*. London: Chambers.

Collins, Jock. 2002. "Chinese entrepreneurs: The Chinese Diaspora in Australia". *International Journal of Entrepreneurial Behavior and Research* 8, 1/2: 113–133.

Commonwealth Bureau of Census and Statistics (Australia). 1906–1917. *Trade and Customs and Excise Revenue of the Commonwealth of Australia*. Commonwealth Bureau of Census and Statistics.

Cornish, Selwyn and William Coleman. 2014. "Making a land fit for a gold standard: Monetary policy in Australia 1920–1925". Discussion Paper of Centre for Economic History. Canberra: Australia National University.

Curthoys, Ann. 2001. "Men of all nations, except Chinamen: Chinese on the New South Wales goldfields", in Iain McCalman, Alexander Cook, and Andrew Reeves, eds, *Gold Forgotten Histories and Lost Objects of Australia*. Cambridge: Cambridge University Press, pp. 103–124.

Dai, Yifeng 戴一峰. 2003. "Wangluo hua qiye yu qianru xing: Jindai qiaopiju de zhidu jianguo (1850s–1940s)" 网络化企业与嵌入性：近代侨批局的制度建构 (1850–1940) [Networked enterprise and embeddedness: The systemic construction of the modern remittance office (1850s–1940s)]. Zhongguo shehui jingji shi yanjiu 中国社会经济史研究 [Research on Chinese Social and Economic History] 1: 70–78.

Denzel, Markus A. 2010. *Handbook of World Exchange Rates, 1590–1914*. Burlington, VT: Ashgate Publishing.

Du, Guifang 杜桂芳.1995. "Chaoshan qiaopi: yiwu yu quanli-yi qianglie de xinli xuqiu wei tezheng de jiazu guanian" 潮汕侨批：义务与权利 – 以强烈的心理需求为特征的家族观念 [Remittance in qiaoshan: obligation and right-familism characterized by strong psychological needs]. Huaqiao huaren lishi yanjiu 华侨华人历史研究 [Overseas Chinese History Studies] 4: 42–49.

Fitzgerald, Shirley. 1977. *Red Tape, Gold Scissors: The Story of Sydney's Chinese*. Sydney, Australia: State Library of New South Wales Press.

Frost, Warwick. 2002. "Migrants and technological transfer: Chinese farming in Australia, 1850–1920". *Australian Economic History Review* 42(2): 113–131.

Gock Chin (Guo Quan 郭泉). 1961. *Yong an jingshen zhi faren jiqi chengzhang shilue* 永安精神之发轫及其成长史略 [A brief history of the origin and development of the spirit of Wing On]. Hong Kong: unknown publisher.

Gock Lock 郭乐. 1949. *Huiyilu* 回忆录 [The memoirs]. Hong Kong: unknown publisher.

Hamashita, Takeshi. 2008. *China, East Asia and the Global Economy*. New York: Routledge.

Harris, Lane J. 2015. "Overseas Chinese remittance firms, the limits of state sovereignty, and transnational capitalism in East and Southeast Asia, 1850s–1930s". *The Journal of Asian Studies* 74: 129–151.

Hobsbawm, E. J. 2005. *Industry and Empire: From 1750 to the Present Day*. New York: The New Press.

Hodge, Harry. 1986. *The Hill End Story: A History of the Hill End-Tambaroora Goldfield Book 1*. Third edn, Toorak, Vic: Hill End Publications.

Hsiao, L. L. 1974. *China's Foreign Trade Statistics 1864–1949*. Cambridge, MA: Harvard University Press.

Hsu, Madeline Y. 2000. *Dreaming of Gold, Dreaming of Home: Transnationalism and Migration Between the United States and South China, 1882–1943*. Stanford: Stanford University Press.

Kuo, Mei-fen. 2013. *Making Chinese Australia: Urban Elites, Newspapers and the Formation of Chinese Australian Identity, 1892–1912*. Melbourne: Monash University Publishing.

Lee, Pui Tak 李培德. 2015. "Linking global and local networks of credit and remittances: Ma. Tsui Chiu's financial operations in Hong Kong, 1900s–1950s". In Ulbe Bosma and Anthony Webster, eds, *Communities, Ports and Agency: Shaping Maritime Mercantile Networks in Asia from the Eighteenth Century Onwards*. London and New York: Palgrave Macmillan, pp. 165–178.

Li, Longsheng 李隆生. 2010. *Qing dai de guo ji mao yi: bai yin liuru, huo bi wei ji he wan Qing gong ye hua* 清代的国际贸易：白银流入、货币危机和晚清工业化 [International trade of Qing dynasty: Flow of silver, risk of monetary and industrialization of late Qing]. Taipei: Xiuwei zi xun ke ji gu fen you xian gong si.

Lin, Jinzhi 林金枝. 1982. "Jindai huaqiao zai shanghai diquqi yetou zilishide ruogan wenti" 近代华侨在上海地区企业投资历史的若干问题 [Some issues on history of commercial investments in Shanghai]. *Nanyang wenti yanjiu* 南洋问题研究 [Research on Nanyang issues] 3: 108–120.

Lin, Jinzhi 林金枝. 1987. "Huaqiao touzi dui yanhai chengshi de xingqi yu zhongguo-jindaihua de zuoyong" 华侨投资对沿海城市的兴起和中国近代化的作用 [The impact of Chinese investments from overseas toward the urbanization in the cities alongside oceans and China's industrialization]. *Huaqiao daxue xuebao* 华侨大学学报 [Journal of Huachiao University] 2: 10–23.

Lin, Jinzhi and Weiji Zhuang. 1985. 林金枝, 庄为玑. *Jin dai Hua qiao tou zi guo nei qi ye shi zi liao xuan ji* 近代华侨投资国内企业史资料选辑 [Selected essays on history of Chinese modern enterprises: Guangdang province]. Fuzhou: Fujian ren min chu ban she.

Lipton, Phillip. 2007. "A history of company law in colonial Australia: Economic development and legal evolution". *Melbourne University Law Review* 31(3): 805–836.

Liu, Jin. 2009. *Wuyi yinxin* [Wuyi silver and letters]. Guangzhou: Guangdong renmin chuban she.

Liu, Jin and Wenzhao Li. 2011. *Yinxin yu wuyi qiaoxiang shehui yu* 银信与五邑侨乡社会 [Silver and letters in the wuyi society]. Guangzhou: Guangdong renmin chuban she.

Lydon, Jane. 1999. *Many Inventions: The Chinese in the Rocks, Sydney 1890–1930*. Clayton, Vic: Dept. of History, Monash University, Monash publications in history; no. 28.

Macgregor, Paul. 2012. "Lowe Kong Meng and Chinese engagement in the international trade of Colonial Victoria". *Provenance: The Journal of Public Record Office Victoria*, issue no. 11, available at: http://prov.vic.gov.au/publications/provenance/provenance2012/lowe-kong-meng#sthash.cVOFo08j.dpuf. Accessed 18 June 2016.

Macgregor, Paul. 2015. "Chinese political values in colonial Victoria: Lowe Kong Meng and the legacy of the July 1880 election", in Sophie Couchman and Kate Bagnall, eds, *Chinese Australians: Politics, Engagement and Resistance*. Boston: Brill.

Maddison, Angus. 1995. *Monitoring the World Economy 1820–1992*. Paris: Organisation for Economic Co-Operation and Development.

Magee, Gary B. and Andrew S. Thompson. 2006. "The global and local: Explaining migrant remittance flows in the English-speaking world, 1880–1914". *The Journal of Economic History* 66: 177–202.

McLean, Ian. 2007. "Why was Australia so rich?". *Explorations in Economic History* 44: 635–656.

New South Wales. 1892. *Report of the Royal Commission on Alleged Chinese Gambling and Immorality and Charges of Bribery Against Members of the Police Force*. Sydney: C. Potter.

New South Wales Statistical Register. 1895, 1897, and 1900). Statistician's Office. Sydney: Govt. Printer.

Norton, Robert. 1970(?). *The Story of Wing On*. Unknown printer.

Pei, Yan 裴艳. 2013. "Qiaopi beijing xia de Zhongshan yimin yu jinrong wangluo" 侨批背景下的中山移民与金融网络 [Zhongshan migrants and financial networks against the background of *qiaopi*]. Bagui qiaokan 八桂侨刊 [Overseas Chinese journal of Bagui] 3: 45–50.

Powell, J. M. 1998. *An Historical Geography of Modern Australia: The Restive Fringe*. Melbourne: Cambridge University Press.

Royal Commission on Customs and Excise. 1906–1907. *Progress reports*. Melbourne: Govt. Printer.

Royal Commission on the Fruit Industry. 1913. *Parliamentary paper no. 59 Minutes of evidence and appendices*. Melbourne: Government Printer.

Sawa, Sempei. 1943. "Japanese and British vessels in Chinese water". *Kyoto University Economic Review* 18(1): 18–33.

Shanghai Academy of Social Science. 1981. Institute of Economy. *Shanghai Yongan Gongsi Di Chansheng, Fazhan He Gaizao* (The origin, development and reconstruction of Wing On Company in Shanghai). Shanghai: Shanghai renmin chubanshe.

Sinn, Elizabeth. 2013. *Pacific Crossing: California Gold, Chinese Migration, and the Making of Hong Kong*. Hong Kong: Hong Kong University Press.

Smith, H. A. F.S.S. 1921. *The Official Year Book of N.S.W. 1920*. Sydney: W. A. Gullick, Govt. Printer.

Stephen, A. (ed.). 1997. *The Lions of Retreat Street: A Chinese Temple in Inner Sydney*. Sydney: Powerhouse.

Wang, Sing-wu. 1978. *The Organization of Chinese Emigration, 1848–1888: With Special Reference to Chinese Emigration to Australia*. San Francisco: Chinese Materials Center.

Williams, Michael. 2002. "Destination qiaoxiang: Pearl River Delta Villages and Pacific ports, 1849–1949". PhD diss. The University of Hong Kong.

Williams, Wells. 1856. *A Chinese Commercial Guide*, consisting of a collection of details and regulations respecting foreign trade with China, sailing directions, tables, etc. Canton: Printed at the Office of the Chinese Repository.

Willmott, W. E. 2007. *The Chinese Communities in the Smaller Countries of the South Pacific: Kiribati, Nauru, Tonga and the Cook Islands*. Christchurch, NZ: Macmillan Brown Centre for Pacific Studies.

Wong, Kin. 1913. *International Chinese Business Directory*. San Francisco: International Chinese business directory Co., Inc.

Xian shi gong si guang gao bu (ed.). 1935. Xian shi gong si Aomen zhi hang kai mu ji nian te kan 先施公司澳门支行开幕纪念特刊 [Opening commemoration of the Sincere Co. Ltd. Macao branch]. Hong Kong: Xianggang Zhong huan rong ji yin wu ju.

Xianshi gongshi 先施公司. 1924. "Xianshi gongsi ershiwu zhounian ji'nian ce" 先施公司二十五周年纪念册 [Souvenir publication for the twenty-fifth anniversary of the Sincere Company]. Hong Kong: Xianshi gongshi.

Yao, Zengyin 姚曾荫. 1943. *Guangdong sheng de Hua qiao hui kuang* 广东省的华侨汇款 [Remittance from Chinese overseas to the Guangdong province]. Chongqing: Shang wu yin shu guan.

Yen, Ching Hwang. 1998. "Wing On and the Kwok brothers: A case study of pre-war Chinese entrepreneurs", in Kerrie L. Macpherson, ed., *Asian Department Stores*. Honolulu, HI: University of Hawaii Press.

Yen, Ching Hwang. 2013. *Ethnic Chinese Business in Asia: History, Culture and Business Enterprise*. Singapore: World Scientific.

Yong, C. F. 1977. *The New Gold Mountain: The Chinese in Australia, 1901–1921*. Richmond, Australia: Raphael Arts.

Newspapers

The Age, Melbourne

The Argus, Melbourne.

Ballarart Star, Victoria.

Guangyi huabao 广益华报 (*Chinese Australian Herald*) Sydney.

Minguo bao 民国报 (*Chinese Republic News*) Sydney.

Daily Commercial News and Shipping List, Sydney.

Los Angeles Herald, USA.

Northern Territory Times and Gazette, Darwin.

Register, South Australia.

Sydney Morning Herald, Sydney.

Donghua bao 东华报 (*Tung Wah News*),Sydney.

Donghua xinbao 东华新报 (*Tung Wah Times*), Sydney.

Online sources

Chinese Australian Historical Society: http://chineseaustralianhistory.org/bew-chips-ledger/.

Historical exchange rate data: www.measuringworth.com/datasets/gold/result.php.

Trove: http://trove.nla.gov.au/newspaper?q= National Library of Australia.

Post Office Reports from 1884, in Sessional Papers at Hong Kong Government Report Online 1842–1941, http://sunzi.lib.hku.hk/hkgro/index.jsp.

Index

Page numbers in **bold** denote tables, those in *italics* denote figures.

For Product Safety Concerns and Information please contact our EU representative GPSR@taylorandfrancis.com
Taylor & Francis Verlag GmbH, Kaufingerstraße 24, 80331 München, Germany

www.ingramcontent.com/pod-product-compliance
Ingram Content Group UK Ltd.
Pitfield, Milton Keynes, MK11 3LW, UK
UKHW011014180926
475701UK00004B/737
9780367445102